Routledge Revivals

Mercurius Rusticans

Mercurius Rusticans
A Critical Edition

Ann J. Cotton

First published in 1988 by Garland Publishing, Inc.

This edition first published in 2019 by Routledge
2 Park Square, Milton Park, Abingdon, Oxon, OX14 4RN
and by Routledge
52 Vanderbilt Avenue, New York, NY 10017, USA

Routledge is an imprint of the Taylor & Francis Group, an informa business

© 1988 by Ann J. Cotton

All rights reserved. No part of this book may be reprinted or reproduced or utilised in any form or by any electronic, mechanical, or other means, now known or hereafter invented, including photocopying and recording, or in any information storage or retrieval system, without permission in writing from the publishers.

Publisher's Note
The publisher has gone to great lengths to ensure the quality of this reprint but points out that some imperfections in the original copies may be apparent.

Disclaimer
The publisher has made every effort to trace copyright holders and welcomes correspondence from those they have been unable to contact.
A Library of Congress record exists under ISBN:

ISBN 13: 978-0-367-19863-3 (hbk)
ISBN 13: 978-0-367-19865-7 (pbk)
ISBN 13: 978-0-429-24377-6 (ebk)

GARLAND PUBLICATIONS IN AMERICAN AND ENGLISH LITERATURE

Editor
Stephen Orgel
Stanford University

GARLAND PUBLISHING, INC.

Mercurius Rusticans

A Critical Edition

Ann J. Cotton

GARLAND PUBLISHING, INC.
NEW YORK & LONDON 1988

Copyright © 1988
Ann J. Cotton
All Rights Reserved

Library of Congress Cataloging-in-Publication Data

Mercurius Rusticans. English & Latin
Mercurius Rusticans : a critical edition / [edited by] Ann J. Cotton.
p. cm. — (Garland publications in American and English literature)
English and Latin.
Originally presented as the editor's thesis (M.A.)—University of Birmingham, 1972.
Bibliography: p.
ISBN 0-8240-6383-X
1. College and school drama, Latin (Medieval and modern)—England—Oxford (Oxfordshire)—Translations into English. 2. College and school drama, Latin (Medieval and modern)—England—Oxford (Oxfordshire) 3. English drama—Translations from Latin (Medieval and modern) 4. Theater—England—Oxford (Oxfordshire)—History—16th century. I. Cotton, A. J. (Ann Josephine) II. Title. III. Series.
PA8552.M42E5 1988
882'.02—dc 19   88-17717

Printed on acid-free, 250-year-life paper
Manufactured in the United States of America

Genius Academiæ cum primis Academicis
scuto topicis et lauro rosis, lilijs coronatis.

Cognoscite me Genium vestræ Academiæ
Quem mater alma peperit nobis vobis.
Est alius vobis, alius Academiæ Genius,
Et dispar ortus contrarij mores, differens status
Unde mihi et illi non satis aliquando ca...
Mihi vita cæpit quum primum studuit domus
Musis sacravit, [...] sedulus domi
Quicquid deinceps [...] quatuor [...]
Annis [factum?] usq ad hodiernum diem
Memoriâ teneo. Jam autem visibilis appareo
non ut scholodum [...]; et monumenta virtus,
sed facta quondam pelara, pelaros viros
Exponerem audias. Levior me [...] protulit,
Lusus, iocisq, iuvenilis ætatis lubrico
Et quicquid [...]
Et [...] morsaevij petulantior dolus
Erit vestra a fabulam videbis quasi speculo
Non facta sed ficta, non vera, sed veri similia:
Strident [...] poeticâ licentiâ, nec legis Comicæ
[...] autoris verborum modi.
Dispensare p diuarum horarum absentiâ
A serijs negotijs, causa est, quia Genius vester
Jam agendum saturnalia, sint omnes hilares non solemni
Ex alienis molestijs vestra voluptas nascitur
Quis ordens placeat, vobis fauere sed facile
[...], animisq, fausto, fausto vultis oculis
Haustu auribus acceptis, et porrectis frondibus
Pro gratiâ vestrâ reponite gratiam, nobisq, ut vero a [...]
facilem licentiam et pedibus visu du [...]

CONTENTS

THE PROLOGUE OF <u>MERCURIUS RUSTICANS</u> (FROM THE
    ORIGINAL MANUSCRIPT)   Frontispiece

                                                                        PAGE

ABBREVIATIONS

INTRODUCTION:

    I. Academic Drama in England during the Renaissance . . i
    II. Authorship and Date of <u>Mercurius Rusticans</u> . . . ix
    III. The Plot of the Play xviii
    IV. <u>Mercurius Rusticans</u> A Critical Study of its Humour . xx
    V. Songs in <u>Mercurius Rusticans</u> xlvii
    VI. Vocabulary lxv
    VII. Syntax. lxx
    VIII. Literary Form lxxvii
    IX. The Manuscript of <u>Mercurius Rusticans</u>. . . lxxx
    X. Treatment of the Text lxxxii

<u>MERCURIUS RUSTICANS</u> (TEXT AND TRANSLATION) . . . I

NOTES 257

CHANGES OF PUNCTUATION 470

BIBLIOGRAPHY. 507

ABBREVIATIONS

The following abbreviations have been used to save space:

General

ap.	apud: in
c.	chapter; and also circa: about
cf.	confer: compare
comp.	compiled by
ed.	edited by
ext.	extract
f.	and following lines, or, and following pages
fl.	floruit: flourished, was active
ibid.	ibidem: in the same book or passage
op. cit.	opus citatum: the work already mentioned
sc.	scilicet: to wit, namely
s.v.	sub voce: under the heading
trans.	translated by
v.	verse
vol.	volume

Periodicals and Standard Works

A.D.B.	Allgemeine Deutsche Biographie
A.J.P.	American Journal of Philology
Boas	Boas, F.S., *University Drama in the Tudor Age* (Oxford, 1914).

C.E.	Chambers's Encyclopaedia
D.G.R.B.M.	Dictionary of Greek and Roman Biography and Mythology
D.N.B.	Dictionary of National Biography
E.B.	Encyclopaedia Britannica
G.D.M.	Grove's Dictionary of Music and Musicians
Lily	Lily, W., A short introduction to grammar (commonly call'd the Accidence)...and of the Latin tongue. Followed by Brevissima institutio. (Corrected and enlarged by Erasmus and others (? London, 1719).
Mallet	Mallet, C.E., A history of the University of Oxford, 3 vols. (London, 1924-27; reprinted New York, 1968).
N.B.U.	Nouvelle Biographie Universelle
O.C.C.L.	Oxford Companion to Classical Literature
O.C.D.	Oxford Classical Dictionary
O.C.E.L.	Oxford Companion to English Literature

O.C.F.L.	*Oxford Companion to French Literature*
O.C.M.	*Oxford Companion to Music*
O.E.D.	*Oxford English Dictionary*
O.E.P.M.	*Old English Popular Music* by W. Chappell, 2 vols. (London, 1893).
Ong	Ong, W.J., *Ramus, method and the decay of dialogue. From the art of discourse to the art of reason* (Cambridge, Mass., 1958).
P.M.L.A.	*Publications of the Modern Language Association of America*
Scot	Scot, R., *The Discoverie of Witchcraft*, introduction by H.R. Williamson (Arundel, Centaur Press, 1964).
T.L.R.B.	*Thesaurus Linguae Romanae et Britannicae, 1565* comp. by T. Cooper, English Linguistics, 1500-1800, 200 (Menston, 1969).
V.H.C.	*Victoria History of the Counties of England*
Ward	Ward, G.R.M., trans., *The Foundation Statutes of Bishop Fox for Corpus Christi College A.D. 1517, with a life of the founder* (London, 1843).

INTRODUCTION

I. ACADEMIC DRAMA IN ENGLAND DURING THE RENAISSANCE.

"The Elizabethan world looked back with reverence on the days
'when Roscius was an actor in Rome'."

W. BEARE, The Roman Stage.

Mercurius Rusticans is one in a long series of academic plays, generally in Latin, but occasionally in English, which were performed at the colleges of Oxford and Cambridge, during the sixteenth and seventeenth centuries. Not only were these plays - about one hundred and fifty in all[1] - written by members of the University, but they were also acted by them: Masters, Bachelors and undergraduates, alike, took part. The plays were usually staged in the college hall,[2] and both private and public performances were given: private, when only the members of the college were present, and public, when important guests, such as doctors of the University, or - sometimes - town dignitaries,[3] were invited to attend. On very special occasions academic plays were performed in the presence of the Sovereign, as in 1564, when Queen Elizabeth toured the colleges of Cambridge, and again in 1566, during the royal visit to Oxford. Indeed, the great interest which Elizabeth - a monarch with an inborn love of the theatre - showed in all forms of dramatic entertainment throughout her reign, soon spread to the academic stage, and prompted the writing and performance of a large number of plays.

The growth of University drama in England during the Renaissance was the result of a combination of several different factors. In its narrowest sense, the academic play can be seen as a natural transition from the rudimentary religious dramas, enacted at the University colleges towards the end of the fifteenth century. These were morality plays, interludes and 'shews', which took place on all the major feasts in the Church calendar, such as Christmas and Easter. Gradually, the morality play progressed to the interlude, and the interlude to comedy or tragedy, modelled on classical drama. In most respects, however, the academic play was essentially a product of the Renaissance. Throughout this great revival of learning, those who had a deep absorption in the history of the stage, were possessed with an overwhelming desire to recreate, but in a new form, the glories of the ancient Greek and Roman theatre. They sought to achieve this aim by writing plays, original in themselves, yet either adapted from, or based on, the works of classical authors. The outcome was a unique blend of the classical and the romantic, of precision of form and light jeu d'esprit, of mediaevalism and humanism, of the past and of the present.

Moreover, the increasing interest being taken in the tragedies of Seneca, and the comedies of Plautus and Terence, in schools and universities on the continent, as indicated by the frequency with which the plays were performed there, and the numerous imitations of them, written by French and German scholars, extended, before long, to academic circles in England. It is possible, too, as Boas[4] points out, that the institution of the 'Christmas Lord', or 'Lord of Misrule' did much to further the writing of University plays. This was an old, established tradition in the Oxford colleges, whereby every year, at Christmas or thereabouts, a senior Fellow was elected to be 'Lord of Misrule'. His 'reign', during which he held mock authority over his juniors, usually lasted from Christmas to Candlemas (February 2nd.) and was proverbially a time for great merry-making. One of the official duties which the 'Christmas Lord' had to carry out, was to provide the students with some form of entertainment. This normally took place in January, towards the end of the 'Lord's' rule, and was to include tragedies and comedies, both in Latin and English, as well as various 'shews'. This more or less meant that new plays had to be written for this occasion each year. Finally, the fact that by the beginning of the sixteenth century, the sons of gentlemen, and other high-born and wealthy youths, who, like a great many Englishmen of the Tudor period, had an inbred passion for the theatre, were being admitted to the colleges of Oxford and Cambridge, created a demand for more plays, and also furnished the Universities with a large number or budding new actors and play-wrights.

Within the academic community, itself, the function of college plays was three-fold. Firstly, they gave the students, who for the

greater part of their time at University, led a rather enclosed
life, governed by stringent rules, with a healthy outlet for
their youthful exuberance and high spirits. Secondly, the plays had
immense educational value. Based, as so many of them were -
particularly those written in Latin - on the works of Seneca, Plautus
and Terence, and abounding in quotations from many famous poets and
philosophers, they were instrumental in familiarising the students
with several classical authors; while from the actor's point of view,
learning to deliver one's lines with correct pronunciation and
emphasis was a useful exercise in rhetoric and declamation. Thirdly,
when august foreign visitors came to the University, it was possible,
through the medium of Latin academic drama, to set before them a fine
piece of theatrical entertainment, which they could both enjoy and
fully understand - Latin being, of course, at that time, an
international language.

The themes of the plays were wide and varied. Some authors chose
to write biblical dramas, in which they adapted for the stage stories
from the Scriptures. Nicholas Grimald's _Christus Redivivus_ (c.1540),
a play about the Resurrection, and his _Archipropheta_ (1546/7), the
subject of which is the career of John the Baptist, are good examples
of what could be achieved when the rules laid down for the writing of
pagan drama were applied to a Christian concept. Other writers

preferred to draw their inspiration from the vast well of ancient mythology, as preserved in the works of Homer, Vergil and Ovid: the results can be seen in such plays as William Gager's <u>Meleager</u> (1581/2), <u>Dido</u> (1583) and <u>Ulysses Redux</u> (1591/2), and in James Calfhill's <u>Progne</u> (1566).

Sometimes University dramatists had recourse to the political history of ancient times, and even to the history of mediaeval England, in which they found many episodes with great theatrical possibilities. Richard Eedes, for instance, wrote a play with the assassination of Julius Caesar as its theme - <u>Caesar Interfectus</u> (1581/2), and Thomas Legge, donning the buskin of high tragedy, produced a work for the academic stage on the life of King Richard III, entitled <u>Richardus Tertius</u> (1579/80), to which Shakespeare may in some measure be indebted.[5] There were also plays harking back to the old Moralities, in which abstract and allegorical characters appeared, such as Thomas Artour's <u>Microcosmus</u> (1520/32) and <u>Mundus Plumbeus</u> (1520/32); and others dealing with the early history of Christianity, like Nicholas Grimald's <u>Protomartyr</u> (c.1540), a dramatization of the story of St. Stephen, now no longer extant.

Occasionally, college plays were used as a vehicle for satire. In <u>Ignoramus</u>, for example, which was acted in 1615, the Recorder of Cambridge is held up to ridicule, while the butt for much of the burlesque humour in <u>Pedantius</u>[6] (1580/1) is Gabriel Harvey. Similarly,

J. Hacket's <u>Loiola</u>, acted in 1622/3, contains much anti-Jesuit and anti-Puritan feeling. Some academic drama was based on tales from popular literature: the plot of Richard Edwardes' <u>Palamon and Arcyte</u> (Parts I and II),[7] (1566), to name but one, was taken directly from Chaucer's <u>Knight's Tale</u>. Later, Italian literature began to make its influence felt: the romantic comedies, such as Abraham Fraunce's <u>Victoria</u> (1579/83), and Walter Hawkesworth's <u>Leander</u> (1602/3) and <u>Labyrinthus</u> (1602/3) are all adapted from Italian originals.[8] A decidedly Italian flavour also surrounds those plays written in the pastoral genre, like Samuel Brooke's <u>Scyros</u>[9] (acted in 1612/3), Phineas Fletcher's <u>Sicelides</u> (acted in 1614/15), and the anonymous <u>Pastor Fidus</u> (c.1595/1600), modelled on Guarini's <u>Pastor Fido</u>.

The most interesting class of academic stage-plays, however, are undoubtedly those which treat of contemporary student life, shedding light on the conditions in which University students of the sixteenth and seventeenth centuries, lived and worked. These include <u>The Pilgrimage to Parnassus</u> (1598), <u>Club Law</u> (1599/1600), and <u>The Return from Parnassus</u> (Parts I and II) (1601/2).[10] It is into this last category that <u>Mercurius Rusticans</u> falls.

NOTES

[1] A full list of titles can be found in *The Cambridge History of English Literature*, VI, 469-87.

[2] When Queen Elizabeth visited King's College, Cambridge, in 1564, a stage had to be erected at the Queen's expense in the antechapel, since the hall was not large enough to accommodate the royal party *and* all the members of the college.

[3] The Mayor of Cambridge, together with other civic officials and their wives, attended the performance of *Club Law* at Clare Hall in 1599/1600.

[4] *University Drama in the Tudor Age*, p.7.

[5] See Boas, pp. 130-1.

[6] This play has been ascribed to Anthony Wingfield.

[7] This play is no longer extant, but a summary of the plot is given by J. Bereblock in his *Commentarii*.

[8] Luigi Pasqualigo's *Il Fedele*, and G.B. della Porta's *La Fantesca* and *La Cintia*, respectively.

[9] This was a version of Bonarelli's *Filli di Sciro*.

[10] All the Parnassus plays are anonymous. *Club Law*, however, may have been written by George Ruggle. (See *Club Law*, edited by G.C. Moore Smith (Cambridge University Press, 1907) Introduction, section V.).

II. AUTHORSHIP AND DATE OF MERCURIUS RUSTICANS

> "The chief glory of every people
> arises from its authors."
>
> SAMUEL JOHNSON

Of the authorship and date of Mercurius Rusticans very little is known. The play may well be regarded as anonymous, and is described as such in all the catalogues in which its name appears. In E. Bernard's Catalogi Librorum Manuscriptorum Angl. et Hibern, (1697), the entry is simply '8557.95. Mercurius Rusticus,[1] Comoedia ab Oxoniensi quodam scripto, cujus Scena est Hinxey'. This entry was exactly repeated in William Huddesford's Catalogue, (1761).[2] Falconer Madan, in his Summary Catalogue of Western Manuscripts (II, pt.2, 1183), speaks of it thus: '8557. Mercurius Rusticanus,[3] a Latin play, of which the scene is laid in Hinksey by an Oxford man'. In "A Census of Anglo-Latin Plays", P.M.L.A., 53, pp.624-9, Alfred Harbage lists it among anonymous plays, as he also did in Annals of English Drama 975-1700, (1964).

Most of the cataloguers are unanimous on one point: namely, that Mercurius Rusticans was written by 'an Oxford man', i.e. a student, or scholar, at Oxford University. This fact, of course, is obvious from the very subject-matter of the play. Who, but an Oxford student, would be so intimately acquainted with college life, as portrayed in the play? Who, but a University scholar in the sixteenth or seventeenth century, would have such a command of Latin, and such a knowledge of classical literature? And who, but a person who had spent part of his life in Oxford and its neighbourhood, would choose the little known village of Hinksey as the setting for his play?

Having established, therefore, that the author of <u>Mercurius Rusticans</u> was a student at Oxford University, of which college was he a member? Here we are not entirely without help. At the end of the play, beneath the Epilogue, we find a very interesting, short, doggerel rhyme. It is written in quite a different hand from the rest of the play, and is composed by a "Mr. Sellar of C.C.C." (Corpus Christi College). The rhyme reads as follows:

"Mr. Sellar of C.C.C. in jeere of this play

Of old leathern thongs
And other mens songs
They patchd us up a play
Th' were so often out
we began to doubt
whether th' were Hincksie men or they."

This little verse tells us quite a lot. It seems that the author of Mercurius Rusticans, whoever he was, must at some time in his life have been a student at Corpus Christi College. Otherwise, how would Mr. Sellar have had access to the manuscript of the play, or have seen it performed so frequently - "Th' were so often out/ we began to doubt, &c."? Furthermore, the rhyme suggests that the play was extremely popular, if it was staged so often. It would probably have been put on at Christmas, since there are several references to Christmas in the play: for example, the Genius Academiae (Prologue, l.24) explains, "Iam aguntur Saturnalia"; Doulerus (I,2) complains of not being allowed to go home "nativitatis festo", and at the end of the play it is again Doulerus who remarks (V,243) that there is no harm in laughing and being merry, but once in the year, and that on the Feast of the Nativity - "Nativitatis festum". Finally, it is interesting to note that Sellar uses the word "They". Does this, in fact, mean that more than one person had a hand in writing the play? If so, they obviously worked well together as a team, since there are no inconsistencies in the play, itself, which such a combined effort might conceivably have produced. Perhaps Sellar simply means that someone other than the author of the play composed the songs? Or does the "They" refer to the company of actors taking part? It is difficult to be certain about any of this, especially when there is no record of such a play ever having been performed at Corpus Christi College.

We shall very likely never discover the true identity of the author of Mercurius Rusticans. He probably thought it wiser not to put his name to a work which depicts students behaving in such an unruly manner and so flagrantly breaking all the college statutes. But, whoever he was, he certainly had a flair for writing comedy, and it would be most interesting to know if he went on to distinguish himself in the field of English literature.

While we can be reasonably sure that the author of Mercurius Rusticans was a student at Oxford, it is well nigh impossible to assign any definite date to the play. Harbage, in his Annals of English Drama 975-1700, has this to say regarding the date of Mercurius Rusticans: "According to Madan, 'written in 1663'". Indeed, Madan does state categorically in the Summary Catalogue of Western Manuscripts (II, pt.2, 1183), that the play was written in 1663. But on what evidence? My own examination of the manuscript revealed an important clue. On a small slip of paper inserted between the last leaf of MS.8537 and the first leaf of Mercurius Rusticans are written the words:

> Wilson a
> M[anuscri]pt writer living
> neare Chester 16[6]3
> &c. qu. cat. 6

- xiii -

Since this piece of paper was obviously inserted in the book of MSS. a long while after it was bound, and has, moreover, been glued in at an angle, it is, unfortunately, quite impossible - without damaging the page - to ascertain whether there is an initial preceding the name 'Wilson', and to transcribe exactly the word which comes before 'writer'. Also, the second '6' of the date, 1663, is a very badly formed figure, and could quite easily be an '0'. The date would then read 1603. Madan, however, clearly thought that the year mentioned was 1663, and that the information recorded on this slip of paper related directly to Mercurius Rusticans. But no reference is made to the play, itself, and it is feasible that the words on this piece of paper have no bearing whatsoever on the date of the play's composition. They may, in fact refer to an entirely different work, and have been inserted between the two manuscripts at random, for it seems strange that someone "living neare Chester", should be making a copy of a play written by someone at Oxford. Madan's date, therefore, appears to be erroneous. He also transcribes the title of the play incorrectly, calling it Mercurius Rusticanus. This suggests, perhaps, a somewhat hurried and incomplete inspection of the MS.. Furthermore, 1663 would be a rather late period for the play's composition, when we consider that most academic drama was written between 1537 and 1603. It would make the play post-Restoration, and this is highly unlikely, since it seems to have more in common with the type of college plays written in the early part of the seventeenth century.

Is there any evidence within the play, itself, to suggest a possible date for its composition? We can, I think, dismiss as poetic fiction the Genius Academiae's statement in the Prologue[4] that, at the time the play is being performed, he is eight hundred years old - having first come to life when King Alfred founded the University of Oxford in 873 A.D..[5] This would mean that the play was written in about 1673, and while it places it fairly and squarely in the seventeenth century, this date poses the same problems as Madan's suggestion of 1663: it is rather late.

Perhaps it would be more constructive to try and identify the "Mr. Sellar of C.C.C.", who has added his criticism of the play to the bottom of the MS.. This is not a difficult task. According to Foster's *Alumni Oxonienses*, p.1333, there were only three[6] people by the name of Sellar, who were students at Corpus Christi College, between 1500 and 1714. They were: (i) John Sellar, who was a member of C.C.C., 1568-1561; (ii) John Sellar, Jnr. (John Sellar's son), who was a student at C.C.C. 1608-1614, and (iii) his brother, Henry Sellar, who studied at the college from 1611 to 1618. From what our Mr. Sellar says, the play had clearly been performed several times before he wrote his comments on it. He may even have been present at the very first performance. This probably means that quite a few years had elapsed between the play's 'first night' and Mr. Sellar's putting pen to paper. John Sellar, Snr. left Corpus Christi College in 1581, to become vicar of Eastry, so if we assume that it was he who was responsible for the rhyme at the end of the play, Mercurius Rusticans would then have to have been written at least some years prior to 1581. This makes the date a little early. There are strong indications that it is one of John Sellar's two sons who is voicing his criticism of the piece.

Does Mercurius Rusticans contain any topical allusions which may suggest that it was written between 1608 and 1618, or at any time during the early part of the seventeenth century? The only contemporary figure mentioned in the play is Simon Forman,[7] the astrologer and quack doctor. However, the author of Mercurius Rusticans obviously looked upon Forman as a necromancer, since the scene[8] in which we find the reference to him is that where Nichades pretends to conjure up the devil. Now Forman did not begin publicly to practise necromancy until 1588 (seven years after John Sellar, Snr. had left Corpus Christi College). Forman's reputation then seemed to grow steadily until his death in 1611. Ben Jonson alludes to him in his play Epicene (1609). These facts would appear to show that Mercurius Rusticans was written after 1588, - and if its composition is to coincide with the years spent at C.C.C. by John Sellar, Jnr. and Henry Sellar - possibly, even later than 1608.

There is another clue in the play, itself, which points to its date of composition as being somewhere between 1608 and 1618. In Act III, 1.259, Nichades mentions the name "Dulcinea". This could only refer to Dulcinea del Toboso, the sweetheart of Don Quijote, in Cervantes' famous novel, Don Quijote de la Mancha. The first part of

Don Quijote, in which Dulcinea figures, though not very prominently, was not published until 1605, and although the book was extremely popular, it was not translated into English before 1612. Whether the author of Mercurius Rusticans was familiar with the original Spanish version of the story, or whether he knew it only in translation, this still makes the date of the play post-1605.

Furthermore, in the first scene of the third act, a discussion takes place between the students about the evils of tobacco and smoking, strongly hinting that this was an important social issue round about the time that the play was written. Now the great tobacco controversy may also be said to have reached its peak around 1604/5, with the publication of King James' A Counterblaste to Tabacco (1604).

Finally, "French crowns" (coronati Gallici) are often mentioned[9] in the play, and so were obviously in current use at this time. French crowns, however, did not become legal tender in England until the very end of the sixteenth, and beginning of the seventeenth, century. In 1595, England began to export to France on a large scale and this commerce, together with the reimbursement of the large sums which Elizabeth had sent to Henry IV, drew a great quantity of French money to England.

It seems likely, therefore, but by no means certain, that Mercurius Rusticans was written sometime between the years 1605 and 1618.

NOTES

[1] Surprisingly few cataloguers have succeeded in transcribing the title of the play correctly.

[2] This was a catalogue of the MSS. then housed in the Ashmolean Museum, Oxford.

[3] Again the title of the play has been incorrectly transcribed.

[4] 11.6-10.

[5] See also Commentary, p. 264.

[6] There was, in fact, a fourth person by the name of Seller at C.C.C., 1577-1587 (?). However, as the Mr. Sellar who composed the rhyme at the end of the play, spells his name 'ar', and not 'er' it seems unlikely that there is any connection.

[7] See Commentary, p. 415.

[8] $\overline{V}$, i, 10.

[9] e.g. $\overline{IV}$, vi, 333; $\overline{V}$, iv, 198.

III. THE PLOT OF THE PLAY

"Lusus, iocusque iuvenilis aetatis lubricae,
Et quicquid invidus carpit, aulicus superbus crepat,
Et rusticantis mercurii petulantior dolus,
Erit nostra fabula:"

MERCURIUS RUSTICANS, Prologue, 14-17.

Mercurius Rusticans tells the story of the escapades of three, penniless, Oxford clerks, down in the country. Left behind at their college, during the Christmas vacation, when most of their friends have returned home, Doulerus, Nichades and Philopinus make up their minds to seek fun and adventure in the village of Hinksey, not far from Oxford. So off they set.

Once arrived in Hinksey, the students take up residence at the village inn, and soon become acquainted with several of the local inhabitants: Thomas Pigeon, the innkeeper, Anna, his wife, and Joanna, his daughter; Robert Dawson, a farmer, who has a nagging, ill-tempered wife, called Caecilia, and Richard Cullie, the blacksmith. It quickly becomes clear to the three scholars, as they listen to the villagers' conversation and watch them going about their daily lives, that the countrypeople are extremely boorish and greatly their intellectual inferiors. With their innate sense of humour and love of revelry, the students decide to take advantage of this fact. For their own amusement - but more especially that of the audience - they embark on a series of elaborate confidence tricks and practical jokes: the villagers, needless to say, prove ready dupes...

First, Doulerus, professing himself to have fallen desperately in love with Joanna, promises to marry her, - a promise, however, which he has absolutely no intention of keeping. Next, he poses as a lawyer and attempts to settle some trifling suit between Dawson and Cullie. Nichades, meanwhile, masquerading as a sorcerer, pretends to turn Dawson invisible, and to conjure up the devil. He also makes off with a solid gold punchbowl belonging to Pigeon, which he later <u>sells</u> back to him! Philopinus, too, is no mean scholar when it comes to trickery and deceit. He gulls Caecilia into thinking that he is a physician, and prescribes a cure for her barrenness - with disastrous results! All three students quite unashamedly make love to Susanna, the maid-servant; Doulerus plays a final trick on Joanna, by giving her what he claims is a love-potion, but what she discovers -too late - is really a powerful laxative, and Pigeon is swindled of the entire sum of money which the students owe him for their bed and board!

All ends happily, however. Caecilia has been taught a lesson; Dawson has been made a laughing-stock, as he rightly deserves; Pigeon has derived great amusement from observing the antics of the three scholars, and Doulerus, Nichades and Philopinus have had a riotous and most enjoyable holiday - free of charge!

IV. MERCURIUS RUSTICANS: A CRITICAL STUDY OF ITS HUMOUR

"Fun", said Garrick, the great eighteenth-century actor, "gives you a forcible hug, and shakes laughter out of you, whether you will or no." This statement could not be more true than of the fun in which Mercurius Rusticans abounds. For the space of some 1,500 lines the author leads us through a delightful maze of situation comedy, knockabout and slapstick humour, burlesque, parody, social satire, sexual innuendo, puns and double entendres. The play, of course, is no great literary masterpiece. At worst, it is a patchwork, as Mr. Sellar[1] sneeringly points out, of songs, classical tags and jest-book type practical jokes, all strung together without any real unifying force. At best, the play explores in a humorous vein the relationship between the sophisticated world of the intellectual and the simple world of the rustic, and describes what happens when the two clash - when the irresistible force meets the immovable object. And the play has the happy knack of producing laughter; enormous, great belly-laughs, one imagines, if it were well acted, and even many a titter from the reader who is only acquainted with it on the written page.

Humour is like wine: it does not always travel well. Yet somehow the fun in Mercurius Rusticans seems to have remained remarkably fresh down the ages, and the play is as amusing to us, today, as it must have been to those students, who, so many hundreds of years ago, sat watching it in their college hall. Any stand-up comic, or television script-writer will tell you that it is the hardest thing in the world to be funny, so exactly how did the author of Mercurius Rusticans, whoever he was, manage to succeed so brilliantly, where others have failed?

The humour in the play can be divided into three main categories. Firstly, there is that humour which is derived from the characters, themselves, from the personalities, idiosyncrasies, and psychological traits, which the author has seen fit to give them; secondly, there is that which is derived from situations external to the characters: buffoonery, trickery, practical jokes, misunderstandings and the like; finally, there is that which is derived from the language of the play: wit, double entendres, puns, parody and proverbs, alliteration and assonance. In these respects Mercurius Rusticans could be said to resemble Plautine comedy. However, here, in the grouping of humour into different classes, the similarity begins and ends, for the way in which the author of Mercurius Rusticans and the author of the Menaechmi, Casina, Rudens, - employ these various types of humour in their respective plays are quite distinctive.

The characters in Mercurius Rusticans fall into two groups: (i) the students, and (ii) the countrypeople. Unlike so many of the characters in Roman comedy, they are rounded, living people, universally recognizable. Gone are the stock types, like the cunning

servant, the angry father, the love-sick youth and the
unscrupulous bawd. In their place we have characters and situations
which could occur in any age. They did not exist only in the author's
time: they could have existed long before, or long after. We can
still see them today. They are based on real, living models, dwelling
in their natural surroundings, reacting to circumstances in which they
find themselves in the way one would expect them to do. One can say
of the author of <u>Mercurius Rusticans</u> what someone once said of the
celebrated French dramatist, Molière, "il peint d'après nature".

For models on which to base the students, - Doulerus, Nichades
and Philopimus - the author did not have far to look. All he had to do
was to turn and observe the person sitting next to him at the
Scholars' table in hall, or, for that matter, to take a long and
critical look at himself in the mirror. He is intimately acquainted
with the lives of students, their joys and woes, as only a student
can be. Doulerus, Nichades and Philopimus are the three anti-heroes
in the story: they are not eligible to be called heroes, because they
do not possess any of the qualities, like honesty, bravery and
integrity, which one associates with heroes, yet, nevertheless, they
are the three protagonists. It is they who carry the action forward,
speaking in witty, colourful language, filled with comparisons and
allusions to classical literature, and interspersed with the
occasional proverb. They are an extremely likeable trio, and right
from the very beginning of the play, one feels endeared to this

rebellious, high-spirited and fun-loving crew. They possess that priceless quality of being able to take nothing seriously: Doulerus, obliged to stay at college over Christmas, when most students go home, and with not a penny in his pocket, can only reflect upon his sorry state in lines that fairly drip with puns and double entendres;[2] and when Pigeon threatens to report the students to the University authorities for failing to pay him the money which they owe him, they can only answer him with jokes and word-play.[3]

Doulerus, Nichades and Philopinus drink, gamble, womanize, keep animals in their room, and carry shot-guns around with them. In short, they break every rule in the book, but this is one of the many sides to their personality which makes them appealing and at the same time convincing. They appear so utterly human: everyone is a rebel at heart, and a set of petty rules, made by some jumped-up bureaucrat, are there for the breaking. It is delightful, nay, even cathartic, in a way, to see someone actually breaking the rules and getting away with it. It must have given untold pleasure to the students watching Mercurius Rusticans, to see those statutes, which were so much part and parcel of their lives, neatly swept aside and trampled on! If Doulerus, Nichades and Philopinus were around on the campuses of today, they would be the first to organize a 'sit-in', or take part in a student demonstration. The challenge of authority did not begin in this century: Doulerus and company had already thrown down the gauntlet four hundred years ago. There is nothing new under the sun.

We also feel drawn to the students' side because, above all, they take us into their confidence. They 'let us in', as it were, on all their secrets, and on all the jokes, which they intend to play on the poor, unsuspecting inhabitants of Hinksey. This, in its turn, gives us, the audience, a great feeling of superiority over the countrypeople because we know something which they do not. We can almost see Philopinus winking at us, as he talks of prescribing a medicine to cure Caecilia's barrenness,[4] or Nichades giving us the 'thumbs-up', as he pretends to call forth the devil,[5] and Pigeon falls for it so readily.

The fact that there are <u>three</u> students instead of just one, as there conceivably might have been, also adds greatly to the scope and humour of the play. There is obviously something special about the number three: there were, for example, three musketeers, three men-in-a-boat and three fiddlers at the court of Old King Cole. And whereas three is sometimes said to be a crowd, here it is company, for besides exactly balancing the three chief characters amongst the countrypeople - "Nos tres sumus, vos estis tres, tria sunt omnia"[6] - it also means that the students can share their jokes and plans with one another, and have a good laugh, when the others' backs are turned. Similarly, since two heads are better than one, and, therefore, by the same analogy, three heads must be better than two, it enables the three students to hold the stage for quite long intervals on their own - the humour stemming from the witty repartee which they constantly exchange with one another, as, for instance, in Scene 2 of Act I, or in the first scene of Act III. With _three_ main characters, one can never grow tired. Doulerus, Nichades and Philopinus each take it in turn to perform their particular rôle and to steal the lime-light: Doulerus as lady-killer par excellence, Philopinus as quack doctor, and Nichades as magician-cum-sorcerer. This gives the author the opportunity to develop the action of the play along three different channels.

Doulerus, Nichades and Philopinus, therefore, are living, breathing characters. They have not been forced under the glass of some scholastic, or academic, hothouse into the stereotyped figures which appear in so much neo-Latin drama: they are plants which have been allowed to grow wild and free in their natural surroundings.

But if the students are true-to-life, the countrypeople are nothing if not more so. One might argue that no one, not even in the seventeenth century, could be so superstitious, so gullible, so ignorant, so incredibly stupid as the villagers of Hinksey, but the fact is, people were, - and still are. How many times do we not pick up the newspaper and read of various confidence tricks and practical jokes having been perpetrated against the general public? It was not so very long ago that someone tried to sell London Bridge to an American tourist; while, to a lesser extent, people are being continually 'taken in' by front-door salesmen, and advertising gimmicks.

Cullie, Dawson and his wife, Pigeon and his family, are acting out 'an everyday story of countryfolk': their pace of life is slower than that of town-dwellers; they have their own homespun philosophies; they are not interested in what some obscure Roman poet wrote, thousands of years ago; here and now is what matters to them; they are happy with little - a pouch of 'baccy and a jug of barley-mow. We grow to love the villagers of Hinksey because they are simple and genuine, and because (and this is probably most important of all) they give a boost to our ego. Their ignorance and lack of knowledge, which makes them such ready dupes, gives us an air of intelligence and learning, since we and the students feel that we know so much more than they do - but do we? We learn from books, they learn from life - "quod rustici discunt experientia / Id hauriunt ex libris docti".[7]

The rustic characters in the play do not appear until the third scene of the first act. After the witty, intellectual badinage of the previous two scenes, it comes as rather a shock to be suddenly catapulted into the snug of some little village inn, but the shock soon subsides into acute pleasure as we feel the tempo slowing to a more leisurely pace. Once inside the 'pub', we are confronted by two of the locals, Dawson and Cullie, (Hinksey's answer to Walter Gabriel and Ned Larkin) propping up the bar, as they 'talk of many things' with Thomas Pigeon, the landlord.

It is clear from the first that Dawson is by far the most foolish and dim-witted of all the countrypeople who appear in the play. He has been reduced to a state of near idiocy by his nagging, domineering wife, Caecilia. He is the original hen-pecked husband. His only means of retaining his sanity is to escape from her as often as possible: his refuge is the village 'pub', where he drowns his sorrows in pint after pint of Pigeon's ale. It is largely his fear of his wife which drives Dawson to believe that the students really do possess magic powers which can turn him invisible, and cure Caecilia's barrenness. He will try anything, but anything, to gain a moment's peace from Caecilia's prating tongue:

"Oh, adest uxor! Obsecro, me illico reddatis invisibilem."[8]

We can feel absolutely no sympathy for him. Cullie is right when he says of him,

"Non est eius tam miseranda quam ridenda stultitia"[9]

and later,

"Dignus est haberi ludibrio, quum sit adeo fatuus."[10]

Cullie is altogether one of the shrewder inhabitants of
Hinksey. He knows what students are, how they behave. We get the
impression that he has seen it all before - and enjoyed it! He
speaks of "omnis hilaritas, quae placebat antiquitus."[11] Because
he is thus forewarned, Cullie is very wary of the students - he is,
in fact, the only character whom Doulerus, Nichades and Philopinus
never really succeed in getting the better of. Time and again the
students enquire after his wife, but Cullie realizing the danger in
introducing her to them, replies,

"non videbitur a Marti vel Arti deditis."[12]

The scholars are impressed, and possibly even a little taken
aback, by the blacksmith's apparent knowledge of classical mythology.
Here is a man who can meet them on their own ground.

"Sed unde tantum rusticis?"[13]

they ask, surprised. Quick as a flash back comes the answer,

"   Qui fieret aliter?
Literatus urbis vestrae nos afflat odor."[14]

Cullie is also extremely sceptical about the so-called magic
powers which the students say they possess,

"   loquantur magica, et describant circulos.
Forsitan quidem diabolus latet crumenis, quum careant cruce."[15]

Later, Doulerus tries to persuade Cullie to lend him his clothes, so that he can dress himself up as Cullie and put his wife's chastity to the test, but Cullie 'ain't bitin'',

"Nequaquam, sic lubens et libens
Fabricarem mihi cornua."[16]

Finally, when the students see they are fighting a losing battle, they ask Cullie to join them, since they cannot beat him, and so at the point in the action where Nichades deceives Dawson into thinking that he has made him invisible, Cullie gives the scholars his full support and enters wholeheartedly into the spirit of the thing:

DAWSON: Nonne me vides, faber?
CULLIE: Ubi es? Vocem quidem audio. O artis prodigium!
         Iam posset uxores corrumpere, suffurari et admittere
         Quodvis facinus impune."[17]

In the author's portrayal of Pigeon there is more than just a touch of social satire. Pigeon is, no doubt, meant to represent the kind of dishonest retailer, against whom the University was always appealing to the Crown for protection.[18] The students imply that he charges high prices for his liquor, sells sub-standard food, is in the habit of giving his customers half-measure, and is running a bawdy-house on the side! Strangely enough, though, there are no complaints from his regular customers, - a fact obviously intended to suggest that it is only students whom Pigeon attempts to swindle. In the eyes, therefore, of Doulerus, Nichades and Philopinus, the trick which they play on him is a form of poetic justice: like being repaid by like.

Pigeon, however, is not as gullible as the students would like us to think. In one of his rare asides, Pigeon remarks,

"Habent et suam stultitiam academici."[19]

He appears to know what is going on in the minds of Doulerus and his friends, their motives and intentions. That is why we are surprised - and, perhaps, a little disappointed, too, - when Pigeon allows himself to be made a fool of in such a ridiculous manner. We had expected more of him. The fact is, of course, that Pigeon, like so many countrypeople, is, by nature, very superstitious: the students realize this, and play upon it, until Nichades' boast that he can call up the devil, finally breaks down all Pigeon's defences, and his curiosity overcomes him. Up until then he displays a fine contempt for the students' smooth, pretentious talk; having been young himself, once, he is particularly quick to warn Joanna against taking Doulerus' ardent professions of love too seriously, saying to her,

"Filia, non nosti adolescentium mores, arrident et derident simul."[20]

Mention of Joanna brings us to the female characters in the play. All these, of course, would have been played by men, and, no doubt, it must have caused the students in the audience great amusement to see their contemporaries capering around the stage in skirts and flounces. Indeed, we still laugh at pantomime dames and female impersonators today. Mercurius Rusticans, with its preponderance of rustic female characters, would certainly have given the opponents of University drama several grounds for complaint, since one of the chief objections raised to academic plays was that they encouraged men to dress up as women, and for a man to put on a woman's clothes, - especially the clothes of a 'low' woman - was looked upon as the height of sinfulness.[21]

All the female characters in Mercurius Rusticans are essentially comic. Anna, Pigeon's wife, is the perfect example of the scheming mother. She sees in Doulerus just the man for her daughter, and is determined to throw the pair of them together at any price. She dangles all kinds of carrots in front of Doulerus' nose, saying that when her daughter marries, she will receive as her dowry one hundred pounds and a precious family heirloom - a solid gold punchbowl - to boot![22] It is not often that such an eligible young man as Doulerus appears in Hinksey, so naturally Anna must make the best of the opportunity when it arises. Besides giving Doulerus plenty of encouragement, Anna also has some words of wisdom to offer her daughter. Each time that she and Joanna are alone on stage, she asks for a progress report on how the affair is going, and makes suggestions as to how to trap Doulerus well and truly. She hints that Joanna should 'play hard to get', but, at the same time, not _that_ hard to get,

> "   lasciva protervia
> Negando affirmes, quod mox affirmando neges:"[23]

Anna is obviously an expert on handling the opposite sex.

Joanna, herself, is a typical, strapping country wench: she runs races with the other village girls, plays at tennis,[24] and - one gets the impression - is not averse to the occasional romp in the nearest hay-stack with one of the village lads, but soon 'fetches him a clip round the ear', if he steps out of line. She tells Doulerus,

"Si quis colonus posthac me tentabit osculari,
Impingam ei colaphum et me reservabo tibi."[25]

She is possessed of all the accomplishments which it was thought necessary for a young lady to possess in the seventeenth century: that is, she can both sing and dance. She is, however, modest about her talents - "non possum bene", she confides, when asked to give a solo, and we feel there may be some truth in what she says, as she adds,

"   et tamen die Dominico
Omnes me respiciunt cantantem."[26]

Joanna quickly succumbs to Doulerus' pseudo-wooing, and within the space of some fifty or so lines, has drifted into a betrothal with him.[27] Whereas Anna regards Doulerus as a means of getting Joanna off her hands, Joanna sees in him a passport to the big world outside: if she were to marry Doulerus, she could escape from her rustic back-water, and live the life of a lady in high society. As soon as Doulerus has told Joanna (with no intention of fulfilling his words, of course) that he would like her to be his wife, she immediately begins to get ideas above her station. She talks of dressing in silken gowns, and wearing myriads of jewels.[28] Evidently, no one has ever told her that the academic is the lowest paid of the higher professions, and that scholars, like Doulerus, are dedicated, rather than worldly! She imparts her hopes and dreams for the future to the serving-maid, Susanna,

"   Parum aestimo,
Quid fiat de patre, matre, vobisque omnibus, si contingat maritus,
Tum enim quadriiugo curru per plateas ferar,
Tum epulabor ad mediam noctem, ut dominae solent,
Tum famuli crinibus tortis, et vestibus nitidissimis
Domum reducent a spectaculis, ut dominae solent.
Tum non obliviscar Susannae, sed eris mihi pedisequa
Et te ducet uxorem ditissimus cliens."[29]

Joanna, however, is soon brought low by the shameful trick which Doulerus plays on her, but even this does not dampen her spirits for very long, for as she remarks drily,

"Et dominae et reginae non possunt non pedere."[30]

In the character of Susanna we have Cullie's female counterpart. Like Cullie, Susanna is shrewd and sharp-witted; she knows precisely what the students are thinking. She warns Joanna that Doulerus is probably only 'pulling her leg', by saying he wants to marry her - "solent enim fallere."[31] But Joanna, of course, is too blind to see this. Susanna is also quick to catch the students out in their trickery, when, one by one, they come to her and ask her to admit them to her bed-chamber that same night.[32] She agrees to do so, although she has no real intention of carrying out her promise, since she knows full well that Doulerus, Philopinus and Nichades have no intention of carrying out theirs. Next morning she tells them,

" locuta sum tantum ioco."[33]

Not for nothing was this shrewd serving-wench christened Susanna, after the chaste and virtuous lady whose story is told in the Apocrypha!

Last, but by no means least, there is Dawson's scolding, ill-tempered wife, Caecilia. Here we have a sort of feminine Punch, who seldom ever appears without she is waving a big stick, and screaming in her own fashion, 'That's the way to do it! That's the way to do it! That's the way to treat a husband who stays out drinking till all hours of the day and night.' Caecilia is the classic example of a husband-beater. With the torrents of abuse she rains down upon Dawson's head,- "Barde, blennue, ebrie,"[34] with her sudden and unexpected entrances, and her graphic descriptions of her husband's apparent inability to provide her with children, Caecilia is certainly one of the most amusing, - if not the most amusing - of all the rustic characters in the play. Caecilia does not have a major rôle, it is true, but one feels that if the part were well acted, the student playing Caecilia might well steal the show, as did Robert Helpmann in his portrayal of Dr. Pinch in the London Old Vic's production of <u>The Comedy of Errors</u> (1957).

We have seen how much of the humour in the play is derived from the distinctive personalities and psychological traits of the different characters, but what of the humour which arises out of the comic situations in which these characters find themselves? In a sense, of course, each practical joke which Doulerus, Nichades and Philopinus play, precipitates in its turn, a comic situation, and provides an opportunity for some real knockabout humour. Much of the comedy here is visual, and so one has to imagine the dramatic possibilities of the situation as presented on the stage. Take, for example, the scene[35] in which Joanna re-enters after Doulerus has given her the so-called love-potion, which Doulerus and his companions know, which we know, but which Joanna does not know - contains a powerful laxative. She comes on to the stage all unsuspecting, and starts billing and cooing with Doulerus, but suddenly the 'potion' begins to take effect. The forces of nature prove too much for Joanna, but at the same time she does not want to be torn from Doulerus' side, especially when they are getting on so well. She is obliged to leave the stage, however, for, as everyone

knows, 'when you've gotta go, you've gotta go!' ? The actor playing
Joanna would probably show this acute frustration by a series of
agonised facial expressions. So Joanna makes a hasty exit. We can
imagine Doulerus meanwhile pacing up and down, chuckling to himself.
A few minutes later, Joanna returns and resumes the conversation
where she left off. But no sooner has she uttered two lines, than the
medicine starts working again; Joanna has to depart once more, and
the whole process is repeated. To heighten the humour of the situation,
Doulerus (although he knows the answer only too well) keeps asking
Joanna the reason for her sudden, inexplicable exits, and Joanna in
her girlish modesty is unable to tell him!

Further situation comedy is provided in the fourth scene of
Act IV, where Nichades and company pretend to turn Dawson invisible.
The whole scene is one of high-spirited nonsense. Dawson is made to look
and act like a complete fool: the students sit him on a chair, tell him
to hold his left shoe in his right hand, and insist that he wears a
ring, which - they allege - has magical properties, on the end of his
nose, so that he closely resembles Edward Lear's 'Piggy-wig', and
place a hunting-net over his head. Nichades utters the magic words, and
then informs Dawson that he is beginning slowly to disappear. The
farmer, now convinced that no one can see him, starts moving the
furniture around as proof positive that he is still in the room, while
Philopinus and the others, with a nod and a wink, marvel at chairs that

take to the air. The fun is just at its height, when suddenly the door opens, and in storms Caecilia, screaming at her husband to come home at once. With the forthrightness of the little boy in the fairy story of The Emperor's New Clothes, she cries to Dawson,

> Abi domum! Nihil nisi te ludificant."[36]

And the illusion is shattered.

Another very amusing sequence in the play is that in which Nichades pretends to conjure up the devil, and succeeds in giving Pigeon a very nasty fright.[37] The entire scene burlesques the practice of witchcraft, and again much of the humour is visual. Nichades prances round the stage, like a male version of Madame Arcati (but without the bicycle), drawing circles, waving wands and uttering rules from William Lily's Latin Grammar, mingled with a few abracadabras. All he eventually manages to summon forth, however, is his accomplice and friend dressed as the devil, and uproarious laughter from the audience. Nichades has, of course, told the spectators in a previous scene exactly what he intends to do, and so we are prepared for some riotous comedy. Pigeon, nevertheless, is fooled by the whole charade, and this makes us laugh all the louder to think that anyone could be deceived by such blatant trickery.

However, perhaps one of the greatest sources of fun in Mercurius Rusticans is the play's verbal humour. Much of this appears quite spontaneous, but it must be borne in mind that the author, being a student, would have undergone - in his University career - a strict training in rhetoric, in the ways and means of using words to emphasize and persuade, and to exhibit verbal eloquence and wit. He would have been familiar with thousands of figures of speech, devices of style and processes of thought. The great facility with which he writes springs, therefore, from his rigorous schooling in the art of speech.

The author uses several different verbal devices to shake laughter out of his audience. First of all, there is the pun. When Doulerus throws his cap in the air, Philopinus remarks, "Pileum tu pilam facis";[38] when Cullie tells Philopinus that he is a "faber ferrarius" by trade, the latter exclaims, "De Ferrara? Italus es";[39] and when Pigeon bewails the fact that he has lost a considerable amount of money, "perdidi plus quam duos bonos angelos"(coins), Philopinus reassures him with these words, "Interea vidisti plus quam tres malos angelos"[40] (spirits). These are just a handful of the countless puns which occur throughout the play. Occasionally, the author will employ the two meanings of a word at the same time, often a word is repeated with a second meaning, and sometimes a word may have the meaning of a word of similar sound imposed upon it. Today, we tend rather to frown on the pun as a comic device, and consider it to be the lowest form of wit. Kellett[41] has shown, however, that the pun was used very successfully by such writers as Isaiah and St. Paul, and by the Greek dramatists while the greatest punster of all time was, of course, the immortal bard, himself. If puns were good enough for Shakespeare, then they are quite good enough for the author of Mercurius Rusticans. In the eyes of sixteenth and seventeenth-century audiences, the pun would have appeared as an example of intellectual brilliance and verbal dexterity, and when we read Pigeon's 'tour de force' at the close of the first scene of Act II, we are inclined to agree,

"Est enim mea occupatio, cuppatio: meum servitium, cervisia.
Mea oratio, oris ratio. Doctores sunt mihi coctores
Nec paginas lego, sed patinas lingo et denique
Totum vivere nihil aliud est quam bibere."

The proverb, too, is employed with comic intention. Anna warns her daughter about the ways of young men by telling her, "Fugientem sequitur iuvenis, sequentem fugit";[42] Doulerus, after he has heard the musician sing and play in Act IV, Sc.I, states that it is obvious how badly the fellow performs, because "ex ungue leonem"; and it is also Doulerus who remarks with mock-solemnity, when Susanna has seemingly deceived all three of the students with her feminine wiles, "Apis mel ore, aculum cauda gerit;".[43] The proverbs are not always amusing in themselves: they are, for the most part, scraps of philosophy, containing an element of truth, but it is the situations in which the proverbs are applied, and the characters who utter them, which give them such comic force. The proverbs used in Mercurius Rusticans are particularly interesting because they are a curious blend of Roman and English: some can certainly be traced to the works of classical writers, whilst others occur only in English literature, and so have had to be rendered into Latin by the author. For instance, the well-known saying 'The devil dances in my pocket', which appears in various forms in the works of many sixteenth and seventeenth-century writers, such as Skelton, Greene and Massinger, is what Cullie is alluding to, when he says of the students, "Forsitan quidem diabol s latet crumenis, quum careant cruce."[44] This notion of the devil dancing in one's pocket was, of course, an entirely English concept. The proverb meant, in effect, "I have no money", since during the sixteenth century pennies were engraved with a cross,[45] and crosses were thought to drive away the devil: if one had no money in one's pocket, one had no cross, and so the devil could creep in.

Parody, however, is undoubtedly the comic device which the author uses most frequently, and to the best advantage. Doulerus, for example, indulges in the very commonplace pastime of 'chatting up a bird', by taking up the stance of a tragic actor, and quoting passages from the great Roman epic poet, Vergil.[46] The spectators, of course, would be expected to recognize the quotations immediately, much as the audience

at a Whitehall farce would (one hopes) notice if one of the
characters suddenly began talking in Shakespearian, or Miltonic,
strains. The incongruity would be immediately noticeable and
laughable. In the dialogue between Doulerus and Joanna, however, the
humour is heightened even more by the fact that Joanna - not
surprisingly - has absolutely no idea what Doulerus is saying!
Similarly, Dawson, when describing the row which he has just had with
his wife, launches into something which sounds suspiciously like a
mixture of phrases pilfered from Juvenal's *Sixth Satire*.[47] But Dawson,
being one of the 'low' characters, would not, of course, be allowed to
get his quotations word perfect. Anna, too, is a mistress of mis-quotation
with a gay abandon that would make Horace turn in his grave, she declares,
"amor aequali pede / Turres et tebernas pulsat".[48] Even Nichades, who
ought to know better, announces, "Et diabolus intererit, si nodus dignus
vindice"[49]; and Doulerus, when asked what he would like for supper,
recites, parrot-fashion, the list of delicacies upon which - Suetonius
tells us -[50] the Emperor Vitellius once dined.[51]

Add to this mixture of puns, proverbs and parody, just a pinch of
sexual innuendo, a few lavatory jokes, and a liberal seasoning of
assonance and alliteration, and there are the ingredients for some
extremely witty and amusing dialogue. The results can be seen
particularly clearly in Nichades and Philopinus' conversation with
Doulerus (Act I, Sc.2); in Doulerus' dialogue with Joanna (Act II, Sc.3);

and in Doulerus' interlude with Susanna (Act III, Sc.5). It is as well that the dialogue in Mercurius Rusticans is so racy, colloquial, and yet, at the same time, interspersed with elegant literary mannerisms, for many of the scenes contain little real dramatic action, and so the lively exchange of wit between the characters prevents the interest of either the audience or the reader from flagging.

Mercurius Rusticans, therefore, is pure farce from start to finish: it is a mélange of comic characters, ridiculous situations and humourous language. What a welcome change this play must have been from the dull routine of college life! What a great favourite this play must have been with the students - both those who took part in it, and those who only sat and watched - in our modern phraseology, a 'smash hit'! And what a ready target this play must have provided for the opponents of the University stage, for there is very little in it which can be called truly edifying! Mercurius Rusticans is, in short, a superb example of seventeenth-century Oxford students 'doing their own thing'!

[1] See above, section II.

[2] I, i, 1-20.

[3] IV, v, 300-4 and 308.

[4] III, iv, 173f..

[5] V, ii, 72f..

[6] II, i, 49.

[7] III, iv, 154-5.

[8] III, iv, 166.

[9] II, i, 3.

[10] IV, iv, 202.

[11] I, iii, 114.

[12] II, ii, 78.

[13] II, ii, 80.

[14] II, ii, 80-1.

[15] III, iii, 127-8.

[16] III, iv, 204-5.

[17] IV, iv, 250-3.

[18] See also Commentary, p. 439.

[19] III, vii, 331.

[20] III, iii, III.

[21] See Boas, pp.228-9.

[22] II, iii, 120-1.

[23] II, iv, 203-4.

[24] IV, iii, 173-4.

[25] IV, iii, 179-80.

[26] II, iii, 151-2.

[27] II, iii, 167f..

[28] II, iii, 191.

[29] II, iv, 220-7.

[30] IV, v, 285.

[31] II, iv, 217.

[32] III, v, 241f..

[33] IV, i, 16.

[34] I, iv, 135.

[35] IV, iii.

[36] IV, iv, 275.

[37] V, iif..

[38] I, ii, 81.

[39] II, ii, 67.

[40] V, iv, 201.

[41] <u>Fashion in Literature: A Study of Changing Tastes</u>, (London, 1931).

[42] II, iv, 205.

[43] III, vi, 269.

[44] III, iii, 128.

[45] See also Commentary, p. 355.

[46] II, iii, 126f..

[47] II, i, 8-10.

[48] III, iii, 116-17.

[49] III, v, 215.

[50] See Commentary, p. 356.

[51] III, ii, 90-1.

V. SONGS IN MERCURIUS RUSTICANS.

"It is the best of all trades, to make songs, and the
second best to sing them."

HILAIRE BELLOC

Songs play an important part in Mercurius Rusticans, and for this reason an entire section of the Introduction has been devoted to them. There are seven songs in all, plus a few ale-house catches. Some of these songs occur near the beginning of the play, some at the end, while others break in at various points throughout the action with a delightful freshness and spontaneity. The themes of the individual songs are wide and varied: there are drinking-songs, love-songs, hunting-songs, songs about food, songs about the weather, and even songs about natural phenomena.

Almost every character in the play has his, or her, own song, and these are so designed as to fit perfectly the mood of the singer or the situation. They underline, as it were, the feelings of the character on any given occasion. What, for example, could be a better way of conjuring up the true atmosphere of a seventeenth-century English country 'pub', than the roistering catches "Alii sectantur forum"[1], and "Canis, vetus canis antro dum iacet suo",[2] sung by Cullie, Pigeon and Dawson, in the early part of the play? What could be a more suitable means of expressing a young girl's desire to marry, than Joanna's rendering of the tender and wistful "Caelibi Diana lare"?[3]

What could be a more effective mode of conveying to the audience the excitement of the hunt, than Doulerus, Nichades and Philopinus' enthusiastic performance of "Lustrate lata Botliae prata"[4] - in which one can almost hear the hare scampering across the fields, and the steady rhythm of the hound's paws beating on the ground, as it gives chase? And what could be a happier way of ending the play, than with a song which recounts - almost with a hint of nostalgia for something lost that can never be recaptured - the adventures of the three fun-loving students in Hinksey, and which begins "Scholares hic fuere,"?[5]

Sometimes, of course, the songs have a precise rôle to fulfil within the action of the play. In Act III, Sc.6, for example, Doulerus and Nichades entertain the audience with a song entitled "Iam fremit Boreas", while Philopinus goes off to prepare the 'medicine' for Caecilia. Here, the song is being used as a stop-gap, so to speak: the plot of the play, itself, cannot be furthered at this particular stage until Philopinus has returned with his concoction, and thus the song provides a necessary, but nevertheless, enjoyable, musical interlude. Similarly, in the first scene of the fourth act, the songs and music which the lute-player offers Doulerus, Nichades and Philopinus as entertainment, gives them an opportunity to sharpen their wits against his, and to make him and his vocal talents the butt for their jokes.

Just as the songs, themselves, differ in theme and purpose, so the tunes to which they are directed to be sung are quite distinct from one another. The stage-directions in Mercurius Rusticans indicate that the majority of the songs in the play can, in fact, be sung to the tune of certain well-known ballads and airs. This, in itself, must have added greatly to the charm and fascination of the songs, for, although the words were new, all the tunes were very popular in the late sixteenth and early seventeenth centuries, and so would have been instantly recognizable to the audience. Even today we prick up our ears if we hear a song which we know well, being sung in a foreign language: strange new words seem to give an old and familiar tune fresh vitality, and we listen all the more appreciatively.

Indeed, Mr. Sellar,[6] in his comments on the play, claims that the songs are "other mens'". However, it is not clear what exactly is meant by this statement. Sellar may merely be endorsing what is already quite obvious, that the author of Mercurius Rusticans did not write the tunes for the songs, but re-wrote in Latin popular songs to be sung to the original tune. On the other hand, he may be implying that someone other than the author wrote the words - an interesting theory, but one which, unfortunately, there is no means of either proving or disproving.

The musical accompaniment to the songs and dances in the play would, no doubt, have been supplied by the 'fidicen', and also by the musician who appears at the end of Act III, and plays a dance tune on his pipe and tabor. The soft, sweet music of the lute, for instance, would have exquisitely matched the sentiments expressed in Joanna's love-song in Act II, Sc.3, while the louder, more rhythmic sound of the pipe and drum would have been exactly suited to the dancing and capering of the three 'satyri' in the fourth scene of the last act.

There can be no denying that the songs and music in <u>Mercurius Rusticans</u> contribute very largely to the success of the play as a piece of theatrical entertainment. They greatly increase its general light-heartedness, and in so far as they serve to emphasise the emotions of the various characters, they have a certain choric quality, too. But most important of all they provide melody and verse in an era that was pre-eminently one of music, song and poetry, thus following the taste of the age, and appealing to the 'children of the times'.

Here are some notes on the words and music of the more interesting songs, in the order in which they occur in the text.

II. iii, 153 <u>Caelibi Diana lare</u>

<u>Diana</u>, of course, was the Roman goddess of virginity and hunting.

It is constructive to compare the thoughts expressed in the first four lines of the second stanza of this song with ll.26-9 of the Latin poet, Nemesianus'[7] fourth eclogue:

"cerva marem sequitur, taurum formosa iuvenca,
et Venerem sensere lupae, sensere leaenae
et genus aerium volucres et squamea turba
et montes silvaeque, suos habet arbor amores."

(In my quotations from classical authors, I use the standard Loeb edition, unless otherwise stated).

The stage directions state that this song is to be sung to the tune of Dulcina. This was a very popular ballad in the seventeenth century. The earliest mention of it can be found in the registers of the stationer's company, where its transfer from one printer to another is recorded as having taken place on May 22nd., 1615. The ballad is also alluded to in Izaak Walton's The Compleat Angler (1653), where the Milk-woman asks, "What song was it, I pray? Was it 'Come Shepherds, deck your heads', or 'As at noon Dulcina rested'?"[8]

The words and music of Dulcina are printed in Chappell's O.E.P.M., I, 160f.. The first verse runs as follows,

"As att noone Dulcina rested, in a sweete and shadie bower,
Came a shepard and requested in her lap to sleepe an hour.
But from her looke, a wound he tooke, soe deepe that for a
farther boone
The Nimphe hee pray'd, whereto she say'd, forgoe mee nowe,
come to mee soone."

III. i, 4 <u>Lustrate lata Botliae prata</u>

    For place names see Commentary, pp. 324-7.

There is also a hunting-song in another Latin academic play, the comedy, <u>Silvanus</u>, (1596/7).[9] In the opening scene, Silvanus, the hero, is about to set off on a hunting expedition, and asks his friends to join him, as he sings a hymn to Diana, patron goddess of the chase,

> "Cantemus omnes Cynthia,
>   (Hei, ho, Cynthia)
> Venationis domina,
>   (Sic incipit melodia).
> Quae habitas in saltibus,
>   (Hei, ho, Delia)
> Ornata nostris laudibus,
> Adsis nobis bellula."

According to a note written in the margin of the MS., the words of "Lustrate lata Botliae prata" can be sung to the tune of <u>Whoop, doe me noe harme</u>. This apparently was a well-known ditty round about the end of the sixteenth, beginning of the seventeenth, century. We find mention of it in Shakespeare's <u>The Winter's Tale</u>, (IV,iv, 198), and in Ford's <u>The Fancies Chaste and Noble</u> (III, iii), where Secco,

addressing it to Morosa, sings, "Whoop! do me no harm, good woman."
There is also a ballad in The Famous History of Friar Bacon and
Friar Bungay[10] to be sung to the tune of O do me no harme, good man.

The melody was still popular towards the close of the
seventeenth century, for in the second part of Westminster Drollery
(1672) there is a ballad, entitled Of Johnny and Jinny, which, it
seems, was intended for this tune. It begins like this,

"The sweet pretty Jinny sate on a hill,
　Where Johnny the swain her see,
　He tun'd his quill, and sung to her still,
　Whoop, Jinny, come down to me."

The tune of Whoop, do me no harm, good man is printed in
Chappell's O.E.P.M., I, 96.

III. vi, 279 Iam fremit Boreas
　Boreas is another name for the north wind.

The sentiments voiced in this song - namely, the idea that one
can derive great pleasure and satisfaction from watching the elements
rage outside, if one is safe and sound indoors, and secure in the
knowledge that no harm can come to you - are very similar to those
which can be found in Tibullus, I, I, 45-8,

"quam iuvat immites ventos audire cubantem
　　et dominam tenero continuisse sinu
　aut, gelidas hibernus aquas cum fuderit Auster,
　　securum somnos imbre iuvante sequi!"

and Vergil, Eclogues, VII, 49-52,

"Hic focus et taedae pingues, hic plurimus ignis
　semper et adsidua postes fuligine nigri:
　hic tantum Boreae curamus frigora, quantum
　aut numerum lupus aut torrentia flumina ripas."

The stage-directions suggest that this song should be sung to the tune of *Virginea*. Unfortunately, I am unable to find any reference to a song or tune of this name in any of the standard works on sixteenth or seventeenth-century music. There were, however, it appears, a great many songs, popular about this time, which had the word 'virgin' in the title. These include: Mad Moll, or The Virgin Queen, or Yellow Stockings (O.E.P.M., II, 74); The Kind Virgin's Complaint (Roxburghe Ballads, VI, 253); The Virgins' Happiness (Douce, II, 237); The Virgin's Constancy (Pepys Collection of Ballads, IV, 55). The title *Virginea* could refer to any one of these.

III. vi, 31 <u>Labebitis armum ovis</u>

The author may here be giving a Latin treatment to a song of local origin. The countryfolk of Berkshire seem to have had a particular preoccupation with food: Hearne,[II] for instance, records how, on a Shrove Tuesday, the children of Sunningwell (a village not far from Hinksey), used to go round the neighbourhood at dusk, singing, "Beef and Bacon's out of season / I want a Pan to parch my Peas on." He explains that these words were repeated several times, and that stones were then thrown at the front doors of all the houses, "which makes people generally shut their doors that evening!"

IV. i, 49 <u>Non hino diebus undecim</u>

<u>Lutetia</u> is the Latin name for Paris.

<u>Et peperit murem denuo / Parturientes decennio</u>: cf. Horace, <u>Ars Poetica</u>, 139,

"Parturient montes, nascetur ridiculus mus."

This was a well-known proverb in classical times. Athenaeus (XIV, 6, 616d), tells of how Tachos, the king of Egypt, derided Agesilaus, who was of small build, by quoting ὤδινεν ὄρος, Ζεὺς δ' ἐφοβεῖτο, τὸ δ' ἔτεκεν μῦν ("The mountain was in labour, and Zeus was frightened, but it brought forth a mouse.")

It seems just possible that this song may indeed contain some allusion to a topical event. There is mention of a definite place - Paris, of a definite person - a "princeps", and of definite lengths of time - "undecim diebus", "decennio" and "quinque ferias". Furthermore, Doulerus remarks, after hearing the song, "Credidit hoc maxime placere nobis Oxoniensibus",[12] as though it ought to have great interest, or relevance, for Oxford students.

All these points seem to indicate that the song is something more than just a nonsensical rhyme. Could it, in fact, be a reference to a recent visit made by the then President of Corpus Christi College to the University of Paris? This is difficult to prove, however, without being able to establish the exact date when the play was written.[13] Also, the word normally used to translate "President" in Latin, and that used in all the statute books, and other documents relating to the college, is "praeses", <u>not</u> "princeps". "Praesidem" (accusative case of "praeses") would have fitted the line of the song just as well as "principem", for it has the same number of syllables and the same ending: "princeps" is not, therefore, being employed as a substitute for "praeses". It is unlikely, too, that the verse is alluding to the President of the college, since the lines are not particularly complimentary. The words "Et peperit murem denuo /Parturientes decennio" imply that the person, about whom the song is written, promised to do great things, but, in fact, accomplished little, or nothing.

Who, then, is the "princeps" referred to? There is a slight chance, if we assume the date of the play's composition to be post-1603 (i.e. after the accession of James I to the throne), that it is a "prince", namely, Charles, who became hair-apparent in 1616. Could this song, therefore, be an allusion to the expedition made by Charles and the Duke of Buckingham to Spain in 1623 to seek the hand of the Infanta Maria?[14] The prince and Buckingham spent some time at Paris en route, and achieved very little whilst in Spain.[15] This means, however, that the play would have to have been written after 1623, and this seems rather late.

"Non hinc diebus undecim" is directed to be sung to the tune of Bonny Nell. This is believed to have been a very popular ballad in the sixteenth and seventeenth centuries. However, the music entitled Bonny Nell which is preserved in the 1670 edition of Apollo's Banquet for the Treble Violin, is probably quite different from the original ballad tune, since this is expressly a piece of dance music. Also, Dr. Corbet, later Bishop of Norwich, composed some words to the tune of Bonny Nell, which could not successfully be sung to this melody. The verses are printed in Nicholls' Progresses of King James, (III, 66).

The ballad, itself, as well as the original tune, is, unfortunately, now lost. It is, however, referred to in The Anatomie of the English Nunnery at Lisbon, published "by authoritie in 1622". The nuns of that convent obviously had a particular affection for the song.

English writers of the period also mention the ballad. Massinger speaks of some "Bonny Nell", in his Old Law (IV, i), where the Cook says, "That Nell was Helen of Greece too"; and Gnotho answers, "As long as she tarried with her husband, she was Ellen; but after she came to Troy, she was Nell of Troy, or Bonny Nell, whether you will or no."

In the Pepys Collection (III, 124), there is a song "to an excellent new tune, or to be sung to Bonny Nell," which commences,

"As I went forth one summer's day,
To view the meadows fresh and gay, " &c.

The dance tune music of Bonny Nell can be found in Chappell's O.E.P.M., II, 23.

IV. i, 58 Vapores Phaebus bibit

Phaebus was a poetical name for the sun in Roman literature.

Vapores luna sorbet: An allusion to the moisture of the moon. It was commonly believed in the sixteenth and seventeenth centuries that the moon - probably because it controls the tides - was a watery planet. There are several references to this notion in the plays of Shakespeare. In <u>Hamlet</u> (I, i, 118-20), Horatio describes how

> "   the moist star
> Upon whose influence Neptune's empire stands
> Was sick almost to doomsday with eclipse;"

Similarly, Titania, in <u>A Midsummer Night's Dream</u> (II, i, 103-5), says,

> "Therefore the moon, the governess of floods,
> Pale in her anger, washes all the air,
> That rheumatic diseases do abound."

This belief is also referred to in the works of other, much earlier writers. Newton,[16] for example, in his <u>Direction for the Health of Magistrates and Studentes</u> (1574), tells us that "the moone is ladye of moisture"; while Bartholomaeus,[17] in <u>De Proprietate Rerum</u>, speaks of the moon as being "mother of all humours, minister and ladye of the sea."

<u>Aqua, a qua sunt cuncta, /Orbem connectit totum</u>: cf. Apuleius, <u>De Platone</u>, I, viii,

> "mundumque omnem ex omni aqua totoque igni et aëris universitate cunctaque terra esse factum"

(For Apuleius, see Teubner edition).

According to the stage-directions, this song may be sung to the tune of *The Bedlam* (sometimes called *Tom a Bedlam*). This was an extremely popular ballad during the 1600s, and later. The words are as follows:

"From the hagg and hungrie Goblin, that into raggs would rend yee:
And the Spirit that stands by the naked man in the booke of
                                                    moones defend yee.
That of your five sound senses, you never be forsaken:
Nor wander from your selves with Tom abroad to beg your bacon.
While I doe sing any foode any feeding, feedinge, drinke or
                                                    clothing:
Come dame or maid, be not afraid poore Tom will injure nothing.

Of thirty bare years have I twice twenty bin enraged,
And of forty bin three times fifteene in durance soundlie
                                                    caged:
On the lordlie lofts of Bedlam, with stubble softe and dainty,
Brave braceletts strong, sweet whips ding dong, and wholesome
                                                    hunger plenty.
And now I sing any foode, any feedinge, feedinge, drink or
                                                    clothing:
Come dame or maid, be not afraid, poore Tom will injure nothing."

Countless different versions of the ballad exist, but most of them are written in the same measure. In the <u>Roxburghe Collection</u>, (I, 42), for instance, can be found a song about the tricks and disguises of beggars, entitled <u>The Cunning Northern Begger</u>, and directed to be sung to the tune of <u>Tom a Bedlam</u>. Similarly, in <u>Wit and Drollery</u>, (1656, p.126), and <u>Pills to purge Melancholy</u> (1700 and 1707, II, p.192), two more versions of <u>Tom of Bedlam</u> are printed. Also, in <u>Pills to purge Melancholy</u> (1707, III, p.13), there appears an amusing song "on Dr. G[ill?], formerly master of St. Paul's School", which is exactly fitted to this particular tune, and which begins thus,

"In Paul's Churchyard in London,
There dwells a noble firker,[18]
    Take heed, you that pass,
    Lest you taste of his lash,
For I have found him a jerker:

Still doth he cry, take him up, take him up, sir,
    Untruss with expedition;
O the birchen tool
Which he winds in the school
    Frights worse than the Inquisition."

Even as late as 1731, in <u>Loyal Songs written against the Rump Parliament</u>, (II, 272), there is a ballad set to this very tune, and there are two more among the King's Pamphlets in the British Museum.

Other versions of <u>Tom of Bedlam</u> include <u>Loving Mad Tom</u> (<u>Wit and Drollery</u>, 1682, p.184); "Tobacco's a musician and in a pipe delighteth" (Nicholls' <u>Progresses</u>, or Rimbault's <u>Little Book of Songs and Ballads</u>, p.173) and "All in the land of Essex" (Sir John Denman's <u>Poems</u>, 1671).

The song of <u>Tom of Bedlam</u> is also referred to in Jonson's <u>The Devil is an Ass</u>, (1616), (V, 2, 35), where Pug, wishing to be considered mad, says, "Your best song's Thom. o' Bet'lem."

The music of <u>Tom of Bedlam</u> is printed in Chappell's <u>O.E.P.M.</u>, I, 175.

(For further information about any of the traditional tunes mentioned above, see Chappell's <u>O.E.P.M.</u>, I and II.).

NOTES

[1] I, iii, 118f.

[2] II, i, 17f.

[3] II, iii, 153-64.

[4] III, i, 4-18.

[5] V, iv, 216-31.

[6] See above, section II.

[7] Nemesianus was a Roman poet, born in Carthage, who wrote in the latter part of the third century A.D.. His works include the Eclogae, Cynegetica and De Aucupio.

[8] The Complete Angler, edited by 'Ephemera', or 'Bell's Life in London' (London, 1853) Third Day, c.4.

[9] See Boas, pp.298-303.

[10] Written by Robert Greene.

[11] Remarks and Collections of Thomas Hearne, edited by C.E.Doble (and others), 11 vols., Oxford Historical Society, 2, 7, 13, 34, 42, 43, 48, 50, 65, 67, 72 (Oxford, 1885-1918), VIII, (Sept.23rd., 1722 - Aug. 9th., 1725), 330.

[12] IV, i, 55.

[13] Assuming that the play was written between 1605 and 1618 (see above, section II), the date of its composition would fall within the presidencies of John Rainolds (1598-1607), John Spenser (1607-1614) and Thomas Anyan (1614-1629): there is, however, no record of any of these men having made an historic, or memorable, visit to the University of Paris.

[14] See *The Cambridge Modern History*, III, 575f.

[15] Although a marriage contract was, in fact, signed between Charles and the Infanta Maria in July, 1623, it proved null and void, for, on Spain's refusal to support the restitution of the elector Palatine, war was urged with Spain.

[16] Thomas Newton (1542? -1607), poet, physician and divine.

[17] A thirteenth-century writer.

[18] A noun derived from the verb 'to firk', meaning 'to lash, whip, beat, trounce, drub.'

VI. VOCABULARY

"For words, like Nature, half reveal
And half conceal the Soul within."

ALFRED, LORD TENNYSON

The vocabulary of <u>Mercurius Rusticans</u>, perhaps more than any other aspect of the play, serves to emphasize its strange, hybrid nature, its combining of the classical and the mediaeval to form an entirely new mode of literary expression. For the most part, the Latin spoken in the play is basically classical: the students, for example, speak in a lucid, at times even poetical,[1] language, peppered with quotations from many famous, Roman authors. The rustics, on the other hand, are made to talk in the colloquialisms and slang of the 'low' characters of Plautine comedy. This two-tier system of language, which continues throughout the play, is extremely effective in stressing the fundamental differences between the two social classes represented, and we are reminded that Shakespeare uses a similar device in several of his comedies.[2]

In the vocabulary of <u>Mercurius Rusticans</u>, however, there are quite a number of departures from pure classical usage. Sometimes, no doubt, the author discovered that no classical Latin word existed for the particular idea, or concept, that he wished to express. On such an occasion many possible courses of action lay open to him: he could use a classical Latin word, but with a different meaning; an exclusively mediaeval term; a coinage, or word of his own invention, or simply an English phrase.

There are numerous examples in the play of classical Latin words being employed with unusual meanings. "Fenestra", for instance, is used for "a lamp", II, 36. "Cervisia" means "ale", I, 84. "Aulicus" = "a courtier", Prologue, 15; "farta" = "mincemeat", I, 3; "pileum" = "a student's cap", I, 81; "fascia" = "a garter", II, (stage-direction at 175); "procurator" = "a proctor", II, 200; "villa"= "a village", III, 97; "herba"= "a herb", III, 316; "typus"="print", IV, 104; "cloaca" = "a privy", IV, 176.

There are mediaeval terms, like "festum Nativitatis", I, 2; "pictae chartae", I, 10; "bombarda", I, (stage-direction at beginning of Sc.2); "archiepiscopus", I, 26; "presbyter", I, 28; "diabola", I, 47; "monarchus" and "fraterculus", I, 76; "anglice", I, 168; "rixatrix" and "baptizo", I, 175; "bursa", II, 20; "compotator", II, 42; "reiuvenesco", II, 116; "sortilegium", II, 120; "dies Dominicus", II, 151; "periscelis", II, 176; "saccharum", II, 188; "ars chymica", II, 192; "ullibi", II, 291; "cacodaemon", II, 294; "lupulus", III, 43; "tobacchus", III, 49; "organizo", III, 188; "embryo", III, 189; "almanacta", III, 230; "panis tostus" and "nux muscata", IV, 12; "aqua rosacea", IV, (stage-direction at end of 136); "mesenterium", IV, 148; "pila palmaria", IV, 174; "antrorsum", IV, 206; "retrorsum", IV,

207; "purgatorium", V, 71; "heptarchia", V, 76; "Iesuita", V, 136; "archidiabolus", V, 189.

Some words have been invented by the author, himself, - either for humorous effect, or because a Latin equivalent, either classical or mediaeval, did not exist for his purpose. These include: "alla"(ale), I, 108; "vas urinarium" (chamber-pot), I, 148; "Actaeonius" (like Actaeon), I, 162; "ignorama" (an ignorant person), I, 167; "Hincksianus" (Hinksonian), I, 187; "cuppatio" (potation), II, 31; "cervisiarius" (of ale) II, 44; "in particulari" (in particular), II, 113; "equina solea" (horseshoe), II, 233; "potifex" (maker of drink, a brewer), III, 44; "nicotianus" (of nicotine), III, 53; "recipe" (recipe), IV, 131; "contratenor" (contratenore), IV, 160; "semiputris" (half-mouldy), V, 140; "fityr" (a type of fairy), V, 165; "Europa" (Europe) and "Polyphemicus" (of Polyphemus), Epilogue, 28; "Chinenses"(Chinese), Epilogue, 29.

Among the English phrases which have found their way into the dialogue of the play, are "tittle tattle" and "hoddy doddy", I, 167; "a wispe, et cucking stoole", I, 168; "penylesse bench", III, 332.

There are also several words of Greek origin, such as "artocreas", I, 3; "stratagema", I, 75; "geometra", I, 82; "gyrus", I, 173; "pera", II, 20; "symbolus", II, 175; "crystallinus", II, 178; "nepenthes", II, 188; "thema", III, 29; "syllaba", III, 35; "zythum", III, 45; "poema", III, 47; "euge" and "poeta", III, 57; "cometa", III, 66;

"cercopithecus", III, 77; "epigramma", III, 92; "nectar" and "ambrosia", III, 93; "ephippium", III, 122; "mysterium", III, 147; "maechus" and "basiliscus", III, 200; "zelotypus" and "apage", III, 201; "bibliotheca", IV, 103; "hypotrimma", IV, (stage-direction at 127); "eclipsis", IV, 171; "colaphus", IV, 180; "mysticus", IV, 234; "character", IV, 235; "hieroglyphicus", IV, 236; "comaedia" and "tragaedia", IV, 279; "phantasticus", V, 23; "planeta", V, 55; "barathrum", V, 91; "zona", V, 129; "mimicus", V, 157; "obolus", V, 218.

Finally, many rare and unusual words occur in the text, which are normally only found in the works of ante-classical or post-classical writers. Examples of these are "helluo", I, 4; "macilentus", I, 28; "phlegmaticus", I, 41; "coronis", I, 56; "auscultator", I, 64; "quadratura", I, 83; "marsupium", I, 88; "suboleo", I, 106; "propino", I, 107; "corculum", I, 134; "bardus" and blennus", I, 135; "bibaculus", I, 141; "potilis", II, 46; "amasia", II, 166; "praestigiator", II, 180; "levipes", III, I; "radicalis", III, 50; "septipes", III, 71; "trituro", III, 168; "matrix", III, 180; "debitum", III, 273; "septimana", III, 320; "punicans", IV, 5; "vilesco", IV, 27; "modulamen", IV, 39; "decennium", IV, 52; "destinor", IV, 167; "efficacia", IV, 236; "numella", IV, 307; "terriculamenta", V, 23; "masculosus", V, 44; "circulator", V, 54; "muccosus", V, 61; "pupus", V, 184; "bibones", V, 204.

NOTES.

[1] e.g. II, vi, 270-276; III, v, 255-261; III, vi, 267-271; IV, ii, 96-113; IV, iii, 114-118; V, v, 234-244.

[2] e.g. *A Midsummer Night's Dream, As you Like It,* and *Twelfth Night.*

VII. SYNTAX

"Why care for grammar as long as we are good?"

ARTEMUS WARD

A close examination of the syntax of <u>Mercurius Rusticans</u> brings to light, not surprisingly, several deviations from true, classical Latin grammar. Whereas the <u>vocabulary</u> which the author uses, is, in the main, classical,[I] his syntax is decidedly that of late, or mediaeval, Latin writers: the canons and laws laid down for the composition of classical Latin are repeatedly broken, or ignored.

The subjunctive mood, for example, is employed very loosely, with little regard for the rules which govern it. Often it is used in the wrong tense: in a final clause, where the main verb of the sentence on which it is dependant, is Primary, we frequently find the imperfect subjunctive being used in the subordinate adverbial clause of purpose: "Iam autem visibilis appareo:/Non ut...praeclaros viros/ Exponerem ordine", Prologue, 10-13; "sed adveniat filia,/ Ne imprudens violaret edictum Claudii/ Et sic in morbum incideret", IV, 163-165. Sometimes, where one would normally expect to find the subjunctive, recourse has been had to the indicative. This is particularly true of indirect questions: "Satis apparet quam pessime canis" IV, 56; "videbis quid Nichades efficiet", IV, 333; "Dic vero qualis apparebit" V, 43; "Revocetur in memoriam quam iniqua postulant" Epilogue, 13.

Again, in conditional sentences, the use of the subjunctive is somewhat erratic. In an unfulfilled condition, referring to past time, where, in classical Latin, the pluperfect subjunctive would be used in both clauses, here we have a curious combination of the imperfect subjunctive and the pluperfect indicative: "Melius esset mihi si trunco aut stipiti nupseram", I, 149; "Quod si res bene successerat, ego in aulas principum/ Me insinuarem, inter heroicos luderem/ Secretiora consilia nullo vidente cognoscerem", IV, 270-272. Similarly, in an unfulfilled condition that refers to present time, the author of *Mercurius Rusticans* substitutes the present subjunctive in the protasis, instead of employing the imperfect subjunctive in both clauses: "Si ad numerum literarum (ut solent) possis bibere,/ Facile provocares, et vinceres omnes Bataviios", II, 64-65. Also, in improbable conditions, there is a rare mixture of the indicative with different tenses of the subjunctive, where generally the present subjunctive would be used in both clauses: "Si nobiscum eas ad Hincksy, reddemus te phlegmaticum", I, 41; "Si ostenderent mihi suam artem, remunerarem amplissime", III, 124. Frequently, the subjunctive is employed where it is, in fact, quite unnecessary. There are several instances of it being used where the appropriate tense of the indicative would suffice, as in what are clearly open conditions, like "si maritus redeat ad caenam, paratum erit electuarium", III, 194; "Rex Gyges habuit annulum cuius palam si converteret/ Versus palmam, ipse spectaret omnia/ Nulli mortalium spectabilis", III, 161-163.

Likewise, after the adverb "quasi", the tense of the subjunctive used is often contrary to that dictated by the rules of classical Latin; where the pluperfect tense would be more natural to the sense, the imperfect is found: "Genialiter temet ipsum habeas, agricola, quasi hoc praesente die/ Oves tonderentur aut grana conderentur horreo", II, 75-76. Occasionally, the subjunctive is not used at all after "quasi", even though a comparison is being made with something unreal: "Ventrem, ventrem inclamat, quasi possessa fuerat a spiritu", IV, 140.

Another instance of the author not employing the subjunctive when it is required, is the use of "utinam" - in classical Latin normally followed by the subjunctive (Optative Subjunctive) to express a wish or a prayer - with the indicative: "O utinam potui furem deprehendere, aut saltem cognoscere", IV, 325.

Very often the subjunctive is employed - quite in accordance with the laws of classical Latin - after verbs <u>asking</u>, <u>ordering</u>, <u>begging</u>, &c., but "ut" and also the pronoun denoting the person who is being addressed, are frequently omitted, so that the indirect command implied, is not always clearly constructed:"quaeso nobiscum eas", I,71;

"Quaeso feras", II, 59; "Quaeso hanc villam transferas/ Procul ab Oxonio", II, 287-288; "Quaeso ludamus cum cacodaemone tuo aliquantulum", II, 294; "Quaeso habeam", IV, 93; "quaeso numeretur pecunia", V, 19.

Indirect statements, introduced by verbs of saying, thinking, knowing, believing, feeling, &c., are, on several occasions, rendered by a "quod" clause with a finite verb, rather than by the accusative and infinitive (the usual construction in classical Latin): "scio quod succedet", III, 177; "Scio quod vis me decipere", III, 262; "Scio quod pharmaci salsa qualitas sit ingrata stomacho", IV, 210; "Scio quod farta sunt in causa", IV, 284; "sciatur quod sub hoc meo cubiculo,/ Porrigatur cella vetus et inanis quae ignoratur a plurimis", V, 2-3; "Fateor quidem quod plurimi serviunt diabolo", V, 31; "Vidistis autem quod simulata plerumque vitia,/ Nugae dolosae..../Ab invidis obiiciantur", Epilogue, 3-5.

Abundant use has also been made in the play of the perfect of instantaneous action - either to denote the sudden, or the unexpected: "Alea, pictaeque chartae et compotationes crebrae/ Nummos abstulere," I, 10-11; "Et trunco arboris affixere versus maledicos", II, 308; "Intumulant nares quod peperere nates", IV, 194; or simply because this form of the verb was more suited to the author's purpose, as, for example, in V, 216-30, where each line is required to rhyme: "Scholares hic fuere...Et daemonem ostendere".

The historic infinitive, too, occurs quite frequently to show

- lxxiv -

repeated action, or add greater emphasis to certain parts of the dialogue: "Caelibi Diana lare/ Viduum amplexathorum,/ Fugere viros, fugare/ Bestias, ducit decorum", II, 153-6. The infinitive also often does service as a noun, whilst still retaining some characteristics of a verb: "Hoc est meum laborare", II, 30; "Lunae iugales sistere...Haec parva sunt, potest haec quaevis Thessala venefica", II, 270-6.

There are, moreover, in the play, many examples of contracted verb forms: "victitasse", I, 52; "excogitarunt", I, 76; "somniasti", II, 112; "comparasti", II, 119; "illaqueasti", "fascinasti" and "afflasti", II, 189-90; "iactasti", IV, 87.

Other interesting items of syntax include the unusual use of "dispensare" with the preposition "pro", meaning "to give licence, grant freedom to do": Prologue, 22; the occurence of the archaic form of the ablative plural of the pronoun "qui": "queis", Prologue, 26, and IV, 68; the use of the pronominal suffix "met": "nosmet" I, 117; "temet", II, 75; the use of the future imperative of some verbs for emphasis: "introducito" and "reponito", II, 101; "scitote", III, 218; the rare use of the preposition "ad" in connection with liquid measurement: "Afferatur cervisia non ad pintam aut quartam, sed ad congium/ Non ad modum sed ad modium modium", III, 133-134; "oblivisci" taking the dative, instead of the accusative or genitive, case of the noun: "O Xantippe obliviscamur iurgii virgis", III, 170; the use of the verbs "aio" and "inquam" -

in ordinary conversation - when normally they occur only <u>after
quotations</u>: "Sic aiunt scilicet", II, 85; "Inquit enim
Aristoteles in graeco contextu", III, 182. Other strange bits of
syntax are the substitution of the phrase "Nolo ne timeas" for
"noli timere", V, 42, and "Nec fugite" for "nolite fugere",
V, 174; the use of "vale" (2nd. pers. sing. imperative of "valeo")
as a noun, V, 211; and, finally, the declining of "dumus" as
though it were a noun of the third, and not the first, declension,
V, 98.

NOTES

[1] See above, section VI.

VIII. LITERARY FORM

"An prosaicum sit nescio an metricum".

QUEROLUS, Prologue.

Any discussion of the literary form of Mercurius Rusticans must of necessity be rather superficial and incomplete, since at present very little literature is available on the use of metre in renaissance Latin drama - particularly comedy, and there is an urgent need for further research to be carried out in this field. The following observations, however, can be made: firstly, the lines of this particular play will not scan according to the laws governing classical Latin metre, although in a few rare instances an iambic($\cup$ -) 'flavour' can be detected at the end of a line, as in the prologue (ll.1-30); there are also one or two lines which could be said to consist of iambic clausulae: for example,

"Mihi vita caepit quum primum Alfredus domum"
(Prologue, 1.6)

Secondly, there is very little rhyming at the end of lines, yet internal rhyme occurs on several occasions, e.g.,

"Quasi haec studendi non ludendi esset tempestivitas"
(I, 18)

"Est enim mea occupatio, cuppatio: meum servitium, cervisia.
Mea oratio, oris ratio. Doctores sunt mihi coctores
Nec paginas lego, sed patinas lingo et denique
Totum vivere nihil aliud est quam bibere." (II, ll.31-4)

"Nequaquam, sic lubens et libens
Fabricarem mihi cornua."
(III, ll.204-5)

"Seu Panes, aut Manes, seu satyri vel fityri,
Seu lares aut lemures aut Penates vocamini;"
(V, ll.165-6).

All the songs in the play also rhyme, of course, but these cannot really be used in determining the true literary form of Mercurius Rusticans, since they have been specially written to fit the music of certain popular tunes, and, therefore, resemble English, rather than Latin, verse: in other words, their rhythm is accentual instead of quantitative. The words of the songs have been arranged in such a way that it is the naturally stressed syllables - and not the long and short syllables - which form a pattern.

The most, therefore, that can be said regarding the literary form of Mercurius Rusticans is that it is a mixture of prose and metre - and I use the word 'metre' very loosely here. The author, himself, freely admits that in the play,

"nec leges comicae
Stricte tenebuntur aut metrici verborum modi."
(Prologue, ll.19-20)

It would be wrong, then, to look for any definite metrical scheme within the framework of the play, and the reader who does so will be disappointed. The author of <u>Mercurius Rusticans</u> was writing at a time when the rules for the composition of classical metre had been considerably 'bent' by a succession of earlier neo-Latin dramatists. It is more than likely, too, that the play was written in some haste, and that the author, unlike the Roman poets of old, did not have time to polish his work, or to smooth out any metrical difficulties, before presenting it to his audience.

IX. THE MANUSCRIPT OF MERCURIUS RUSTICANS

The manuscript of Mercurius Rusticans is at present housed in the Bodleian Library, Oxford, (shelf-mark MS. Wood, D.18). It originally formed part of a collection of 126 MSS., belonging to the Oxford antiquarian, Anthony à Wood. On Wood's death, in November, 1695, his books and manuscripts passed to the Ashmolean Museum, where they remained until 1860, when they were transferred to the Bodley. The manuscript is written on paper, in what Madan describes as "a 17th.-century hand",[1] It measures $8\frac{3}{10} \times 6^{1}/10$ ins., and consists of 36 leaves. It is bound with three other MSS..[2]

NOTES

[1] <u>A Summary Catalogue of Western Manuscripts in the Bodleian Library at Oxford</u>, vol.II, pt. 2, p.1183.

[2] For further details about these MSS. and their contents, see op. cit., pp.1183-5.

X. TREATMENT OF THE TEXT

In my treatment of the text, I have –

(a) kept the author's spelling,

(b) silently normalised the author's use of upper and lower case,

(c) modernised long s,

(d) expanded abbreviations,

(e) separated ligatures,

(f) adopted the modern usage of v and u,

(g) printed j as i throughout,

(h) removed diacritical accents,

(i) printed abbreviated speech headings in full,

(j) numbered each Act in tens,

(k) retained the author's punctuation, except in places where it seemed obviously wrong, and there was a danger of the sense being obscured. (Any changes of punctuation have been listed on pp. 470 - 506).

MERCURIUS RUSTICANS [1]

Scena: Hynoksey vel Hincksie. [2]

THE STUDENT DOWN IN THE COUNTRY

OR

CARRY ON UP THE ISIS

The scene: Hinksey.

DRAMATIS PERSONAE

GENIUS ACADEMICAE
DOULERUS ⎫
NICHADES ⎬ Academicorum ficta nomina
PHILOPINUS ⎭
PIGEON,[3] hospes
ANNA, uxor
IOANNA, filia
SUSANNA, ancilla
ROBERTUS DAWSON, agricola
CAECILIA, uxor
RICHARDUS CULLIE, faber ferrarius
Puer [4]
Fidicen
Daemon
Tres lamiae,[5] seu satyri cum musico ⎬ κωφὰ πρόσωπα
Puer
Pastor

CHARACTERS

THE GENIUS OF THE UNIVERSITY

DOULERUS ⎫
NICHADES ⎬ false names assumed by the students
PHILOPINUS ⎭

PIGEON, an innkeeper

ANNA, his wife

JOANNA, his daughter

SUSANNA, a maid

ROBERT DAWSON, a farmer

CAECILIA, his wife

RICHARD CULLIE, a blacksmith

A boy

A lute-player

The Devil

Three boggarts, or satyrs with musical accompaniment ⎫ Personae
⎭ Mutae

A boy

A shepherd

GENIUS ACADEMIAE[6] cum armis academiae [7]
scuto depictis, et lauro, rosis, liliis coronatus.

Cognoscite me genium vestrae academiae,
Quae mater alma praebuit vobis ubera.
Est alius urbis, alius academiae genius,
Et dispar ortus, contrarii mores, differens st$\overset{a}{y}$tus,
Unde mihi et illi non satis aliquando convenit.
Mihi vita caepit quum primum Alfredus domum
Musis sacravit, inchoans Athenas novas:
Quicquid deinceps bis quater centum fuit
Annis peractum usque ad hodiernum diem,
Memoria teneo. Iam autem visibilis appareo: 10
Non ut recludam urnas, et monumenta veterum,
Aut facta quondam praeclara, praeclaros viros
Exponerem ordine. Levior me causa protulit:
Lusus, iocusque iuvenilis aetatis lubricae,
Et quicquid invidus carpit, aulicus superbus crepat,
Et rusticantis mercurii petulantior dolus,
Erit nostra fabula: videbitis quasi speculo,
Non facta, sed ficta, non vera, sed veri similia.
Utar autem poetica licentia, nec leges comicae
Stricte tenebuntur aut metrici verborum modi.   20
Viri ter venerabiles et egregii, gratiose quaesamus
Dispensare pro duarum horarum absentia
A seriis negotiis: causa est, quia genius rogo.

The GENIUS OF THE UNIVERSITY bearing a shield
on which is depicted the University coat
of arms, and wearing a garland
of laurel, roses and lilies.

Be it known that I am the Genius of your University, which, like some kindly foster mother, has given you nourishment. The City has one Genius, the University another, but because of our unequal birth, diverse customs and differing rank, he and I sometimes don't agree very well. My life began as soon as Alfred dedicated a temple to the Muses, thereby founding a second Athens: all that has come to pass in the eight hundred years which have elapsed since then, up until this very day, I know by heart. But now I am here before you in visible form, not to break open the urns and tombs of those who have gone before, nor to set forth in order the noble deeds and famous heroes of long ago. Less serious is the reason for my coming: sport, the lively jests of headstrong youth, and whatso'er the envious man carps at, whatso'er the proud courtier prattles of, and the more wanton mischief of the student down in the country, shall be the theme of our play. You shall behold, as if 'twere in a mirror, not fact, but fiction, not the veritable, but the verisimilar: poetic licence, moreover, will I employ, and neither the rules for the writing of comedy, nor the metrical quantities of words will be strictly observed. Sirs, thrice reverend and distinguished, let us with a good grace endeavour to give licence for a few hours' absence from more serious pursuits. Why? Because I, the Genius of the University, request it.

Iam aguntur Saturnalia, sint omnes hilares, non saturnii:
Ex alienis molestiis vestra voluptas nascitur,
Queis arduum placere, vobis favere sed facile.
Linguis, animisque favete, favete rectis oculis,
Favete auribus arrectis, et porrectis frontibus.
Pro gratia vestra rependam gratias, vobisque interea precor
Facilem lienem et pectus risu turgidum.   30

Now is the Saturnalia being celebrated: let every man be jovial, not saturnine! 'Tis out of others' trouble that your enjoyment is born; hard it is for them to please you, but easy for you to show them favour. Support them with your tongues and hearts, support them with eyes unblinking, support them with ears pricked up and brow unfurrowed. For your indulgence I shall return thanks, and I wish you meanwhile a merry spleen and sides bursting with laughter.

ACTUS I. SCENA I.

DOULEHUS togatus et pileatus cum
literis in manu.

Duri parentes, sed matre sed durior pater,
Qui nativitatis festo me noluit accersere,
Ne farta et artocreas (puto), devorarem nimis.
Iudicor enim liborum magis, quam librorum helluo.
Prudenter itaque cautus est, sic enim scripserit:
Fili manendum est tibi Oxonii his feriis,
Sedulo studendum et parcendum sumptibus, vale.
Quasi haec studendi non ludendi esset tempestivitas!
Sed maius instat malum: defecit pecunia.
Alea, pictaeque chartae et compotationes crebrae   10
Nummos abstulere. His scopulis feci naufragium;
Diebus hisce festis vel potius infestis, meum
Liquefactum est argentum, et expertus sum has ferias
Fuisse nummorum inferias. Quid igitur nunc faciam?
Ab amicis plura petere non sinit pudor,
Nec oppidani mutuo dabunt drachmas decem
Sine faenore, testibus, cera, sigillo, vade.
Optimum est in musaeum me condere et cum hirundine
Per reliquum hyemis dormire aut non vivere
Donec pecuniae sol ver reduxerit meum.   20

(Obambulat)

ACT I. SCENE I.

DOULERUS dressed in cap and gown, with a letter in his hand.

Alas! what strict parents I've got! But father's stricter than mother: although it's Christmas, he's still refused to send for me. I think he's afraid I might guzzle too many pies and puddings - for I'm deemed more of a glutton for what comes out of the cookshops than out of bookshops! And so conditions have been wisely laid down, for he's written me this letter:

"Son, you are to remain at Oxford this holiday. Work hard and keep a tight rein on your purse-strings. Yours ever, Father."

As if this were the season for studying, not for having some sport! But I'm threatened with even greater misfortune: I have no money left. Dice, cards and frequent carousings have made off with all my cash. These are the rocks on which my vessel has indeed foundered; in the course of these holidays, or should I say unholy days, my silver has just melted away, and these jollifications have proved grave for my money! So now what am I to do? Shame forbids me to ask my friends for more, and the townspeople won't lend a brass farthing without interest, witnesses, wax, seals and surety. It's best for me to hide myself away in the University, and, like the swallow, sleep for the rest of the winter, or else not survive until the sun of money brings back my spring.

(he walks up and down)

ACTUS I. SCENA 2.

NICHADES cum cane Gallico;
PHILOPINUS cum bombarda.

PHILOPINUS: Ha, ha, he! Perge.
NICHADES: Deinde in somnio
Mihi videbar magno dolore coarctatus irrepere
Per angustum orificium in furnum tenebrosum et sordidum.
Sed ecce preter spem, aut magis preter metum,
Inibi palatium splenduit aureis tapetibus micans,
Et statim elevatus sum in archiepiscopum nolens volens,
Ornatus et oneratus magno insignium cumulo.
Mox ingreditur macilentus transmarinus presbyter
Et quasi salutaturus se incurvans, calceum dextrum rapit
Seque in pedes coniicit. Iratus surgo de cathedra, 30
Stans pede in uno. Immobiles rident famuli;
Huic magis irascor, dumque clamare volui, somnus abit.
PHILOPINUS: Ha, ha, he! Haec sunt atrae bilis, et soporis ludibria,
Sed quemnam videmus? Nonne nostrum sodalem veterum?

ACT I. SCENE 2.

NICHADES with a hunting dog;
PHILOPINUS with a shot-gun.

PHILOPINUS: Ha, ha, he! Pray, do continue.

NICHADES: Well, then in my dream it seemed as if I was being forced with considerable discomfort to crawl through some narrow opening into a dark and dirty oven. But lo and behold! Unlike what I had hoped, or rather feared, there shone forth in that place – a palace, gleaming with golden tapestries, and straightway was I raised willy-nilly to the office of Archbishop, crowned and drowned in a great mass of insignia. Presently, in walks some skinny priest from across the sea, and, bowing low, as though he were about to pay me homage, he snatches hold of my right shoe and throws himself at my feet. Angrily I get up from my throne, "standing on one foot." The servants, keeping stock-still, begin to titter. At this I grew more and more angry, but before I could shout aloud, the dream had vanished.

PHILOPINUS: Ha, ha, he! These are tricks played on the mind by black bile and sleep. But who's that over there? It's our old friend, is'nt it?

NICHADES:	Ipsus est nec diu videram. O charissime,
	Laetus sit tibi hic dies!
DOULERUS:	Et tibi laetior!
PHILOPLIUS:	Et tibi laetissimus!
NICHADES:	O festiva gradatio!
	Nil habet ulterius, quod nostris moribus addat
	Posteritas: sumus adeo morati probe.
	Sed heus! Dic, bona fide, cur sic ambulas melancholicus? 40
	Si nobiscum eas ad Hinckey, reddemus te phlegmaticum.
DOULERUS:	O utinam! Sed animus vobiscum ambulabit meus.
PHILOPLIUS:	Quid impedit, quaeso?
DOULERUS:	Illud impedimentum maximum:
	Deest argentum vivum, optimus, rusticorum deus,
	Ille mercatorum mercurius, faeneratorum meretrix,
	Quam comprimunt clanculum, dum faenus ut faetus editur:
	Deest, amici, pecunia, pecunia illa diabola.
PHILOPLIUS:	Piah! Hoc nihil est, malo virum habere indigentem
	Pecuniae quam pecuniam viro.
	Paupertas Musarum comes est: ego pariter aestimo 50
	Divitem et Ditem Plutum et Plutonem nihili.

NICHADES: Why, so it is! It's a long time since I last saw him. My dear fellow, may this day be a happy one for you!

DOULERUS: And happier for you!

PHILOPINUS: But happiest for you!

NICHADES: Oh, what a merry gradation! "Posterity hath nothing more to add to our ways." We did well to tarry so long. But come, tell us, for pity's sake, why you're walking up and down, looking so melancholy? Now, if you were to come with us to Hinksey, we'd make you a phlegmatic man again.

DOULERUS: Would that I might! Still, I shall go with you in spirit.

PHILOPINUS: Pray, what is it that stands in your way?

DOULERUS: That greatest of all obstacles: quick silver is wanting, my dear fellow, that idol of countryfolk, that Mercury of merchants, that whore of money-lenders, whom they force in secret until interest, like an infant, is brought forth. Money's lacking, friends, money, that root of all evil.

PHILOPINUS: Pish! That's nothing. "I'd rather have a man without money than money without a man." Poverty goes hand in hand with the Muses. In my opinion, Dives is equal to Dis, and Plutus to Pluto, and both are worthless.

MICHADES:	Audivi quendam satrapam victitasse cerebellis passerum.
	Et nos non valemus vivere nostrorum ope?
	Animo sis parato, non denegabis tuum consortium.
DOULERUS:	Sed num certum est ire?
PHILOPINUS:	Certissimum.
	Iam sumus exituri, ut scilicet imponamus coronidem
	Festis diebus, et veteres renovemus iocos.
DOULERUS:	Sed quid agemus apud Hinoksy?
PHILOPINUS:	Quid agendum rogas?
	Bibamus, et ludamus et ludificemus rusticos.
	Iocemur hilares, et magno gaudeamus gaudio, 60
	Venemur etiam et aucupemur, si quid supersit otii.
	Linguam sinamus libere quidvis loqui,
	Quam hic coercet fraenum rationis stupidae,
	Aut criticus auscultator. Non amo pueros senes,
	Ut neque senes bis pueros. Semel insanivimus omnes.
	O terque quaterque foelix, qui iunior furit,
	Nec ad senectam nuces et nugas reiicit!

NICHADES: I've heard tell how a certain eastern ruler kept himself alive on sparrows' brains, yet _we_ can't live off our own resources! Be of stout heart, you shan't deny us the pleasure of your company.

DOULERUS: But have you really made up your minds to go?

PHILOPINUS: Of course, we're just about to set off, so that we can - not to mince matters - put the finishing touch to this holiday, and get up to our old tricks again.

DOULERUS: But what shall we do at Hinksey?

PHILOPINUS: You ask what we shall do! Why, we shall drink and sport and make fun of the country yokels. We shall merrily jest and rejoice with great joy. We shall hunt, too, and go fowling - that is if there's any time left. We shall allow our tongues to utter freely whatever they choose, for here they're curbed by a set of senseless rules, or by those who listen to us with too critical an ear. I dislike precocious children, but I dislike old men in their second childhood twice as much. We've all gone mad at one time or another. O three and four times blessed is he who runs wild in his youth, and doesn't save his rattle and toys for his old age!

NICHADES: O Socrates, et tertius Cato, quam graviter philosopharis!
            Sed, (mi amicissime) nos instructi sumus ad hoc iter:
            Ecce hic Laelaps canis meus, ecce illic bombarda optima, 70
            Et tu iam satis expeditus quaeso nobiscum eas.
DOULERUS: Ibo, quamvis haud satis paratus.
PHILOPINUS: Lepidum caput te amo.
            Nunc exopto ut in nostrum cerebrum influat
            Quicquid olim Bacon, Scoggin, et reliqui boni socii,
            Quicquid facetiarum et ludorum et stratagematum
            Excogitarunt monachi, et iocosi fraterculi,
            Quos omnes invocamus ut nostros secundent iocos.
NICHADES: Nil dubites, astutias suppeditabit occasio,
            Et nosti quibus mercibus et nugis implentur loculi.
DOULERUS: Heigh! Vale Oxonium! Veni Hinckey!   80

                            (Pileum rotat)

PHILOPIRUS: Pileum tu pilam facis:
            Ut sic rotatum, quod nequeant omnes geometrae,
            Quodammodo reddat quadraturam circuli.

NICHADES: O Socrates, O Cato the third, how seriously you philosophize! But, my dear friend, we've equipped ourselves for the journey. See, here's Trouncer, my dog, and there's my best fowling-piece. And I entreat you, now quite lightly laden, to come with us.

DOULERUS: I will, though I'm not very well prepared.

PHILOPINUS: Oh, I love you for a pleasant companion! Now I pray that whatever Bacon, Scoggin, and their other good friends devised long, long ago, that whatever strokes of wit, sport and practical jokes, the monks and mischievous friars have thought up, may flood our brains. Let's call upon all of them to further our jests.

NICHADES: Have no fear, there'll be plenty of opportunities for us to show our cunning, and you know what wares and trash our wallets are crammed with!

DOULERUS: Heigh-ho! Farewell Oxford, Hinksey here we come! (He whirls his cap round)

PHILOPINUS: Why, with that "ball" you've scored a hat trick! Whirling your cap round like that, you're demonstrating in a certain way what none of the mathematicians can do - how to square the circle!

DOULERUS: Eamus itaque ut curas iugulemus risu et cervisia,
Non est vivere, sed ridere vita. Vos videbitis de pecunia?

PHILOPINUS: Maxime. Ego habeo solidum, ille sex denarios;
Hoc pecuniae sufficiet.

DOULERUS: Heu non amplius?

PHILOPINUS: Est satis superque. Nos freti sumus in genio, non marsupio.
Prestat habere crumenam vacuam, quam inane cerebrum;
Insuper ad victum sufficient lepores, et alites capiamus. 90
Eamus autem, eamus cito!

DOULERUS: Nonne conveniens sit
Mutare nomina, ut ludentes ignoremur postea?
Quod si placet, vocabimur: Primus, Secundus, Tertius.

NICHADES: Non sed doctiora nomina conveniunt academicis;
Ego ero Nichades, quasi inferno imperans.

DOULERUS: Et ego Doulerus, quasi puellas ambiens.

DOULERUS: Let's be off, then, so that we can banish care with laughter and ale! Life's not for living, but for laughing! Er...you'll look after the money matters will you?

PHILOPINUS: Yes, of course. I have a shilling, and he's got sixpence. That should be quite sufficient.

DOULERUS: Dear me! Is that all?

PHILOPINUS: It's enough and more than enough. We're relying on our wits, <u>not</u> on our purses. It's better to have an empty money-bag, than an empty head. Besides, the nares will do for food, and we should catch some game-birds as well. But let's away! Let's away quickly!

DOULERUS: Wouldn't it be a good idea to change our names, so that people won't take us for the tricksters afterwards? If you like, we could call ourselves First, Second and Third.

NICHADES: No, no, no. More learned names befit scholars like us: I shall be Nicnades, as though I'm the ruler of hell!

DOULERUS: And I shall be Doulerus, as if I'm always chasing the wenches!

PHILOPINUS: Et ego Philopinus, quasi potum amans.

                              (Rident)

　　　Iam memores sint singuli, ut suas agant partes.
　　　Hei dery, dery, dery, dery! Hei down a down, down dery!
　　　Vultisne cum domino per vadum ferri? Ambulemus!   100

                         (Exeunt)

PHILOPINUS: And I shall be Philopinus, just like a man who's fond of his liquor!

                                             (They laugh)

Now see that each one remembers what part he has to play.

    Hei dery, dery, dery, dery. Hei down a down, down dery!
    D'ye want to be carried o'er the stream with your
        master in the ferry?

Let's be off!

                                             (Exeunt)

ACTUS I. SCENA 3.

DAWSON. CULLIE. SUSANNA sequitur
cum cervisia.

CULLIE: Hospes! Hoe! Ubi es? Ubi dormis? Num te retinet
Lectus, aut cibus? Ubi es? Huc ades!
Herum tuum vocites, Susanna, ut nobiscum bibat.

(Exit SUSANNA; intrat PIGEON)

PIGEON: O sodales bibuli, ut se res habet hodie?
DAWSON: Bene se res habet, sed ego non bene habeo rem.
PIGEON: Oh, suboleo te, hodie obiurgavit obiurgavit uxor;
Sic per rem intelligis uxorem. Ambobus propino.

(Bibunt)

CULLIE: Haec est alla nobilissima. Haec guttur pluit,
Confortat stomachum, et cerebrum calefacit.
Ad salutem uxorum.
DAWSON: Mihi non placet;   110
Ego potius cibam ad uxoris aegritudinem.

(Bibit)

PIGEON: Miror academicos rarius huc advenire, quam sunt soliti;
Aliquot iam mensibus non aliquem accepi hospitio.

ACT I. SCENE 3.

DAWSON. CULLIE. SUSANNA follows, carrying a jug of ale.

CULLIE: 'Ei, landlord, where be you? Where be you a-sleepin'? Surely it ain't your bed or your food what's keepin' 'e? Come 'ere! Susanna, go tell your master to come an' 'ave a drink wi' us.
(Exit SUSANNA. Enter PIGEON)

PIGEON: Ah! Me ole boozin pals! An' 'ow is't wi' you to-day?

DAWSON: It be well, but I ain't well wi' it.

PIGEON: Oh, I smells you! The wife's bin scold, scold, to-day, 'as 'er? By "it" you means the missus. Well, 'ere's an 'ealth to you both!
(They drink)

CULLIE: This be an excellent ale! It wets the whistle, strengthens the stomach and warms the brain. Good 'ealth to all wives!

DAWSON: I ain't in favour. I'd rather drink to the wife's ill-'ealth.
(He drinks)

PIGEON: I'm surprised the students doesn't come 'ere as often as they used to. 'Tis many a long month since I gave any of 'em 'ospitality.

CULLIES: Ibi periit omnis hilaritas, quae placebat antiquitus,
Et omnia iam tendunt ad mores et studia,
Et sedulo nocte dieque omnes incumbunt studiis.
Sed simus hilares inter nosmet ipsos, et canamus aliquid;
Ego incipiam:

    Alii sectantur forum,
    Alii Martis favorem,
    Alii maris furorem,   120
       Ego potum diligo!

PIGSON: Iam ergo potum habens: si tu potum diligas,
Hoc poculum haurias, dum cantamus ha, ha, he!
Ha, ha, he! Ha, ha, he! Dum cantamus ha, ha, he!

OMNES:
    Quamvis sit profundum,
    Quamvis sit rotundum,
    Attamen est iucundum,
    Ut semper videas fundum!

    Tres pelles ovium reversas,
      Nebulo et meretrix,   (Ter)   130
    Qui potu dicit mersas.

CULLEN: Ay, that good 'umour, which in times gone by didn't come amiss, now be completely dead over yonder. These days they gives all their attention to rules an' larnin', an' they is all bent eagerly over their books both night an' day. But let's be merry 'mongst ourselves, an' sing a catch. I'll begin:

    Some the lawyer's life pursue,
    Others for Mars' favour sue,
    Others the ocean's fury value,
        But me - I likes to drink!

PIGEON: Well then, now a drink you gain -
If you do not drink disdain.
May you now this goblet drain!
While we do sing ha, ha, he, ha, ha, he, ha, ha, he,
While we do sing ha, ha, he!

ALL: Though deep it be,
Though round it be,
Nevertheless, pleasant it be,
So that always the bottom you see!

Three sheeps'skins reversed,
An idle rascal and a whore,   (Three times)
Who says they are in drink immersed?

PIGEON: O suavissimae merulne! Tibi, Roberte, quam raucus est larynx!

PIGEON: O you sweet song-birds! But, Robert, what a raucous voice you 'as!

ACTUS I. SCENA 4.

Intrat CAECILIA.

CAECILIA: Ubi est maritus? Ubi latitat? Numquamne cessabis ad
Popinam currere?
DAWSON: Quaeso, meum corculum, tace.
CAECILIA: Taceam? Barde, blennue, ebrie, taceam? Potius moriar;
Mes pereunt domi, et ingenium tuum hic perit.
Quando nuper agna recens enecta est frigore,
Ubi fuisti? Apud popinam. Quando subgravida
Proiecit faetum abortivum, ubi fuisti? Apud popinam.
Quotidie inebriaris, et domum redis titubans,   140
Stertisque totam noctem brumalem: et taceam, bibacule?
CLELIUS: Indulgeas ludenti paululum, ut fortius labores ferat.

ACT I. SCENE 4.
Enter CAECILIA.

CAECILIA: Where's my 'usband? where's 'e skulkin'? Will you never leave off runnin' down to the ale-'ouse?

DAWSON: Dear 'eart, 'old your tongue, I pray you.

CAECILIA: 'Old my tongue? Why, you dunce, you block'ead, you drunkard! 'Old my tongue? I'll die fust! Things is goin' to rack an' ruin at 'ome, an' your wits is goin' to rack an' ruin 'ere! When that new-born lamb froze to death not long since, where wus you? At the ale-'ouse! When that ewe in lamb gave birth afore 'er time, where wus you? At the ale-'ouse! Ev'ry day you gets drunk, an' comes reelin' 'ome, an' snores all the winter's night; an' you tells me to 'old my tongue? You drunken sot!

CULLIE: An, go on, let 'im sport a while, so's 'e can bear 'is troubles more bravely!

CAECILIA: Etiam vos otiosi combibones eum corrumpitis;
Si vult ludere, ludat mecum, ludat domi;
Tota vicinia me deridet ut sterilem et inexpertam viro;
Nec ille curat, nec aliquod quaerit remedium.
Iubebam ut iret Oxonium, ut urinam ostenderet medico,
Sed ille perlapsus ad limen fregit vas urinarium.
Melius esset mihi, si trunco aut stipiti nupseram!
Cur non properas domum? Quid stas lapis?   150
Si adessent vires, et illum et omnes vos verberarem!

            (Trudit foras; se subducunt PIGEON
             et CULLIS, et inter se annunt
                  ut iterum conveniant)

Ego sum omnium faeminarum miserrima, quae maritum habeo
Et stolidum et ebrium! Nec adsunt liberi
Quibuscum colludens tempus et otium fallerem.
Sed si non cavebit posthac, non lingua sed manibus agam!

CAECILIA: Ay, 'tis you, the idle, good-for-nothin' cronies 'e drinks with, as leads 'im astray. If 'e wants to 'ave some sport, why don't 'e 'ave some sport wi' me? Why don't 'e 'ave some sport at 'ome? I be the laughin'-stock of the 'ole neighbour'ood, jest as if I wuz barren or still a virgin, an' 'e don't give a straw, nor does 'e bother to find any cure for't neither. I tells 'im to go t' Oxford to show 'is water to a phy-physician, but 'e trips over the doorstep an' smashes the chamber-pot! I'd 'ave bin better off, if I'd wed a stock or a tree-stump. Why don't you 'urry 'ome? Why be you standin' there like a stone? If I 'ad the strength, I'd beat the livin' daylights out o' 'im <u>an'</u> the lot o' you!

          (She bundles him out of the door:
          PIGEON and CONLIN steal away, giving
          one another the nod that they will
          meet again)

I be the most wretched woman alive, 'avin' an 'usband what's both a fool an' a drunkard! I ain't even got any little 'uns as I can play wi' to beguile me time an' leisure. But if 'e don't look out after this, I'll get to work – <u>not</u> wi' me tongue, but wi' me fists!

ACTUS I. SCENA 5.

PHILOPINUS. NICHADES. DOULERUS.

PHILOPINUS:	Haec est villula parvula, rusticula, sordidula!
CAECILIA:	O cavete, vicini, veniunt scelares Oxonii!
	Vicini, cavete, veniunt scelares Oxonii!
DOULERUS:	Imo tu, quavis ansere loquacior, tace!
CAECILIA:	Cavete de gallinis, cavete de anseribus! 160
NICHADES:	Hoc potius clamandum est: cavete de uxoribus!
	Cavete, mariti, de uxoribus! Nam vos Actaeonios
	Et cornutos possumus facere, quandocunque volumus.
CAECILIA:	Vos impuri nebulones, et lemures nigri, quid hic facitis?
PHILOPINUS:	O tu Furiarum maxima, et Alecto huius oppidi!
CAECILIA:	O vos carnifices cruce dignissimi et patibulo!
DOULERUS:	Tu tittle tattle, tu hoddy doddy, utque cum ignorama loquar,
	Te nulla dignior, anglice, a wispe, et cucking stoole!

ACT I. SCENE 5.
PHILOPINUS. MICHADES. DOULERUS.

PHILOPINUS: This is a tiny little, boorish little, dirty little, village!

CAECILIA: O beware, neighbours! 'Ere come some o' them students from Oxford! O neighbours, take care! 'Ere come some o' them students from Oxford!

DOULERUS: Nay, woman, you cackle more loudly than any goose! Peace, I say!

CAECILIA: Look to your chickens! Look to your geese!

MICHADES: Nay, rather this is what you ought to shout: look to your wives! Husbands, look to your wives! For we can turn you into Actaeons and cuckolds, whenever we please!

CAECILIA: You dirty rascals! You dark fiends! What be you doin' 'ere?

PHILOPINUS: O thou greatest of all the Furies! Thou Alecto of this village!

CAECILIA: Why, you varmints! You deserves to be strung up on a gibbet!

DOULERUS: You do nothing but tittle-tattle and hoddy-doddy, so since I am addressing a numskull, there is no one worthier than you, madam, - in plain English - of the wisp and the cucking-stool!

CAECILIA:	O caelum! O terra! Utinam haberem aquam fervidam	
	Aut lotium, ut capita vobis ungerem!	170
	Abite vos rabulae, et diabolorum progenies!	
NICHADES:	Si non nauseam mihi excitaret, te cogerem	
	Saltitare nudam, et repetere gyros instar simiae!	
CAECILIA:	Nudamne me? Non potes, non potes, trifurcifer!	
PHILOPINUS:	Solent nobiscum rixatrices baptisari fluvio,	
	Et meretrices magnifice per populum curribus vehi.	
CAECILIA:	O quid agam? Non feram amplius! Ite omnes in malam crucem!	

(Exit CAECILIA; intrat puer)

DOULERUS:	Proh facinus immortale! Vicimus mulierem rixando!	
	Et morietur spero, ut luscinia cum cantu vincitur!	
	Heus, puer! Ubi est domus nequitiae, suburbanum	
	prostibulum,	180
	Scylla et Charibdis scolarum, gentis togatae	
	dedecus?	
PUER:	Quid malum dicitis?	

CECILIA: O 'eavens! O earth! 'Ow I wish I 'ad some boilin' 'ot water or some piddle to pour over your 'eads! Be off wi' you, you scoundrels, you devil's offspring!

NICHADES: If it wouldn't cause me to vomit, I'd make you leap up and down with not a stitch on, and turn somersaults like a monkey!

CAECILIA: me? wi' not a stitch on? You...you...you couldn't, you vile wretch!

PHILOPINUS: We make a practice of dipping scolds in the river, and carting whores through the streets for all to hurl abuse at.

CAECILIA: O-oh! What be I a-goin' to do? I can't bear it no longer! Go 'ang all of you!

(Exit CAECILIA: enter a boy)

DOLLERUS: Wonders 'll never cease! We actually got the better of a woman in quarrelling, and she'll die, I hope, like the nightingale when it's vanquished in song! Hey there! You, boy! Where's that den of iniquity, that suburban bawdy-house, that scholars' Scylla and Charybdis, that slur on the race that wears the gown?

BOY: What evil place be you a-speakin' of?

PHILOPINUS: Ubi est spelunca latronum,
Nebulonum asylum, fornix mendicantium?
PUER: Ego dico quid dicitis? Quid vultis?
PHILOPINUS: Popinam volumus.
PUER: Oh, hoc aliud est! Ite ad sinistram, et ad dextram vertite.
Et nasus erit dux viae.
PHILOPINUS: Flagitium, siccine loqueris?

(Puer fugit insequentem)

Tu es Hincksiana soboles verissime!
Contemplemur villam, et deinde adeamus hospitium.

(Exeunt)

PHILOPINUS: Where's that robbers' cave, that idlers' refuge, that beggars' haunt?

BOY: What be you a-speakin' of, I say? Where do you want?

PHILOPINUS: We want the ale-house.

BOY: Oh, so that's it! Go left, turn down on the right hand, then follow your noses.

PHILOPINUS: I'll teach you to answer me like that, you knave!

(The boy runs off as PHILOPINUS tries to catch him)

You're a true Hinksionian, bred and born! Well, let's go and have a look at the village, then make our way to the inn.

ACTUS 2. SCENA I.
PIGEON. CULLIE.

PIGEON: Ubi est miser ille Robertus cui uxor imperat?
Vix redibit hodie adeo territus est.

CULLIE: Non est eius tam miseranda quam ridenda stultitia
Et iam necesse ut iugum quod libenter accepit, ferat.
Sed ecce clanculum se praeripuit.

(Intrat DAWSON)

Quomodo valet uxor?

DAWSON: Utinam valeret ut valedicerem
Et ingestus agger linguam coerceret garrulam!
Facile superat omnes rhetores, causidicos, anseres.
Tota domus iurgiis personuit, evertuntur vascula,
Vapulat ancilla, verberatur canis, perturbantur omnia. 10
Tandem deficiente voce secuta est tranquillitas.
Et dum coagulum cogit; ago aquam hausturus exeo.

CULLIE: Potius allam hausturus, dabo tibi τὲ ἕλου.

DAWSON: Fac ut videam vel potius ut non videam,
Bibas supernaculum, respondebo similiter.

ACT 2. SCENE I.

PIGEON. CULLIE.

PIGEON: Where be poor ole Robert, the one whose wife's got 'im under 'er thumb? T'ain't likely 'e'll come back 'ere to-day, - 'e'll be too scared!

CULLIE: 'Is folly's more to be laughed at than pitied. An' now 'e's got to bear the yoke which 'e wus once glad t'accept. But look, 'e's slipped away without 'er noticin'!

(Enter DAWSON)

'Ow fares your wife?

DAWSON: Wud that 'er fared so well as I could bid 'er a last farewell, an' that the earth lay 'eavily upon 'er to curb 'er pratin' tongue! 'Er could easily outdo all speechifiers, lawyers an' geese! The 'ole 'ouse were filled with the sound of 'er scoldin': the crocks is smashed, the maid gets a thrashin', the dog - a beatin', an' ev'rythin' is turned topsy-turvy. At last 'er loses 'er voice, an' silence reigns. So, whilst 'er was makin' 'erself some curds, I came out fur to swill some water.

CULLIE: Swill ale rather! I gives you the 'ole lot.

DAWSON: Make sure that I sees, or rather that I doesn't see. Drink it down to the last drop, an' I'll reply in like manner.

CULLIE: Canamus alternatim quemadmodum soliti sumus.

> Canis, vetus canis antro dum iacet suo
> Baugh, waugh, baugh a waugh a waugh   (Ter)
> antro dum iacet suo.

> Videtisne Scoti saccum
> pendulum de muro?   (Ter)

> Ollam, peram, bursam, saccum
> pendulum de muro?   (ter) 20

CULLIE: O laetam paupertatem omnibus divitiis redimendam!
Sed cantemus aliud et aliud:

> En pica sedet in arbore
> Quam hilaris, hilaris saltat   (Ter)
> Et bis quam hilaris saltat

> Iam malleus tacet, ho! Non diligo agros, ho!

DAWSON: Iam sarculum iacet, ho! Non diligo fabros, ho!
PIGEON: Iam poculum placet, ho! Non diligo macros, ho!

CULLIE: Let's sing a roundelay, like us usually does:

> There was an old dog, in 'is kennel lay 'e,
> Baugh, waugh, baugh a waugh a waugh,   (Thrice)
> In 'is kennel lay 'e.
>
> The sack that 'angs on the wall, O Scots, d'you see?
> Baugh, waugh, baugh a waugh a waugh,   (Thrice)
> O Scots, d'you see?
>
> A jug, bag, purse, sack, that on the wall 'angin' be,
> Baugh, waugh, baugh a waugh a waugh,   (Thrice)
> That on the wall 'angin' be.

CULLIE: O blessèd poverty that 'as to be bought back with all our riches! But let's sing somethin' else:

> Look at the magpie sat in yon tree,
> 'Ow merrily, merrily capers 'e!   (Thrice)
> And doubly 'ow merrily capers 'e!
>
> Now the 'ammer no sound doth make, ho! Farmlands I do not like, ho!

DAWSON: Now the 'oe a rest it doth take, ho! Blacksmiths I do not like, ho!

PIGEON: Now the cup itself welcome doth make, ho! Lean men I do not like, ho!

OMNES: Sic transit honor, sic manet dolor, sic omnia
                    sunt in malo.
CULLIS: O utinam hoc esset laborare!
PIGEON: Hoc est meum laborare: 30
Est enim mea occupatio, cuppatio: meum servitium,
                                        cervisia.
Mea oratio, oris ratio. Doctores sunt mihi coctores
Nec paginas lego, sed patinas lingo et denique
Totum vivere nihil aliud est quam bibere.
DAWSON: Pulchre, ubi haec didicisti Thoma?

                            (Bibunt)

ALL: Thus glory passes away,

                        Thus sorrow it comes to stay,

                        Thus all rests on misfortune—o!

CULLIE: Oh, wud that this was workin'!

PIGEON: Well, this be _my_ work:
for my vocation be potation; I serves ale, an' ale serves
me; my prayer be the bill of fare; doctors is to me
concocters; I does n't scribble on slates, but I does
dribble on plates, an', in short, the 'ole of livin' is
nougnt but bibbin'!

DAWSON: Well said! Where did you learn them
things, Thomas?

                        (They drink)

ACTUS 2. SCENA 2.
PHILOPINUS. DOULERUS. NICHADES.

PHILOPINUS: Video nefastum buxi signum, et fenestras rubram.
DOULERUS: Cur hic color cauponas denotat?
PHILOPINUS: Quia capita
Rixantibus ebriis comminuta saepe rubent sanguine.
Praeterea, efficit alla vultum rubicundum et purpureum.
               Hinc est conveniens potibus iste color.   40
Sed Nichades et Doulere adeamus domum.
Oh, sedete hilares, compotatores strenui,
Viri boni, et veraces, in potu enim veracitas!
NICHADES: Salvete poculorum triumviri, equites cervisiarii.
PIGEON: Gratissime advenistis, vultisne sedere si placet?
DOULERUS: O vos potiliorum nobilis sanguis, salvete simul.
CULLIN: Vultisne accumbere generosi si placet?
DAWSON: Si placet.
PIGEON: Placetne bibere? Hoh, ollam, et allam cito!

                         (Ancilla cum cervisia)

ACT 2. SCENE 2.

PHILOPINUS. DOULERUS. NICHADES.

PHILOPINUS: I can see the wicked box-wood sign, and the red lamp!

DOULERUS: But why does _that_ colour symbolize ale-houses?

PHILOPINUS: Well, because in drunken brawls heads often get split open and grow red from the blood. Besides, ale makes the complexion red and ruddy. That's why this colour is particularly appropriate to drink. But, Nichades and Doulerus, let's go up to the inn.

Oh, sit you merrily down, my staunch drinking-companions, good men and true, – for in liquor there is truth!

NICHADES: Good-morrow to you, triumvirs of the cups, Knights of the Royal Order of Tipplers!

PIGEON: A thousand welcomes! Be seated, I pray you.

DOULERUS: O you noble line of revellers! I, too, wish you good-day.

CULLIE: Gen'lemen, pray take your seats at table.

DAWSON: I pray you.

PIGEON: You'll 'ave a drink? Ho! A jug of ale, quickly!

(Enter the maid with a jug of ale)

PHILOPINUS: Incipe. Nos tres sumus, vos estis tres, tria sunt omnia,
Erimus itaque hilares simul, bibamus simul;   50
Sed dicite quaeso nomina, ut propriis alloquar,
Sicutque mos est, inde componant iocos,
Vel potius iocos frangam. Quod nomen tibi?

PIGEON: Thomas Pigeon.

PHILOPINUS: Pigeon? Id est columbus.
Ergo tua uxor erit columba, quasi lumbos colens,
Et Cyprias dicat Veneri. Quod nomen tibi?

DAWSON: ~~Minime~~ Robertus Dawson.

PHILOPINUS: Monedulae filius vivitne pater?

DAWSON: Minime.

PHILOPINUS: Tum ipse eris monedula.

DAWSON: Ferenda est academicorum protervia.

PHILOPINUS: Quaeso feras.
Quod nomen tibi?

CULLIE: Ricardus Cullie.

PHILOPINUS: To begin: there are three of us, and three of you, — everything goes in threes, so therefore we shall be merry together, and drink together. But tell me, I pray you, what your names are, so that I may call you by them. For, as is the custom, they may then form the butt of a joke, or rather, I may crack jokes about them! What's your name?

PIGEON: Thomas Pigeon.

PHILOPINUS: Pigeon? In other words, — dove. So your wife must be Mrs. Dove, just as though she were a real lovey-dovey, and could talk to Cyprian Venus! What's your name?

DAWSON: Robert Dawson.

PHILOPINUS: Jack Daw's son, is your father still alive?

DAWSON: No, indeed 'e ain't.

PHILOPINUS: Then you, yourself, must be Jack Daw!

DAWSON: Students' impudence be somethin' that 'as to be endured.

PHILOPINUS: Then be a little enduring, I pray you, what's your name?

CULLIE: Richard Cullie.

PHILOPINUS:	Hah.	60

Difficile est in hoc nomine ludere, sed dicendum
est aliquid:
Cullie. C, IOO, v, 5, duplex l, bis 50, i, unum valet.
Proh numerosum nomen!
Si ad numerum literarum (ut solent) possis bibere,
Facile provocares, et vinceres omnes Bataviios.
Sed cuius es occupationis? Quamvis ex habitu satis sciam.

CULLIE: Faber ferrarius.

PHILOPINUS: De Ferrara? Italus es,
Quid hic agis? Cuius tu mi Dawson?

DAWSON: Pauper agricola.

PHILOPINUS: An coniugatus es?

DAWSON: Etiam, heigh, hogh.

PHILOPINUS: Habesne liberos?

DAWSON: Minime.

PHILOPINUS: An agrum colere potes, uxorem non potes?

DAWSON: Ah, non omnis fert omnia tellus: 70
Ager faecundus est uxor autem sterilis.

PHILOPINUS: Ah, hah! That's a difficult name to pun on; still, something must be said. C-v-l-l-i-e: c - that's a hundred, v - ~~g~~ive, double l - that's twice fifty, and i - well, i equals one. Goodness! What a figurative name! Were you able, as is the custom, to drink to the number of letters, you would easily challenge - and beat, - any Dutchman! But what's your trade? Though I know it well enough from the clothes you're wearing.

CULLIE: I be a farrier.

PHILOPINUS: From F-a-rrara? You're an Italian, then? So what are you doing here? What's your trade, Dawson, my dear fellow?

DAWSON: I be an 'umble farmer.

PHILOPINUS: And are you married?

DAWSON: Ay, heigh-ho!

PHILOPINUS: Got any children?

DAWSON: No, none.

PHILOPINUS: So you can make the land yield fruit, but not your wife, eh?

DAWSON: An, but not ev'ry soil brings forth ev'ry kind of crop. The land be fertile, but the missus be barren.

DOULERUS: Bibamus et garriamus libere, sodales,
Nec nos vobis, nec vos irascemini nobis.
Mi hospes exiccavi hunc calicem et bibamus circule.
Genialiter temet ipsum habeas, agricola, quasi hoc
                                    praesente die
Oves tonderentur aut grana conderentur horreo!
Vulcane, scio te habere Venerem domi.

CULLIE: Sed non videbitur a Marti vel Arti deditis.

PHILOPINUS: Nec multum refert, nos Minervam, non Venerem colimus.
Sed unde tantum rusticis?

CULLIE: Qui fieret aliter?   80
Literatus urbis vestrae nos afflat odor.

PHILOPINUS: Ego quidem sum medicus, iste magicus, ille ariolus.
Possumusque pro vobis mira quaedam facere, si non
                                    miracula.

DOULERUS: Mihi credite, Richades perlegit coniurationem Catilinae,
Et evocabit daemones facilé.

CULLIE: Sic aiunt scilicet.
Sed paulisper abeundum est mihi.

DOGLERUS: Let's sup and prattle freely, my friends. We shan't lose our tempers with you, and you must n't lose your tempers with us! Landlord, I've drained this cup dry, and we'll drink in a circle. Be of good cheer, farmer, as though this very day the sheep were being shorn, and the grain stored in the barn! Vulcan, I know that you have a Venus at home!

CULLIE: Ay, but 'er ain't for the eyes of them as is devoted to warfare or the arts.

PHILOPINUS: No matter, it is Minerva, **not** Venus, that we worship. But where did you yokels learn so much?

CULLIE: 'Ow can we do t'otherwise, when the larnèd smell o' your city be waftin' over us?

PHILOPINUS: Indeed, I'm a physician, this fellow's a magician, and he's a fortune-teller, and we can work wonders, nay – miracles, before your very eyes!

DOGLERUS: Take my word, Nichades has read the <u>De Coniuratione Catilinae</u> from cover to cover, and will conjure up devils without any trouble at all!

CULLIE: That's only what they **says**, of course! But I must be off shortly.

DAWSON: Et mihi.
NICHADES: Quid solvendum?
PIGEON: Solidus, si placet.
NICHADES: Ubi est vestra pecunia? Aequale petit Oxonium.
CULLIE: Sed putabam vos voluisse totum deponere apud Hinckey.
NICHADES: Nequaquam; hoc est recentium 90
         Qui se adhuc inter famulos paternos somniant.
         Sed in posterum habeamus perpetuum vestrum consortium,
         Nihilque praeterea dabitis.
CULLIE: Habebitis pro imperio comites assiduos. Interea valete.
PHILOPINUS: Tibi deus tutelaris Vulcanus faveat,
         Tibi Alma Ceres arrideat,

         (Exeunt CULLIE et DAWSON)

         Sed tibi (mi hospes) nemo superorum favet.
PIGEON: Nonne Bacchus?
PHILOPINUS: Piah! Bacchus non noverat cervisiam,
         Forsan temulentus aliquis daemon tutelam suscipiat,
         Qui vocatur Comus. Sed ubi est nostra hospita? 100
         Accersas illico; canes introducito, bombardam
                       reponito.

         (Exit PIGEON)

DAWSON: Me too.

NICHADES: How much do we owe you?

PIGEON: A shillin', please.

NICHADES: Where's *your* money? Oxford demands equal payment.

CULLIE: But I thought you wus wantin' to put all that aside at 'inksey?

NICHADES: By no means; that's for freshmen who dream they're still amongst their father's servants! But let's always have your company in future, and then you won't need to pay anything more.

CULLIE: You shall 'ave steadfast companions, just as you commands. In the meantime, fare you well!

PHILOLINUS: May Vulcan, your guardian god, watch over *you*, and may kindly Ceres smile upon *you*!
(Exit CULLIE and DAWSON)
But none of the gods above is *your* patron, landlord!

PIGEON: Surely Bacchus be?

PHILOLINUS: Pish! Bacchus knew nothing about ale! Still, perhaps some drunken sprite, called Comus, will become your champion! But where's our hostess? Bid her come at once! Take the dog inside, and put the shot-gun away.
(Exit)

ACTUS 2. SCENA 3.
ANNA cum cervisia.

PHILOPINUS: O mea columba, quid fiet ut exhilaremus corda?
ANNA: Iuvenes egregii, et hospites, gratissimi salvete.
Quicquid vultis, imperate, nihil meum non habebitis.
Ioanna filia, filia Ioanna huc exeas!

(Intrat IOANNA)

DOULERUS: Proh hominum fidem, haeocine filia tua? Haeocine tua filia?
ANNA: Quid est negotii? Non est mea, sed nostra filia, et unica.
DOULERUS: O prodigium! Hesterna nocte somniabam me hanc duxisse coniugem.
Talis enim, omnino talis apparuit, talibus superciliis prominentibus,
Talibus oculis flammantibus, talibus labris blandientibus, 110
Tali faceto naso, haec eadem est. Proh hominum fidem!
Sed dic mihi virgo pulcherrima nonne somniasti de me similiter?
IOANNA: Non in particulari, quantum memini, sed de nescio quo academico.

ACT 2. SCENE 3.

ANNA, with a jug of ale.

PHILOPINUS: O my dove, what shall we do to gladden our hearts?

ANNA: Good day to you, gallant young sirs, most welcome guests! Your wish be my command; you shall 'ave anythin' as it be in my power to give 'e. Joanna, daughter, daughter Joanna, come out 'ere!

(Enter JOANNA)

DODERUS: Good heavens! Is this a daughter of <u>yours</u>? Is she <u>your</u> daughter?

ANNA: What be the matter? 'Er ain't <u>my</u> daughter, but <u>our</u> daughter, our one an' only daughter.

DODERUS: But it's a miracle! Why, only last night I dreamt that I married this very girl, for she looked exactly the same. She had the same prominent eye-br͟ows, the same flashing eyes, the same tempting lips, the same dainty nose, - this is one and the same girl! Who'd have thought it! But tell me, fair maid, whether you have n't dreamt about me in a similar way?

JOANNA: Not about you in particular, - so far as I remembers. But I did 'ave a dream about some scholar, or t'other.

ANNA:	Mira dicitis, habent et suos eventus somnia.
	Afferas filia crateram aureum
	(Dat clavem)
	ut his dominis
	Propinemus. Ah, utinam reiuvenescerem vestrum gratia,
	Et saltare et cantare possem, quam bene ut olim potui!
	Ecce craterem, quem nec emi, nec dono accepi,
	Nec inveni nec surripui.
PHILOPINUS:	Quomodo itaque comparasti?
ANNA:	Eduxi nuper e sortilegio, ha, ha, he! Hanc habebit
	filia 120
	Centumque libras pro dote, et aliquid amplius, si
	maritus placeat.
PHILOPINUS:	Vino vendibili non opus est hedera, nec virgini
	Venali opus est dote. Virtus est dos optima.
ANNA:	De virtutibus nisi fallor, et pulchritudine caecus
	indicet,
	Sed ad salutem vestram domini, cur non hilarescitis?

ANNA: These certainly be extraordinary things that you both be a-speakin' of, an' dreams 'as their own consequences. Daughter, fetch the golden punchbowl —

(She hands her a key)

so's we can drink a toast to these gen'lemen. Ah, wud that I cud grow young again f̆or your sakes, an' dance an' sing as well as I once used to! But look at this punchbowl, — I did n't buy it, I were n't given it fur a present, I did n't find it, nor did I steal it neither.

PHILOPINUS: How did you get it, then?

ANNA: I've jest now produced it by sortilege, ha, ha, he! Me daughter shall 'ave this punchbowl an' one 'undred pounds as 'er marriage dowry, an' 'er shall 'ave even more than that, if us takes to 'er 'usband.

PHILOPINUS: Good wine needs no bush, nor does a maid that's for sale, need a dowry. Virtue's the best dowry.

ANNA: Unless I be very much mistaken, even a blind man wud vouch for '**er** virtue an' beauty. But good 'ealth, gen'lemen! Why am you lookin' so gloomy?

DOULERUS:	O quam te memorem virgo, namque haud tibi vultus	
	Mortalis, nec vox hominem sonat, o dea certe!	
	An Phaebi soror? An nympharum sanguinis una?	
IOANNA:	Ego sum Ioanna, domine, filia patris mei.	
DOULERUS:	Chara deum soboles, magnum Iovis incrementum!	130
	Iam nova progenies caelo demittitur alto,	
	Iam rediit et Virgo, redeunt Saturnia regna.	
IOANNA:	Ego non curo has blanditias, non agis rem serio.	
DOULERUS:	O crudelis Alexi, nihil mea carmina curas?	
	Nil nostri miserere? Mori me denique cogis?	
IOANNA:	Profecto ego amarem mutuo, si revera me amares.	
DOULERUS:	An dubitas Galatea? Thymo mihi dulcior Hyblae,	
	Candidior cygnis, hedera formosior alba.	
IOANNA:	Profecto ego non sum formosa, non sum candida.	

DOULERUS: "O maiden, how am I to address thee, for thou hast not a mortal countenance, nor doth thy voice sound human? O thou art a goddess surely! Art Phoebus' sister? Or one of the race of nymphs?"

JOANNA: I be Joanna, sir, me father's daughter.

DOULERUS: "Beloved offspring of the gods, mighty seed of Jupiter! Now a new race is sent down from heaven on high, now the virgin re-appears and the kingdom of Saturn returns!"

JOANNA: I does n't care fur this sort of' flattery, you ain't in earnest.

DOULERUS: "O cruel Alexis, carest thou nought for my songs? Wilt have no pity on me? Dost compel me at last to die?"

JOANNA: To be sure, I wud love you in return, if you truly loved me.

DOULERUS: "Dost doubt it, Galatea? Sweeter to me than Hyblean thyme, whiter than a swan, more beautiful than the pale ivy."

JOANNA: To be sure, I ain't beautiful, an' I ain't white neither.

DOULERUS: Credimus? An qui amant ipsi sibi somnia fingunt? 140
IOANNA: Num vulneravit primo te amor meus in somnio?
DOULERUS: Infandum, regina, iubes renovare dolorem.
PHILOFINUS: Nonne te pudet iuvenem Doulerum amore perdere?
DOULERUS: Non Thomas te, te genuit, sed cautibus horrens
Caucasus, Mircanaeque admorunt ubera tygres.
IOANNA: Profecto moventur mihi praecordia, amo te fideliter.
DOULERUS: Si me ames, mea animula, quaeso saltites.
IOANNA: Profecto non possum saltare, at faciam periculum.

(Saltat)

DOULERUS: Non melius saltat regina lemurum saltantium.
Si me fideliter ames meum corculum quaeso cantites. 150

DOULERUS: "Am I to believe that? Or do those in love fashion their own dreams?"

JOANNA: Surely 'twere in a dream were n't it, that you was first smitten wi' love o' me?

DOULERUS: "O Queen, thou biddest me renew unspeakable grief."

PHILOPINUS: Are n't you ashamed that young Doulerus here is dying of love?

DOULERUS: "'Twas not Thomas who begot thee, no, but the Caucasus, bristling with sharp rocks, and Hyrcanian tigresses gave thee suck!"

JOANNA: To be sure, you 'as melted my 'eart, I loves you truly!

DOULERUS: If you love me, my darling, dance, I pray you.

JOANNA: To be sure, I can't dance, - still, I'll try.

(She dances)

DOULERUS: The queen of the capering ghosts, herself, dances no better. Sweetheart, if you truly love me, sing, I pray you.

IOANNA: Profecto non possum bene; et tamen die Dominico
Omnes me respiciunt cantantem, faciam periculum.

(Cantat)

(Dulcina)

      Caelibi Diana lare
      Viduum amplexathorum,
      Fugere viros, fugare
      Bestias, ducit decorum.
      Mihi, sed arridet omen
      Coniugis, et dulce nomen.

      Diligit nam ulmum vitis,
      Diligit et turtur parem,   160
      Diligit leaena mitis,
      Diligit ursa marem.
      Mihi sic placet cubile
      Continens par iuvenile.

DUULARUS: O luscinias, cygnos, syrenas et sphaerarum cytharas!
O me beatum, qui tales inveni amasias!
PHILOPINUS: Quid diutius impedit, quo minus peragantur sponsalia
Duobus testibus? Num tu cupis esse huius sponsus?

JOANNA: To be sure, I ain't a very good singist,- still, ev'ryun looks at me when I sings on a Sunday, so I'll try.

(She sings)

> Diana in 'er chaste 'ome doth lead (To the tune of "Dulcina")
> A modest life without embraces,
> To mens' advances pays no 'eed
> An' the beasts o' the forest chases.
> But I do not like the single life,
> An' much prefer the sweet name o' wife!
>
> For close to the elm the vine doth cling;
> Beside 'er mate is the turtle-dove;
> The mild lioness 'er jungle king,
> The she-bear 'er consort doth love.
> Thus for the marriage-bed I care,
> That which contains a youthful pair!

DOULERUS: O nightingales! Swans! Sirens! And music of the spheres! How fortunate I am to have found such a sweetheart as this!

PHILOFINUS: what is there any longer to prevent a betrotnal being performed in front of two witnesses? You do wish to become this maid's betrothèd, do you not?

DOULERUS:	Hoc satis novit Cupido.
PHILOPINUS:	Num tu cupis esse huius sponsa?
IOANNA:	Ita mihi Lucina faveat.
PHILOPINUS:	(Iungit dextras) Vivite 170
	Concordes, vivite laeti, Hymen, o hymenaeo Hymen!
DOULERUS:	Sed oportet ut parentes nesciant de sponsalibus
	Donec ego rediero, et omnia sint parata nuptiis.
IOANNA:	Prudentissime mi Doulere.
NICHADES:	Confirmetur vester amor
	Mutuis donis et pignoribus. Habeat hoc amoris symbolum,
	(Solvit fasciam cruri levi)
	Et interim ambules, quasi Eques aureae periscelidis.
IOANNA:	At hoc animadvertent parentes.

DOULERUS: Cupid knows that well enough.

PHILOPINUS: You do wish to become this man's betrothed, do you not?

JOANNA: May Lucina favour me thus.

PHILOPINUS: (joining their right hands) Long may you live in harmony and joy! Hymen, O Hymenaeus Hymen!

DOULERUS: But your parents mustn't find out about our betrothal until I return, and everything's ready for the wedding.

JOANNA: wisely spoke, my dear Doulerus.

NICHADES: Let your love for one another be strengthened by the exchange of gifts and tokens. Let him have this as a symbol of your love.

(He removes the garter from her smooth ankle)

And in the meantime, you'll have to walk as if you were a Knight of the Golden Garter!

JOANNA: But me parents'll notice.

DOULERUS: Prudentissime Ioanna,
         Sed dabo hoc vitrum crystallinum, quod irritum facit,
         Quicquid veneno, vel incantamento machinabitur aliquis,
         Et per quod deprehendas omnes prestigiatorum doles.   180
IOANNA: Quanti constat?
DOULERUS: Pluris quam quatuor minis.
IOANNA: Observabo diligenter rem tanti pretii, sed quid ego dabo?
NICHADES: Surripias illud poculum.
IOANNA: Sed sub clavibus et cista clauditur.
NICHADES: Nocte atque clanculum subducas, nec unquam factum fatearis
         Donec die nuptiarum prebeat risum omnibus.
IOANNA: Profecto faciam hac nocte.
DOULERUS: O campos Elysios!
         At deest adhuc osculum.
IOANNA: Si cupis ego non curo.

                         (Osculatur)

DOULERUS: Wisely spoken, Joanna. But I'll give you this crystal glass, which renders quite ineffectual whatever harm anyone might contrive to bring about through poison or magic spells, and it will also enable you to detect all the tricks that sorcerers play.

JOANNA: Yes, but 'ow much is it worth?

DOULERUS: More than eight pounds.

JOANNA: I'll put it away very carefully, for 'tis a thing of great value. But what shall I give you?

NICHADES: Why, steal that punchbowl.

JOANNA: But 'tis kept in a chest, under lock an' key.

NICHADES: Then take it away secretly at dead of night, and never admit to what you've done until your wedding-day, when it will cause everyone great amusement.

JOANNA: To be sure, I'll do't this very night.

DOULERUS: O Elysian fields! But I have n't had a kiss yet.

JOANNA: If you wants to kiss me, I...I...does n't mind.

(He kisses her)

DOULERUS:	O vinum et saccharum! O mel et favos, o deorum nepenthes!	
	Illaquensti me capillamentis tuis, fascinasti me oculis	
	tuis,	
	Afflasti me spiritu tuo quasi fulmine.	190
IOANNA:	Nonne quotidie auro et serico ornabor ut domina?	
DOULERUS:	Etiam, et forsan arte chymica transformaberis	
	In aurum solidum, ut olim uxor Midae.	
	Habebis togam pensilem quotidie, et, caput	
	Coronabitur tiara Gallica, hoc modo:	

(Imponit pileum)

IOANNA: Nonne me decet? Si haberem vestes pulchriores, essem
                                                 longe pulchrior.

(Intus Ioanna)

                                                 Mater vocat.
DOULERUS: At requiretur ut poculum, sic osculum charitatis.
IOANNA: Iterum
                                                           vis?

DOUGLERUS: O wine and sugar! O honey and honey-combs! O elixir of the gods! You have ensnared me with your hair! You have bewitched me with your eyes! You have breathed upon me with a breath that sets my very soul on fire!

JOANNA: I shall be decked out in gold an' silk ev'ry day, like a lady, shan't I?

DOUGLERUS: Of course, and, who knows, you may even be transformed by the alchemist's art into solid gold, like Midas' wife once was. You shall have a flowing robe for every day of the week, and on your head you shall wear a French coronet, like this:

(He places his cap on her head)

JOANNA: It do suit me, don't it? If me clothes was more beautiful, I would look far more beautiful.

(From within a voice is heard calling "Joanna")

Mother's a-callin' me.

DOUGLERUS: But just as I demand the punchbowl of you, so I demand an affectionate kiss.

JOANNA: You wants to kiss me again?

DOULERUS: An negas mihi basium? Vel tibi sume tuum, vel mihi redde
meum.

(Exit IOANNA. Rident)

DOULERUS: Fice mea, hoc est lupanar, et hae omnes sunt meretrices.
Ego procurabo, ut procuratores haec intelligant.   200

(Exeunt)

DOUGLAS: Do you deny me a kiss? Then either take back yours, or give me back mine.

(Exit JOANNA. They laugh)

Take my word, this is a bawdy-house, and all these wenches are whores. I shall do some procuring myself, so that proctors may come to understand these things!

(Exeunt)

ACTUS 2. SCENA 4.
ANNA. IOANNA.

ANNA: Quid tibi dixerunt et fecerunt academici?
IOANNA: Nil mali.
Sed dominus Doulerus me perdite amat, et uxorem cupit.
ANNA: Stolida ne credas cito: sed lasciva protervia
Negando affirmes, quod mox affirmando neges:
Fugientem sequitur iuvenis, sequentem fugit.
Blanditiis misceantur minae, et iracundiae gratia.
IOANNA: At peribit interea generosus prae amore mei.
ANNA: Verus amor non exstinguitur sed probatur tempore;
Interim quamlibet ansam arripias, qua amores trahas.

(Exit)

SUSANNA: Chara Ioanna, quaeso me adiuves in coquendis fartis. 210

ACT 2. SCENE 1.
ANNA. JOANNA.

ANNA: What did them students say to 'e? What did they do?

JOANNA: On, nothin' wrong. But Master Doulerus be desperately in love wi' me, an' wants me fur 'is wife.

ANNA: Foolish child! Don't be in such an 'urry to believe it! Rather, you must with a gay sauciness declare by denyin', what you must presently deny by declarin': fur 'tis a young man's nature to follow the one as flees from 'im, an' to flee from the one as follows 'im. Threats must be mingled with flattery, an' kindness with anger.

JOANNA: But meanwhile the gen'leman 'll die o' love fur me.

ANNA: The flame o' true love ain't extinguished by the passin' o' time, only proven by 't. But fur the moment seize ev'ry opportunity you can o' prolongin' this love.

(Exit)

(Enter SUSANNA)

SUSANNA: Joanna, be a dear, an' 'elp me bake some puddin's, I pray you.

IOANNA: Nihil aliud quam Ioanna? Api, ego dedignor omnia farta.
Ego posthac manus lavabo, et ad speculum me componam,
Et otiabor, et vocabis me dominam, si placet.

SUSANNA: O domina, si placet quid novi tibi contigit?

IOANNA: Recte, dicam tibi Susanna. Ille dives haeres,
Ille rectus et robustus et formosus generosus me uxorem
cupit.

SUSANNA: O te faelicem, si vera narras, solent enim fallere.

IOANNA: At ego scio, et sentio, et video, et tango eius amorem,
Dedit enim hoc vitrum.

SUSANNA: Nempe signum amoris vitrei,
Sed quid pater et mater interim?

JOANNA: Jest Joanna? Notnin' else? Be off with you! I'll 'ave nought to do with...with...with any puddin's! 'Enceforth I shall wash me 'ands, an' arrange me 'air in front o' the mirror, an' I shall be a lady o' leisure, an' you will please to call me "Madam".

SUSANNA: What's come over you, please, m-a-d-a-m?

JOANNA: That's better. Well, I'll tell you, Susanna. That rich 'eir, that upright an' strong an' 'andsome gen'leman, wants _me_ fur 'is wife.

SUSANNA: O 'appy you, if what you says be true,- fur they scholars is in the 'abit of deceivin' folk!

JOANNA: But I knows, an' I feels, an' I sees, an' I touches 'is love, fur 'e 's given me this glass.

SUSANNA: A token of a glass love, without a doubt! But wnat'll your father an' mother do in the meantime?

IOANNA: Parum aestimo, 220
Quid fiat de patre, matre, vobisque omnibus, si
contingat maritus,
Tum enim quadriiugo curru per plateas ferar,
Tum epulabor ad mediam noctem, ut dominae solent,
Tum famuli crinibus tortis, et vestibus nitidissimis
Domum reducent a spectaculis, ut dominae solent.
Tum non obliviscar Susannae, sed eris mihi pedisequa
Et te ducet uxorem ditissimus cliens.

SUSANNA: Gratias.
Domina - si placet.
IOANNA: Non obliviscar tui.
SUSANNA: Gratias.

(Exeunt)

JOANNA: I does n't give a straw what 'appens to father, mother, or any of you for that matter, if I gets wed, fur then I shall ride through the streets in a carriage, drawn by four 'orses; then I shall feast till midnight, like ladies does; then, with me 'air all in curls, an' dressed in a shinin' gown, I shall be escorted 'ome from the theatre by me servants, like ladies is; then I shan't forget Susanna, fur you shall be me lady-in-waitin', an' me richest vassal shall 'ave you fur 'is wife.

SUSANNA: Thank you, madam, please...

JOANNA: I shan't forget you.

SUSANNA: Thank you.

(Exeunt)

ACTUS 2. SCENA 5.
CULLIE. DOULERUS.

DOULERUS: Tu iactas artem fabrilem, at ego ex philosophis
Non minus cognovi: in aure enim ponuntur incus et
malleus   230
Ubi crebris ictibus tanquam in fornace elaboratur
Species audibilis opere Vulcanino longe subtilior.

CULLIE: Habesne in aure totam officinam meam?
Num forcipem, folles, clavos et equinas soleas?

DOULERUS: Non solum, sed in cerebro habeo et totum equum.
Nam dum intelligo equum, intellectus meus fit equus.

CULLIE: Cur igitur venisti pedes?

DOULERUS: Notandum non fit equus
Materialiter, sed representative Distinctionem repete.

CULLIE: O nugas levissimas!

DOULERUS: Non interest, quid videantur tibi,
Tractent fabrilia fabri.

ACT 2. SCENE 5.

CULLIE. DOLERUS.

DOLERUS: You boast of the blacksmith's skill, but I, being a man of learning, know just as much about it as you do, - for inside my ear are situated an 'anvil' and a 'hammer', and when the one repeatedly strikes the other, as in a smithy, a 'shape' is forged - but a shape that one can hear, a shape far more delicate than anything Vulcan's craftsmanship could produce!

CULLIE: 'Ave you got all my tools in your ear-'ole? Surely you ain't got fire-tongs, bellows, nails an' 'orseshoes?

DOLERUS: Not only have I got all those, but in my brain I have a whole horse as well. For when I think horse, my intellect becomes a horse.

CULLIE: Why 'ave you come on foot, then?

DOLERUS: Take note, it does n't become a horse in the material sense, no. One has to make the distinction by way of representation.

CULLIE: Stuff an' nonsense!

DOLERUS: It's of no importance what you think. "Let the cobbler stick to his Last."

(Intrat DAWSON)

DAWSON: Mi vicine Richarde, dicam tibi quod iamdudum
contigit: 240
Porcus tuus subrufus (salva reverentia) in meum
Irrupit horreum, et grana devorat (salva reverentia).
Ego evocavi Molossum: Moloo! Moloo! Ille apprehendit
porcum,
Et auriculam sinistram, avellit dentibus (salva
reverentia).

CULLIE: Indignum facinus!
DAWSON: Quaeras tibi remedium!
DOULERUS: Amici, stultum est iniurias pati, sed stultius lites
sequi.
Ego inter vos arbiter sedebo, ut custos iustitiae,
Hanc litem dirimam.

(Se componit)

Quid tu quaeris Dawson?
DAWSON: Ut satisfiat pro grano.
DOULERUS: Quid tu Cullie?
CULLIE: Ut satisfiat pro
porco.

(Enter DAWSON)

DAWSON: Richard, me good neighbour, I must tell 'e what 'appened not long since: that red pig o' yours (savin' your reverence) bursts into me barn, an' eats up all me grain (savin' your reverence). So I calls me Alsatian—"Holoo! Holoo!" — an' 'e catches the pig, an' bites off its right ear (savin' your reverence).

CULLIE: Oh, monstrous!

DAWSON: You seek your own remedy!

DOULERUS: Friends! Friends! It's foolish to bear wrongs too calmly, but it's even more foolish to go on quarrelling about them. I'll act as arbiter between you, — to see that justice is done. I'll soon settle this dispute.

(He composes himself)

Dawson, state your case.

DAWSON: I wants restitution fur the grain.

DOULERUS: And you, Cullie?

CULLIE: I wants restitution fur the pig.

DOULERUS: Videor mihi videre in hoc maleficio plurimas 250
Difficultates, quas obtusus iustitiarius non
apprehenderet:
Primo porcus granum, canis porcum mordet; haec
est lex talionis,
In qua actione granum patitur tantum,
Canis tantum agit;
Deinde dente peccavit et dente punitur porcus:
haec etiam
Est lex talionis, ut habuit granum, sic aurem
perdidit.
At maxima difficultas oritur, quomodo puniatur
canis:
An dens excuteretur, quae perpetravit facinus?
An auris abscinderetur, quia membro simili
Facta est iniuria? Utroque modo erit lex talionis.
CULLIE: Quid denique statuis?
DOULERUS: Sic itaque geometrice: 260
Porcus faciebat ut porcus, canis faciebat ut canis,
Nihil est dicendum amplius. Afferatur cervisia,
Eritis amici: ambobus.

DOULERUS: I think I see in this offence several difficulties which a dim-witted judge would not grasp. Firstly, the pig eating up the grain, and the dog biting the pig, - this comes under the law of "An eye for an eye and a tooth for a tooth," since in this action the grain suffered as much harm as the dog inflicted. Secondly, the pig having committed the crime with its teeth, and also being punished by a set of teeth, - this, too, comes under the law of "An eye for an eye and a tooth for a tooth", because the pig lost its ear as a direct result of eating up the grain. But the greatest problem arises when we come to consider what punishment should be given to the dog. Should the tooth which committed the offence be pulled out? Or should the dog's ear be cut off, since the injury caused was to a similar limb? Either way it will come under the law of "An eye for an eye and a tooth for a tooth."

COLLIE: So what decision 'as you reached, then?

DOULERUS: A geometric one, as follows: the pig was acting like a pig, and the dog was acting like a dog. There is no more to be said. Fetch some ale! You shall be friends.

A health to you both.

DAWSON: Totum aut nihil.
DOULEMUS: Datur medium, nequeo vobis respondere in bibendo:
Primus haustus est necessitatis, secundus est hilaritatis:
tertius est ebrietatis.
Non amo haustum tertium; haec est vita fullonis robae,
Haurire semper aquam, et haustam revomere.

DAWSON: All or nothin'!

DOULERUS: Half is _my_ limit, I can't match you in drinking: the first draught is of necessity, the second of jocularity, and the third of ebriety. I don't like the third draught, — it's the life of the fuller's robe to be always soaking up water, and once it's soaked up, to be spewing it back again!

ACTUS 2. SCENA 6.
PHILOPINUS. NICHADES. PIGEON.

NICHADES: Scio quod non credas, quanta sit mihi peritia.
PIGEON: Mallem credere quam experiri.
NICHADES: Lunae iugales sistere, et velo nigro   270
  Phaebum serenum condere, fluvios retro
  Revocare celeres, movere loco montes:
  Sopire tumidos angues; serpentes feras:
  Pallore stellas tingere, ut nocte media
  Lucidum abscondant, luridum promant iubar,
  Haec parva sunt, potest haec quaevis Thessala venefica.
  At ego maiora, quae nec dese, nec Faustus potuit,
  Spiritum habeo illius magici, qui dicitur Rogerus Bacon.
CULLIE: Callesne artem nigram?
NICHADES: Imo et rubram et viridem
  Et per nigram, evocare valeo daemones nigros;   280
  Per rubram, rubros, et sic in feliquis. Nam daemon
                                                callidus
  Omnes colores induit, ut polypus solet,
  Sed ne terremini, nam nihil faciemus mali.

ACT 2. SCENE 6.

PHILOPINUS. NICHADES. PIGEON.

NICHADES: I know you don't believe what great skills I possess.

PIGEON: I'd rather believe 'em, than put 'em to the test!

NICHADES: Halting the moon's car, drawing a dark veil across Phoebus' bright countenance, causing swift rivers to flow backwards, moving mountains from their proper place, lulling to sleep swelling snakes and fierce serpents, making the stars turn pale, so that in depths of the night they hide their shining radiance and give forth a gloomy light — these are mere trifles, any Thessalian witch can do these things. But I can work far greater wonders, wonders which are beyond the power even of the goddesses and Doctor Faustus; for I have the soul of that magician, who is called Roger Bacon.

CULLIL: Does you practise the black art, then?

NICHADES: Yes, indeed, and the red and green art, too! By the black art I'm able to conjure up black devils; by the red art red devils, and so on through the rest. For the Devil is a cunning creature, and can assume different colours, like the Polyp. But don't be afraid, for we shan't do any harm.

CULLIE:	Num infantulos putas, quos terreant lemurum fabulae?
	Ego nequaquam timeo artem nigram.
NICHADES:	Quia tua nigrior!
	Praeterea transferre possum aedificia ex uno loco
	In alium sine machinis.
PIGEON:	Quaeso hanc villam transferas
	Procul ab Oxonio, ut fruamur rebus et uxoribus.
NICHADES:	Hoc est opus nimis ponderosum meo spiritui;
	At hanc domum facile, ubi eam vis collocari? 290
PIGEON:	Ullibi modo removeatur.
NICHADES:	In pontum igitur dabo
	Praecipitem, ita ut solum culmen emineat,
	Scopulusque sit navitis timendus, ut prius viatoribus.
PIGEON:	Quaeso, ludamus cum cacodaemone tuo aliquantulum.

CULLIE: You must think we be little children – to be frightened by ghost stories! I ain't at all scared of the black art.

NICHADES: No, because your art's far blacker! I can, moreover, transport buildings from one place to another without machines of any kind.

PIGEON: Then transport this village far away from Oxford, I pray you, so's we can enjoy our possessions an' our wives in peace!

NICHADES: That's too weighty a task for my spirit. But I can easily transport this house, – where would you like it set down?

PIGEON: Anywhere, – only move it!

NICHADES: Then I shall plunge it straight into the ocean, so that only the roof will be left sticking out, – a reef greatly to be feared by sailors, just as before it was an object of dread to travellers!

PIGEON: Let's sport with your cacodemon a little while.

NICHADES: Non adsunt libri, quibus constringatur ad certum ambitum.
Fieret tuo dispendio; quid si enim abriperet
Fenestram, aut cum fumo et sonitu et sulphure
Erumperet per caminum, totamque terreret villam?
Praeterea si quid ablatum est, restitutum (modo dicas
              nemini).
Tibique ostendam in speculo nebulonis imaginem.   300

PIGEON: Forsan meam intelligis, et me callide nebulonem vocas,
Sed si nihil dicerem, quomodo res recuperarem meas?

NICHADES: Fur ille sudans, et anhelans in manus dabit.

PHILOPINUS: Crede mihi, agricola,
      (In aurem)
            potest figuras erigere.

NICHADES: Praeterea magico carmine possum hortos et pomatia
              cingere.

NICHADES: There are n't any books with which he could be confined within a certain space. It would be at your own risk: for what if he were to make off with the lamp, or amid smoke, thunder and brimstone, were to burst forth through the fire-place and terrorise the whole village? Moreover, if anything's been stolen, I'll restore it, (only don't tell a soul) and I'll show you the thief's likeness in a mirror.

PIGEON: Per'aps you means my likeness, an' is craftily callin' me a thief. But if I ain't to say nothin', 'ow shall I recover me goods?

NICHADES: The culprit, himself, sweating and panting, will hand them over to you.

PHILOPINUS: Take my word, farmer,

(whispering in his ear)

he can raise up ghosts.

NICHADES: In addition, I can give protection to gardens and orchards with the aid of a magic spell.

DAWSON: Utinam sic mihi autumno praeterito fecisses!
Nam aliqui vestrum abstulerunt pyra generosa
Et trunco arboris affixere versus maledicos:

    Abstulimus pyra, ne apud Carfoix vendas;
    Reliquimus arborem, si placet te suspendas. 310

PHILOPINUS: Ha, ha, he! Certe aliqui aptius se suspenderent, si
                           haberent arborem
Ideoque collum aptant vel humili trabi.

      (Intrat ANNA)

ANNA: Pastor huius oppidi invenit leporem in segete:
Num placet generosi, ut cum eo contendat vester canis?
Requirit autem solidum, ut mos est.

PHILOPINUS: Tene, accipiat;
Eo, eamus ut venemur, et aucupemur simul!

      (Exeunt)

      (ANNA aufert craterem et poculum)

DAWSON: 'Ow I wish you'd done that fur me last autumn, - fur some o' your company stole me best pears an' fixed these insultin' lines to the trunk o' the tree:

> "We've stolen your pears, lest at Carfax you sell them to-day:
>
> We 'ave left you the tree: if you want to go 'ang you may!"

PHILOPINUS: Ha, ha, he! Certainly some folk would hang themselves in a more fitting manner, if they had a tree, and so that's why they fit their necks to even a low beam!

(Enter ANNA)

ANNA: A shepherd o' these parts 'as found an 'are in the cornfield. Wud you gen'lemen like your dog to try its strength against it? But 'e asks a shillin', as be the custom.

PHILOPINUS: (Giving her a shilling) Here, give him this. Ho! Let's go hunting, and fowling, too!

(Exeunt)

(ANNA takes away the punchbowl and the goblet)

ACTUS 3. SCENA I.
PHILOPINUS. NICHADES. DOULERUS.

PHILOPINUS: Lepus est nimis levipes, et volucres sunt nimis
                                                    volucres
Quam ut aliquid capiamus. Canamus tamen utcunque
Cantilenam venatoriam.

DOULERUS: Maxime placet.

                                    (Whoop doe me noe harme)

           Lustrate lata Botliae prata
             Qua Cunner altior patet,
           Qua Bagly sylvam iactitat suam,
             Ho! lepus dumo latet.   (Iterum)

OMNES: Ho! lepus —.

NICHADES: Transivit parva levipes arva
             Camposque pervolat laetus;   10
           Iam Laelaps prior, iam lepus prior:
             Ho! citius sylvam pete.   (Iterum)

OMNES: Ho! citius —.

ACT 3. SCENE I.

PHILOPINUS. NICHADES. DOULERUS.

PHILOPINUS: The hare hares off too quickly, and the game-birds are too game for us to catch anything! But, even so, let's sing a hunting-song!

DOULERUS: An excellent idea!

(To the tune of "Whoop do me no harm")

    Hunt o'er the broad tillage of Botley village,
        Where stands forth Cumnor the higher,
    Where the woodlands of Bagley extend rather straggly,
        Ho! The hare lies hid in the brier!   (Twice)

ALL: Ho! The hare lies hid in the brier!

NICHADES: The swift creature flees across the small leas,
        And through the fields bounds joyously;
    Now Trouncer leads, now the hare leads,
        Ho! Seek you the woodlands quickly!   (Twice)

ALL: Ho! Seek you the woodlands quickly!

PHILOPINUS: Iam canis instantis spiritum flantis
                     Sentit et luto sordet,
                  Iam pete sinistrum, repete dextrum.
                     Ho! leporem canis mordet.   (Iterum)

OMNES: Ho! leporem —.

DOULERUS: Cantemus quidem vacui corum latronibus,
            Nam nobis non restat denarius. Quid itaque faciamus? 20
NICHADES: Phu! Quid nisi procedamus in nostris astutiis?
            Nec dubito de solutione, si res succedant prospere.
            Dabo tibi dimidium, Philopine, quia cum Keckermanno
                                          diligo
            Dichotomias.

PHILOPINUS: Now the hare surely feels the dog's hot
        breath on its heels,
    And is spattered with mud off the ground;
    Now to the left run, back to the right run!
    Ho! The hare is caught fast by the
        hound! (Twice)

ALL: Ho! The hare is caught fast by the
    hound!

DOGLERUS: Yes, indeed "let's sing empty-handed in the face of robbers", for we have n't a penny left to bless ourselves with! What are we going to do?

NICHADES: Phew! What can we do — save persist with our cunning tricks? I've no doubts as to payment, if all goes well. I shall give you a half, Philopinus, for in company with Keckermann, I, too, am fond of dichotomies.

- 103 -

PHILOPINUS: Quid? Num et ego iterum subdividam?
Et sic bibemus in infinitum. Sit haec lex bibenti,
Ut distichon componat antequam bibat.
Quod si Prisciani caput frangimus, existimabitur
Poetica licentia, et excusabitur inter pocula.
DOULERUS: Quod erit thema nobis?
PHILOPINUS: Quidvis, laus cervisiae
En atramentum et calamum et chartam! 30
Haec semper loculis arma parata meis.
Accingamur!

(Scalpunt occiput, ungues arrodunt,
mensam caedunt, versificaturi.)

O faecundi calices, vobis habeo gratias! Audite.

Cedat metheglin, concedat usquebach allae,
Cedant vina; hederam nobilis alla cape.

DOULERUS: Sed syllabam producis falso.
PHILOPINUS: Huic detur venia
T nesciebat valorem peregrini soni.

(Bibit)

PHILOFINUS: What? Then I'll be able to subdivide it again, shan't I? And that way we'll go on drinking forever and ever. Let this be the law unto the man who drinks: that he must compose a distich before he swills his ale. For if we break Priscian's head, it will be deemed poetic licence, and will be overlooked since we're in our cups.

DOULENUS: What's to be our theme?

PHILOFINUS: Anything you like...Ale and its praises? See, here's ink, a pen, and some paper — these weapons are always ready in my wallet! Let's arm ourselves.

> (They scratch their heads, bite their nails, and bang on the table, as they prepare to write their verses.)

O cups, rich in inspiration, I thank you! Listen:

Let mead give place to ale; potheen step down!
Wine, too! Noble ale, you bear the ivy crown!

DOULENUS: But you've got a syllable too many.

PHILOFINUS: Excuse me — the syllables did n't know anything about nice proper quantities!

> (He drinks)

DOULERUS: Sed auscultate meis.

    Nobilis alla veni, versusque infunde cerebro,
      Iam bona non scribit carmina potor aquae.

PHILOPINUS: Tu incipis quemadmodum ego desino.
DOULERUS: Bona ingenia
                                coincidunt.   40

Quando perficiet Nichades?

                (Bibit)

NICHADES: Iam ἕρηκα ἕρηκα. Audite tetrastichon:

    Unde novus lupulus vitiavit felle maligno
      Cervisiam veterem? Dicite potifices.

    Sic ego, sic illi, mytho dedit hordea nostro
      Diva Ceres, Cereris sed gener hos lupulos!

                (Bibit)

DOULERUS: But lend an ear to <u>my</u> lines:

    Come, noble ale, do thou my brain

        with songs infuse,

    who water drinks, can't write poems

        through the booze!

PHILOPINUS: You began the same way as I ended.

DOULERUS: Well, great minds think alike! When 'll Nicnades be finished?

                                  (He drinks)

NICHADES: I've got it! I've got it! Hear my tetrastich:

    "Whence come those new hops that with

        bitter gall

    Do mar the ale of old? Tell me, you

        brewers all,"

    So I. But they, "'Tis Ceres' barley

        in our malt,

    The hops?—They're Ceres' son-in-law's

        fault!"

                                  (He drinks)

PHILOPINUS: O dia poemata! Nonne sumus donandi laurea?
　　　　　　At mihi videtur humor cervisiae temperandus
　　　　　　Cum siccitate tobacchi, in his enim duobus vita
　　　　　　Quasi humido radicali et naturali calido.　　　　　50
　　　　　　Habeoque paratum cum infundibulo. Hoh! Lampadem
　　　　　　　　　　　　　　　　　　　　　　　　　cito!

　　　　　　　　　　(Fumum hauriunt)

　　　　　　　　　　　　　　　Magnae sunt vires huius
　　　　　　　　　　　　　　　　　herbae Indicae.
DOULERUS:　At maius est virus, mihi non placet fumus Nicotianus;
　　　　　　Audite autem versus, quos iam excogitavi in hunc fumum:

　　　　　　　Cur fumus Phlegethon? Cur Styx exhalat opacum?
　　　　　　　Quum fumus miseris tetrior iste foret!

MELOMBUS: O what divine poetry! Surely we deserve to be crowned with laurel leaves! But I think the moistness of ale should be tempered with the dryness of tobacco, for both of these depend virtually on moist roots and natural warmth for life! I've some tobacco ready, and a pipe. Hou! A taper, quickly!

(They inhale the smoke)

The charm of this Indian weed is very great.

DOULEJS: Yes, but the harm it does is even greater! I don't like tobacco smoke; listen to the lines I've just thought up against it:

 Why doesrnlegethon? Why does Styx black, cloudy
  billows out-pour?
 This is the smoke that would the poor souls in
  torment vex the more!

PHILOPINUS: Euge poeta! Sed expectes responsionem, nam et tobacchus
                                                            habet
              Patronum suum.

                    Cur redoleat ara superorum thure Sabaeo?
                    Quam fumus superis gratior iste foret!

      Ha, ha, he! Par pari retuli. Et quidem nihil est fere 60
      Quod non in utramque partem sit disputabile,
      Et ancipiti ratione huc et illuc mentem dividat.
      Exempli gratia: Synesius laudat calvitiem
      Et Iulianus excusat capillitium et barbam prolixam
      Et utrinque arguitur. Apollo erat imberbis et Aesculapius
                                                    satis barbatus.
      Inter corpora imperfecte mixta eminet cometa barbatus,
      Inter pecora dux gregis est hircus barbatus,
      Inter pisces mullus aptus est conviviis barbatus,
      Inter rationalia doctissimus Plato satis est barbatus,
      Contra derident alii barbam et capillos,   70
      Quasi sylvam, ubi nutriantur cuniculi septipedes,

PHILOPINUS: Well done, goat! But you must expect your words to be
challenged, for tobacco also has its champion:

> Why do the altars of the gods of Sheban
> incense smell?
> *This* is the smoke that would please the
> more those who in heaven dwell!

Ha, ha, he! I've repaid you with the same coin! Indeed,
there's scarcely any subject which can't be discussed
from two different points of view, and scarcely one
which doesn't cause the mind to wander this way and
that with two-fold reasoning. For example: Synesius
praises baldness, yet Julian excuses hair and long
beards: men argue for and against. Apollo was clean
shaven, yet Aesculapius had quite a growth of beard.
Among imperfectly mixed bodies, there stands out the
bearded comet; among flocks the head of the herd is
a bearded he-goat; among fish the one that's the
most suitable for the dinner-table is the bearded
mullet; among rational creatures learned Plato
had quite a growth of beard.   But, on the other
hand, some folk laugh beards and hair to scorn, as they
would a forest where rabbits, seven foot tall, were reared,

- III -

PHILOPINUS: Quasi virgam vimineam, qua castigentur pueri,
Quasi scopas, quibus repurgetur sentina,
Quasi caudam, in qua Sertorius luculenter ostendat
                              discordiae salum.
   Imo, memini cuiusdam nebulonis tale dicterium,
   In Dromonem barbatum:

       Simia, Dromo, tuis nasum si clunibus indet,
       Tum cauda iuncta Cercopithecus eris!

Nihil est tam eximium, quod non vituperetur;
Nihil est tam sordidum, quod non laudetur;
Est itaque tutissimum in plerisque sic determinare   80
Quod secundum Scotum, Buridanum, Ockamum, Gorhamum,
Et alios magistros subtilissimos, videtur quod sic.
At secundum divum Thomam, Albertum, Caietanum,
Et alios doctores seraphicos, videtur quod non.
Hah! Quid me taciti intuemini? Nonne cogitandum est
                              de caena?
Hoh! Hospita!

PHILOLINUS: as they would a switch, made of osier twigs, being used to flog boys, as they would a broom being used to clean out a drain, as they would the horse's tail by means of which Sertorius clearly showed the evil of discord! Indeed, I remember just such a witty saying which some rascal made up about Dromo and his beard:

> "If a monkey, Dromo, put its nose up to
> your bum,
> By the addition of a tail, a long-tailed
> ape you would become!"

Nothing's so excellent that no fault can be found in it; nothing's so disgraceful that no good can be found in it. So, therefore, it's safest in most cases to determine that a thing is so, because, according to Duns Scotus, Jean Buridan, William of Ockham, Geoffrey of Gorham, and other very shrewd teachers, it is so; and that a thing is not so because, according to Saint Thomas, Albert the Great, Cajetan, and other 'angelic doctors', it is not so. Han! Why are you gazing at me in silence? Surely we ought to be thinking about supper? Ho! Hostess!

ACTUS 3. SCENA 2.
ANNA.

ANNA: Bene sit vobis. Ut valetis mei filii?
Ridete, saltate, potate, hic omnia sunt communia.

DOULEHUS: Sed quid erit ad caenam? Num adest aprugna caro?

NICHADES: Phuh! Aetolus aper non depopulatus est hos agros.

DOULEHUS: Pares scarorum iecinora, phasianorum et pavonum
cerebella, 90
Linguas phaenicopterum, et murenarum lactes;
Adde satyras et epigrammata.

ANNA: Non novi haec bellaria.

DOULEHUS: Volo nectar et ambrosiam pares: nam caenabimus
Iovialiter.
Sed serio quid erit ad caenum?

ANNA: Iuvenes egregii,
Habebitis lautum convivium, si habetis latum marsupium.
Capum parato teneroeque pullos, et nova fartimina,
Et quicquid aliud villa suppeditabit ex tempore.

DOULEHUS: In tempore quaeso, id est, cito, stomachi enim latrant;
Opportune quidem venimus, qui tempore fartorum venimus.

(Exit ANNA)

ACT 3. SCENE 2.

ANNA.

ANNA: May all go well with 'e! 'Ow now, my sons? Laugh, dance, drink your fill, - all things common among friends!

DOULERUS: But what's for supper? There'll be some wild boar's flesh, won't there?

NICHADES: Huh! The boar of Thessaly has n't ravaged <u>these</u> fields!

DOULERUS: Then prepare "pikes' livers, pheasants' and peacocks' brains, flamingoes' tongues, lampreys' milt" and add a pinch of satire and epigram!

ANNA: I knows nothin' about them delicacies.

DOULERUS: I want you to prepare nectar and ambrosia, for we shall dine in a jovial fashion! But, - and I'm in earnest - what <u>is</u> for supper?

ANNA: Gallant young sirs, you shall 'ave a fillin' supper, if you 'as full purses! I shall prepare a capon, some tender young chick'ns, an' some fresh black puddin's, - an' anythin' else as the village can provide, - accordin' to the weather!

DOULERUS: No "whether", please, for our stomachs are rumbling! Indeed, we arrived at just the right moment, - coming as we did in the black pudding season! (Exit ANNA)

NICHADES:	Ego negligo fartum, quia nomen est sordidum;	100
	Deinde rei sordidioris similitudinem gerit.	
DOULERUS:	Cur non itaque turdus displicet avis lautissima?	
	Sed crede mihi, non inest turpitudo vocibus.	
NICHADES:	Mihi crede, inest turpitudo lactibus,	
	Et sordibus nondum egestis saepe ingeritur cibus.	
DOULERUS:	Suum cuique placet; te suum tamen	
	Penitus aversari, credat Iudaeus, non ego.	
NICHADES:	Imo carnem suillam habeat altare Cereris,	
	Non mensa nostra: in hoc Iudaeus sapit.	
	Sed plura garriamus ad focum.	110

(Exeunt)

NICHADES: I don't care for black pudding! It's got a dirty name, and besides it resembles something much dirtier.

DOULERUS: Well, why is it then that you don't find the turd-bird, that most elegant of fowls, displeasing? But, believe me, there's no foulness in words.

NICHADES: There *is*, I warrant you, foulness in pigs' chitterlings, and they're often served as food with the filth still in them.

DOULERUS: Well, every man as he may: but let the Jew, not I, believe that you've got a deep loathing for pork.

NICHADES: By all means let Ceres' altar have its swine's flesh, but not *our* table. The Jew's a wise man in this respect. But let's continue our conversation by the fireside.

(Exeunt)

ACTUS 3. SCENA 3.
PIGEON. IOANNA. ANNA.

PIGEON: Filia, non nosti adolescentium mores, arrident et derident simul.

IOANNA: O pater, me cursitantem observat obliquo lumine,
Amplexus est, suspirat crebro, pene illachrymat,
Orat, pollicetur, et breviter amat me unice.

PIGEON: Quid ais uxor Anna? Quid haec videntur tibi?

ANNA: Forsitan irretitus est, nam amor aequali pede
Turres et tabernas pulsat. Quis nescit quam facile
Illaqueentur iuvenes aetate lubrica?
Interea dum temporis spatio spectatur affectio,
Se facilem et benignam praebeat, et affectum alat. 120

(Exeunt ANNA et IOANNA. Intrant CULLIE et DAWSON)

CULLIE: Ubi generosi? Ubi tot miraculorum artifices?
Qui inequitant daemones ornatos fraenis et ephippiis.

ACT 3. SCENE 3.

PIGEON. JOANNA. ANNA.

PIGEON: Daughter, you doesn't know 'ow young men be'aves: they laughs wi' you an' at you - all in the same breath.

JOANNA: But, father, 'e watches me out o' the corner o' 'is eye as I goes back'ards and fro'ards about me business. 'E 'as kissed me, an' 'e sighs frequently, - nay, 'e almost weeps, - 'e begs, an' promises, an', in short, 'e loves me an' me alone.

PIGEON: 'Ow say you, Anna, my wife? What does you think about all this?

ANNA: Well, 'e may be trapped, fur love "doth strike towers an' taverns wi' impartial foot". Who don't know 'ow easily young men may be ensnared at this dangerous age? But, fur the moment, let 'er be good-natured an' kindly t'wards 'im, an' let 'er nourish this affection.

(Exeunt ANNA and JOANNA.
Enter CULLIE and DAWSON.)

CULLIE: Where be them gen'lemen? Where be them doers o' so many wonders? Them as rides upon devils, fitted out wi' bridles an' 'orse-cloths?

DAWSON: At loquuntur mira quaeque, a talibus dicuntur fieri;
Si ostenderent mihi suam artem, remunerarem amplissime.
CULLIE: Si cupias, ostendent. Sed mihi tardior fides
Quam ut vulgaribus verbis motus faciam periculum.
Interea loquantur magica, et describant circulos.
Forsitan quidem diabolus latet crumenis, quum careant
cruce.

Quaeso, mi hospes, evocentur.

(Vocat et redit PIGEON)

DAWSON: **An'** they speaks of whatever marvels is said to be done by such as them. If they was to show me their skill, I wud reward 'em most 'andsomely.

CULLIE: They'll soon show 'e, if you wants 'em to. But I be too slow a believer to be moved by mere talk to take the risk. Meanwhile, let 'em utter their magic spells, an' draw their circles. Per'aps the devil be indeed lyin' 'idden in their purses, since they 'as no cross! Landlord, call 'em 'ither, I pray you.

(PIGEON calls them and returns.)

ACTUS 3. SCENA 4.
PHILOPINUS. DOULERUS. NICHADES.

PHILOPINUS: Nunc est bibendum, nunc pede libero   130
Pulsanda tellus. Heigh! Sodales optimi, ut est?
Hac nocte vos omnes nobiscum caenabitis.

OMNES: Gratias.

PHILOPINUS: Afferatur cervisia non ad pintam aut quartam, sed
                                             ad congium:
Non ad modum, sed ad modium. Tibi, mi faber,
Utinam esset Falernum, aut Caecubum!

(Bibit largius)

CULLIE: Cur non exemplum praebes?

PHILOPINUS: Sit haec lex inter pocula:
Bibat unusquisque ad libitum, et hilare utamur
                                             consortio.
Ut vitam prorogemus, non acceleremus mortem.

DAWSON: Num vera, generosi, quae vos posse dicitis?

DOULERUS: Verissima.
Habemus enim rerum naturas ad unguem cognitas;   140
Et ego (nec videatur mirum) canes latrantes
                                             intelligo,
Ranas coaxantes, et garrientes aves.

ACT 3. SCENE 4.

PHILOPINUS. DOULERUS. NICHADES.

PHILOPINUS: "Now 's the time to drink, now 's the time to beat the ground with merry foot!" Hey, my good friends, how goes it? Tonight you shall all dine with us!

ALL: Thank 'e.

PHILOPINUS: Bring ale – not by the pint, or by the quart, but by the gallon; not by the flaskful, but by the caskful! Blacksmith, my dear fellow, would that there was some Châteauneuf – du – Pape or some Beaujolais for you!

(He takes a long drink)

CULLIE: Why does n't you give me a bottle, then?

PHILOPINUS: Well, now, let this be the law amid our cups: that each man shall drink to his heart's content, and that we shall enjoy one another's cheerful company, so that we may prolong life, and not hasten death!

DAWSON: Gen'lemen, surely them things as you says you can do, ain't true?

DOULERUS: They most certainly are, for we're intimately acquainted with the workings of the universe; and I (may it not come as too much of a surprise) can understand the barking of dogs, the croaking of frogs, and the twittering of birds!

- 123 -

PIGEON: Quid sub adventum vestrum latravit Molossus meus?
DOULERUS: Te quatuor diebus continuis numquam fuisse ebrium:
At in limine gratulatus est nobis, a quibus expectat
　　　　　　　　　　　　　　　　　　　　　　　　　esse.
DAWSON: Sunt forsitan vera. Sed quomodo haec discatis, dubito.
DOULERUS: Hoc est mysterium, nec vestris dignum auribus;
Habent animalia suas voces, quibus loquuntur ad
　　　　　　　　　　　　　　　　　　　　　　　invicem.
Sic equa pullum novit, et ovis agnum in medio grege;
Haec symbola discant eruditi per artem Apollonii;　　150
Quaedam et vulgus novit; vult pica garrula
Brevi futuros advenas; vult ululans canis
Mortem domestici; et corvus crocitans pluvias vocat.
DAWSON: Certissima sunt.

PIGEON: Well, what were it then that me bull-mastiff barked to you, when you arrived?

DOCLERUS: Why, he told us that you'd never been drunk for four days at a time, and in the doorway he made a great fuss of us because he hoped we'd give him a bone.

DAWSON: Them things may be true, but I 'as me doubts as to 'ow you learns 'em.

DOCLERUS: Ah, that's a secret, and not fit for your ears. Animals have their own language in which they speak to one another: that's how the mare recognises her foal, and the ewe her lamb in the middle of the flock. Scholars learn these signs through Apollonius' art, but even the common folk know some of them: for instance, a chattering magpie means that strangers will arrive shortly; a howling dog foretells the death of a member of the household, and a croaking raven is calling down the rain.

DAWSON: Ay, 'tis very certain true.

DOULERUS: Iam quod rustici discunt experientia,
Id hauriunt ex libris docti. Et longe plura, longe
plura
Miranda sunt, quae Philopinus in re medica et Nichades
in magica
Valeant efficere si tutum foret: possunt gravidas
Reddere quae steriles, possunt quid futurum praedicere,
Et alia difficiliora, quam quae de Fortunati pileo,
Aut Gygis annulo, referuntur.
DAWSON: Quid illud, quaeso? 160
DOULERUS: Rex Gyges habuit annulum cuius palam si converteret
Versus palmam, ipse spectaret omnia
Nulli mortalium spectabilis. Huic similem arte sua
Fabricavit Nichades, qui gestantem reddit invisibilem.
DAWSON: Num loqueris pro certo?
DOULERUS: Si vis, experieris esse
certissimum.

(Intrat CAECILIA. Exit PIGEON)

DOULERUS: Nowadays, what country-folk learn by experience, scholars draw from text-books. But far, far greater are the wonders which Philopinus in the field of medicine, and Nicnades in the field of magic, could bring about, if it were safe to do so; for they can make barren women conceive, predict what's going to happen in the future, and they can do other things, too, far more difficult than those related about Fortunatus' cap, or Gyges' ring.

DAWSON: What's that, pray?

DOULERUS: Well, King Gyges had a ring, and if he turned the collet of the ring towards the palm of his hand, he could see everything, but not a living soul could see him, and Nicnades, through his own skill, has fashioned a ring similar to this one, which also renders the wearer of it invisible.

DAWSON: Be you a-tellin' the truth?

DOULERUS: If you wish, you can try it out for yourself, and see that what I say is indeed very true.

(Enter CAMILLA. Exit PIGEON.)

DAWSON:	Oh, adest uxor! Obsecro, me illico reddatis
	invisibilem.
CAECILIA:	Nihilne agetur hodie? Non repurgabitur stabulum?
	Non triturabitur hordeum? Semperne otiaris
	Et ad cauponam inebriaris? Abi, morio!

(Baculum elevat; trudit foras)

DOULERUS:	Cedant arma togae! O Xantippe, obliviscamur	
	iurgii virgis,	170
	Erimusque tibi multum devincti, si marito faveas.	
PHILOPINUS:	Amat te unice et liberos optat maxime,	
	Ideoque illi dicturus fui medicinam eximiam	
	Quae te praegnantem redderet, si periculum facias.	
CAECILIA:	Quasi vos medici!	

DAWSON: Oh, 'ere's the missus! Make me invisible this minute, I begs you!

CAECILIA: Ain't nothin' goin' to get done to-day? Ain't the stable never goin' to get mucked out? Ain't the grain never goin' to get threshed? Will you forever idle your time away down at the ale'ouse, gettin' drunk? Get out of 'ere, you good-for-nothin' layabout!

(She raises her stick to him, and bundles him out of the door.)

DOULERUS: "Let arms yield to the toga"! O Xantippe, let's forget the rods of contention, and we shall be much obliged to you, if you'll show your husband a little leniency.

FAIDUINUS: He loves you and you alone, and longs to have a family very much. It was for that reason that I was just about to tell him of a remarkable potion, which would help you to conceive, if you'd only take the risk.

CAECILIA: Huh! Pretendin' to be ph-ph-physicians now, am you!

PHILOPINUS: Medicinae dedimus non parum asperae.
Nihil autem erit periculi, etsi non succedat bene.
At scio quod succedet, quia probatum est a doctoribus.
CAECILIA: Sed non videtur verisimile, quod fiat modo medice.
PHILOPINUS: Nonne? Habeo fortem aquam, et herbae cuiusdam pulveres
Quae sic faecundent uterum et matricem aperiant, 180
Ut concipias vel solo Zephyro, tanquam equa
Lusitanica.
Inquit enim Aristoteles in Graeco contextu:
DOULERUS: Tu es insanus
Graecus!
PHILOPINUS: Quod mulieribus maneant καταμήνια μέχρι τῶν
πεντήκοντα ἐτῶν et tu nondum es quadragenaria.
Concipies itaque brevi, si maritus abstineat legumine;
Nempe circa initium Maii secundum regulam:

Marte mares, Februoque canes, Maio mulieres.

PHILOPINUS: Well, we've administered enough of this bitter medicine in the past! But there won't be any danger, even if it is n't successful, - though I know it will be because it's been tested by very learned men.

CAECILIA: But what 'appens by the aid of medicines don't seem natural some'ow.

PHILOPINUS: Of course it does! I 've some strong water and the powder of a certain plant, which together will make the womb so fertile and so open up the matrix, that you'll become pregnant by the west wind alone, like the Lusitanian mare! For Aristotle says, in his Greek treatise, that -

CAECILIA: (Why, you're a raving Greek now!)

PHILOPINUS: "Menstruation continues up until the age of fifty", but you have n't had even your fortieth birthday yet! So, therefore, you 'll conceive in a very short time from now, - if only your husband will refrain from eating green vegetables. Undoubtedly it will be about the beginning of May, according to the saying:

"In March males, in February airedales, in the month of May females!"

                Et post decimum diem octavum organisabitur,
                Et post diem quadragesimum se concutiet embryo:
                Nisi mentiatur Albertus.

CAECILIA: Ille est spurcissimus
                                    nebulo,   190
                Qui obstetricis habitu mulierum secreta noverat,
                Utque audio scriptis patefacit palam omnia.

PHILOPINUS: Haec aqua, et pulvis forte fortuito sunt in loculo;
                Et si maritus redeat ad caenam, paratum erit
                                electuarium,
                Et habebit secum. Dum vero lectum petis,
                Audacter ebibas, nec sit fortior sensus, quam fides.

CAECILIA: Tentato. Valete.

                              (Exit)

CULLIE: Haec est mulier morosissima, nec conveniens est
                Ut habeamus similem eius progeniem?

DOULERUS: Qualis est tua?
                Nonne videbimus?

CULLIE: Nequaquam, nam visu pariter
                Et moechus inficit, et basiliscus interficit!   200

And on the eighteenth day after conception the embryo will begin to develop sense organs, and on the fortieth day after conception, it will start to move about, — that is, unless Albert's a liar.

CAECILIA: This be a vile knave, who in the guise o' a midwife, 'as found out all woman's secrets, an' even while I listens, ' as disclosed quite openly ev'rythin' that be set down in the writin's!

PHILOPINUS: As luck would have it, I've got some of that very water and powder here in my wallet; so if your husband returns at supper-time, the electuary will be ready and he can take it away with him. Then, indeed, as you 're going to bed, drink it boldly down, and don't let your feelings get the better of your faith.

CAECILIA: I'll do me best. Fare you well.

(Exit CAECILIA.)

COLLIE: 'Er's a very bad-tempered woman, — surely it ain't a good idea fur us to 'ave an offspring exactly like 'er?

DODLINUS: What's <u>your</u> wife like? We shall get a look at her, shan't we?

COLLIE: Oh, no, you don't! Fur the adulterer's look be fatal, — like the basilisk's!

DOULERUS: Quam flavus est zelotypus! Apage, num castam putas?
CULLIE: Quid ni?
DOULERUS: Dabo duos denarios ut illud monstri videam.
Sed, amabo, induam ego vestes tuas, et experiar
Eius castitatem.
CULLIE: Nequaquam, sic lubens et libens
Fabricares mihi cornua.
DOULERUS: Unusquisque est suae fortunae
faber.
CULLIE: Potius ego induam vestes tuas, eaeque experiar,
Et faciam periculum sine periculo; sed optimum est
Praesentibus acquiescere, dum satis castam puto.
DOULERUS: Igitur ἢ πίθι ἢ ἄπιθι aut bibe aut abi.
CULLIE: Bibam et abibo, sed ad caenam redibo.   210

(Exit)

DOULERUS: See how the jealous man turns yellow! But come, surely you don't really believe she's faithful?

CULLIE: An' why shouldn't I?

DOULERUS: I'll pay you twopence to gaze upon...this...this... prodigy! But be so good as to let me put on your clothes, and make trial of her chastity!

CULLIE: Oh, no, you won't! Fur then I should be willin'ly an' wittin'ly forgin' me own 'orns.

DOULERUS: "Every man is the forger of his own fortune!"

CULLIE: I'd rather dress in your clothes, an' put 'er to the test, fur then I should be takin' the risk without there bein' any real risk to take! But 'tis best to rejoice in the present, while I still thinks 'er's quite chaste.

DOULERUS: Then either get tiddled or toddle off! Either drink up or slink off!

CULLIE: Well, I will get tiddled an' slink off, but I'll return at supper-time!

(Exit)

ACTUS 3. SCENA 5.

(Manent academici. Rident, et se
invicem amplectuntur)

PHILOPINUS: Deus bone, quam futilia loquimur et inania,
Et quicquid in buccam venit, ut nobis excitetur risus!
Sed iam progrediamur his nugis, Nichades.

NICHADES: Maxime:
Aderuntque et mihi partes, tandemque deludam optime,
Et diabolus intererit, si nodus dignus vindice.

BOULERUS: Sed nonne ludificamus ancillam, quae procul dubio
meretrix est:
Nam ubicunque lepidam puellam videritis in hospitio,
Scitote laqueum dolosum, et hamum illitum cibo.
Tentemus autem eius pudicitiam dictis solummodo,
Non osculis: nam inveniemus credo satis facilem.   220
Volumus igitur eam sigillatim et vicibus oppugnare.
At ecce! Lupa est in fabula! Ego incipiam: secedite.

(Intrat SUSANNA. Exeunt PHILOPINUS et
NICHADES)

ACT 3. SCENE 5.

(The students stay behind. They laugh, and hug one another in turn.)

PHILOPINUS: Good lord! What idle chat we've been indulging in - saying the first thing that came into our heads, just to cause ourselves amusement! But now, Nichades, let's continue with those jests of ours!

NICHADES: Yes, indeed, and I shall play _my_ part; in the end, I shall prove the best trickster of all, and the Devil will intervene, too, "if the situation requires a champion of that kind!"

DOLPHUS: But ought n't we to make fun of the maid, who is, without a doubt, of easy virtue, - for wherever you see that charming wench about the inn, rest assured that _there_ is a cunning trap and a hook spread with bait! But let 's put her chastity to the test with words only - _not_ with kisses - for we shall, I believe, find her easy enough! Therefore, we must try to accost her one by one, taking it in turns. But look, - talk of the devil - I'll begin, you retire.

(Enter JOANNA; exeunt PHILOPINUS and NICHADES.)

SUSANNA: Domine, num opus est tibi aliquo?
DOULERUS: Non sed aliqua.
Do vero tibi non minus quam munus in manus,
Si non vocares dominus.
SUSANNA: Quid ergo? Magister?
DOULERUS: Hoc ter magis displicet.
SUSANNA: Num generosus?
DOULERUS: Si tu speciosa.
SUSANNA: Num igitur patronus?
DOULERUS: Si tu matrona. Sed velim me vocites magis
Familiari nomine, nempe amicum vel dilectum.

(Manum apprehendit)

SUSANNA: Esne si placet astrologus?
DOULERUS: Maxime fiet almanacta 230
Nondum edidi.
SUSANNA: Et potesne fortunas dicere, si inspicias manus volam?
DOULERUS: Etiam nec minus, si inspiciam plantam nudi pedis.
SUSANNA: Nuptura sumne quaeso?

SUSANNA: 'Ave you need of somethin', sir?

DOULERUS: Not of something, but someone! C-e-rtainly, I would present you with a pleasant present, if you would n't address me in so s-u-rly a fashion!

SUSANNA: What am I to call you, then? Teacher?

DOULERUS: Teach y-e-rself that I find that displeasing, too!

SUSANNA: Gen'leman, per'aps?

DOULERUS: If you're a gentle woman!

SUSANNA: Patron, then?

DOULERUS: Only if you'll be matron! But I wish you'd call me by a more familiar name, - friend, surely, or beloved?

(He takes hold of her hand)

SUSANNA: Be you one o' them astrologers, then?

DOULERUS: Yes, I am indeed: an almanac will be compiled, but I have n't divulged its contents yet.

SUSANNA: An' can you tell folks' fortunes, if you looks at the palms o' their 'ands?

DOULERUS: Of course, - no less than if I look at the sole of a bare foot!

SUSANNA: Then am I to be wed, I pray you?

DOULERUS: Etiam mea iuvencula,
Tempus erit quando vacca fies, et bovem feras
Milone melius.
SUSANNA: Num futurus est maritus corniger?
DOULERUS: De hoc Hammonem consule.
SUSANNA: Sed cuius ordinis?
DOULERUS: Erit
Sacerdos, qui desperabit de omnibus caeteris,
                                    ideoque breviter,
Te videbit, visam cupiet, et cupita potietur;
Et sic tenebitur regula Lilliana, sus atque
                                    sacerdos.
Sed mea Sussa mea, te unice diligo, amore
                                    mutuo   240
Compenses amorem, et me hac nocte admittito.
SUSANNA: Phi! Nonne te pudet?
DOULERUS: Amor non novit erubescere
Nec patitur repulsam; veniam ad horam duodecimam.
SUSANNA: Tibi soli negare non possum, sed fiat clanculum.

(Exit DOULERUS. Intrat PHILOPHILUS)

DOULERUS: Yes, my pretty little calf, the time will come when you will grow into a cow, and will carry the bull better than Milo!

SUSANNA: Me future 'usband's goin' to 'ave 'orns, then, is 'e?

DOULERUS: You better ask Hammon about that!

SUSANNA: But what 'll be 'is station in life?

DOULERUS: He'll be a priest, who will renounce all others for you: in a word, he will look upon you, having looked upon you, he will desire you, and desiring you, he will make you his own; and in this way Lilly's rule will be observed - the pig and the priest! But, S-o-wsie, my dearest, I love you and you alone. Return my love, I beg you, with a mutual affection, and let me in tonight.

SUSANNA: You ought to be ashamed of yourself, you did!

DOULERUS: Love knows not how to blush, nor does it brook being rejected: I shall come at twelve o'clock.

SUSANNA: To you alone I can't say nay, but do it quietly.

(Exit DOULERUS; enter PHILOTINUS.)

(Reducit SUSANNAM exeuntem)

PHILOPINUS: Paucis te volo. O Susanna:
altera
Nec pulchrior illa, sed castior spero fuit.
Candidior folio, nivei Susanna ligustri.
Lucidior glacie, natura dulcior una,
Mollior et cygni plumis, et lacte coacto.
Celare nequeo, nec amorem fateri audeo; 250
Sis, obsecro, benigna, et pereuntem amplectere.
SUSANNA: Phi! Nonne te pudet?
PHILOPINUS: Nox est caeca, et amor captus
oculis.
Ingrediar ad horam primam tuum cubiculum.
SUSANNA: Tibi soli negare non possum, fiat clanculum.

(Exit PHILOPINUS. Intrat NICHADES)

(Reducit SUSANNAM exeuntem)

(PHILOPINUS leads SUSANNA back on to the stage
as she is about to go out.)

PHILOPINUS: I must have a word with you: O Susanna, there is none fairer than she, but I hoped she was more chaste. Susanna, "thou art whiter than the leaves of the snowy privet, more shining than ice, sweeter than Nature alone, softer than swan's-down or cream cheese." I can't hide my love, but I don't dare confess it either. Be merciful, I entreat you, and embrace a man that dies for ~~of~~ love.

SUSANNA: You ought to be ashamed of yourself, you did!

PHILOPINUS: The night is dark, and Love is blind. I shall enter your chamber at one o'clock.

SUSANNA: To you alone I can't say nay: only do it quietly.

(Exit PHILOPINUS, enter NICHADES.)

(NICHADES leads SUSANNA back on to the
stage as she is about to go out.)

NICHADES: Hei ho! Amore quanto perculsus
                sum
  Simul ac te videram, testor oculos tuos:
  O arte quanta rotasti fulgidos oculos,
  Petulcos oculos, natos in perniciem meam.
  O mea Violetta, Aramanta, Rosabella, Dulcinea,
  Phyllis et Amaryllis et si quid aliud nomen,   260
  Suggerunt poetae. Habeam te hac nocte usurariam!
SUSANNA: Phi! Nonne te pudet? Scio quod vis me decipere.
NICHADES: Prius unda dabit flammas. Dic qua hora ingrediar
  Tuum cubiculum.
SUSANNA: Tibi soli negare non possum,
  Ad horam secundam venias clanculum.

    (Intus Susanna, Susanna)

Hera vocat, abeundum est.

    (Exit)

NICHADES: Heigh-ho! With what a great love was I smitten the first time ever I saw your face! I call your eyes to witness: O with what great skill you rolled those flashing eyes, those wanton eyes, those eyes born to be my ruin! O my Violetta, Aramanta, Rosabella, Dulcinea, Phyllis and Amaryllis, and any other name which the poets may suggest! Tonight I shall enjoy you!

SUSANNA: You ought to be ashamed of yourself, you did! I knows full well that you wants to deceive me.

NICHADES: Sooner "shall water produce flames"! Say at what hour I may enter your chamber.

SUSANNA: To you alone I can't say nay. Come in secret at two o'clock.

(A voice is heard within, calling, "Susanna! Susanna!")

Me mistress be a-callin' me, I'd better get movin'!

(Exit)

ACTUS 3. SCENA 6.

(Intrant PHILOPINUS et DOULERUS. Rident)

DOULERUS: O impudicum et infidum muliebre genus!
Libido venenata facie formosa latet;
Apis mel ore, aculeus cauda gerit;
Cautosque mulcet Syren, incautos necat;   270
Caute si non caste, est faeminarum regula.
Expectabit ancilla serio, quod nos promisimus 1000,
Sed huiuscemodi debita solvenda sunt ad Graecas
                                        Calendas.

PHILOPINUS: Iam autem medicamentum parandum est pro Caecilia.
Vitrum habeo atramento semiplenum, cui infundam
                                        urinam
Herbamque Nicotianam, et addam aliquantulum sacchari
Ut alliciatur gustus. Hoc bibet mulier morosissima.

NICHADES: Interea cantemus otiosi:

ACT 3. SCENE 6.

(Enter PHILOPINUS and DOULERUS. They laugh.)

DOULERUS: What unchaste and unfaithful creatures women are! Beneath that fair exterior there lies hid a dangerous fickleness! The bee that has honey in her mouth, has a sting in her tail! The siren charms the careful, but kills the careless! "If not chastely, yet charily" is woman's maxim! The serving-wench will await in earnest, what we promised in jest, - still, debts of this sort have to be paid on the Greek Calends!

PHILOPINUS: But now the medicine must be prepared for Caecilia. I have here a beaker half full of ink, into which I'm going to pour some piss and some tobacco, and I'll also add a sprinkling of sugar to make it taste nice! This is what that bad-tempered besom shall drink!

NICHADES: Meanwhile, as we have n't anything else to do, let's have a sing-song:

DOULERUS: Iam fremit Boreas   (Virginea)
                       Nec hilum ego curo: 280
                       Fremat et fremat rapide,
                           Sub tecto sum securo.

                       Tara ding ding ding, tara ding ding dere,
                       Iucundum est a turba procul hilares sedere!

NICHADES: Iam gemit fraxinus
                       Nec hilum ego curo:
                       Gemat et gemat misere,
                           Sub tecto sum securo.

                       Tara ding, &c.

DOULERUS: Iam fluit pluvia   290
                       Nec hilum ego curo:
                       Fluat et fluat turbine,
                           Sub tecto sum securo.

                       Tara ding, &c.

DOULERUS:	Now the North wind is a-roaring,	(To the
	But not a jot care I;	tune of
	Let it roar and roar fiercely,	"Virginea")
	 'Neath a stout roof am I!

	Tara ding ding ding, tara ding ding dere,
	'Tis joy to sit us merrily down from the
	crowd far away!

NICHADES:	Now the ash-tree is a-sighing,
	But not a jot care I;
	Let it sigh and sigh mournfully,
	 'Neath a stout roof am I!

	Tara ding ding ding, tara ding ding dere,
	'Tis joy to sit us merrily down from the
	crowd far away!

DOULERUS:	Now the rain it is a-pouring,
	But not a jot care I;
	Let it pour and pour gustily,
	 'Neath a stout roof am I!

	Tara ding ding ding, tara ding ding dere,
	'Tis joy to sit us merrily down from the
	crowdfar away!

　　　　　　　Iam ruit saeva nix
　　　　　　　Nec hilum ego curo:
　　　　　　　Ruat et ruat grandine,
　　　　　　　　　Sub tecto sum securo.

　　　　Tara ding, &c.

　　　　　　　(Intrat DAWSON)

DAWSON:　　Nunc advenio ab uxore impetrata venia, 300
　　　　　　Iam enim et vobis et mihi et omnibus est benignior:
　　　　　　Sed ubi est dominus Philopinus?

　　　　　　　(Intrat PHILOPINUS)

PHILOPINUS:　O Roberte, accipias medicamentum pro uxoris sterilitate
　　　　　　Quod illico inflabit quasi utrem illius uterum!
　　　　　　Sed quid nobis dabitur, quando baptizabitur filia?
DAWSON:　　Mallem habere filium, si sit possibile.
PHILOPINUS:　At astra pollicentur tibi filiam et mores tui.
DAWSON:　　Die baptismatis invito vos tres ad prandium
　　　　　　Utque vulgo canitur:

> Now the cruel snow is a-falling,
> But not a jot care I;
> Let it fall and fall bitterly,
> 'Neath a stout roof am I!
> Tara ding ding ding, tara ding ding dere,
> 'Tis joy to sit us merrily down from the crowd
>   far away!

(Enter DAWSON)

DAWSON: I've jest this minute come from the missus, — 'avin' sought 'er forgiveness, — for 'er be now feelin' more kindly disposed t'ward you an' me, an' ev'ryun. But where be Master Philopinus?

(Enter PHILOPINUS)

PHILOPINUS: Oh, Robert, here's the remedy for your wife's barrenness. It'll make her womb swell up at once, like a balloon! But what will you give us, when your daughter's baptized?

DAWSON: I'd rather 'ave a son, if't be at all possible.

PHILOPINUS: But the planets and your own constitution indicate that you will have a daughter.

DAWSON: On the day 'er's christened, then, I'll invite the three o' you to dine wi' me, an' like the song says:

>Habebitis armum ovis, 310
>Aut salsam carnem bovis,
>Aut lardum frictum ovis,
>>Aut aliquid bonum.

>Habebitis nigrum fartum,
>Aut lactis summam partem,
>Aut pernam herbis fartam,
>>Aut aliquid bonum.

PHILOPINUS: Iam verum esse video quod toties dici solet:
O vos coloni de Hinoksey! Vae vobis colonis de Hinoksey!
Nam devoratis plus lardi septimana qualibet, 320
Quam nos scholares totius anni circulo!

(Intrat SUSANNA)

SUSANNA: Imposita est caena mensae, vosque manent convivae reliqui.

PHILOPINUS: Eamus itaque caenatum, et a foco petamus cubilia.

> Fur you a shoulder of mutt-on,
>
> Or a side of beef with salt on,
>
> Or some fat of roasted mutt-on,
>
> > Or somethin' else that's good!
>
> You shall 'ave some real black puddin's,
>
> Or from the milk the skimmin's,
>
> Or an 'am with 'erbs as fillin's,
>
> > Or somethin' else that's good!

PHILOPINUS: Now I see that what people so often say, is very true: O you villagers of Hinksey, woe to you, villagers of Hinksey! For you consume more fat in a single week, than we students do in the course of a whole year!

(Enter SUSANNA)

SUSANNA: Supper's on the table, an' t'other guests be a-waitin' fur you.

PHILOPINUS: And so let 's go in to dine, and then, from the fire-side, hie us to our beds.

ACTUS 3. SCENA 7.
(Pastor PIGEON sequens)

PIGEON: O pastor, pastor, ibam te vocatum ut luderes;
Bene est, quod tecum habeas tympanum et tibiam;
                                      convivium est
exangue quod vino, mutum quod musica, caret.
Iam discubuerunt nostri scholastici, quos cupio
Omni voluptatis genere perfundere.
Rideant ad dolorem usque, ludant, saltent, bibant,
Dominentur in aedibus, nos stultos dicant et
                                        putant.   330
Habent et suam stultitiam academici. Non inulti
                                        ferent.
Sed crumenis vacuis per penylesse bench redibunt
                                        domum!
Hoh! Domini, si saltare velitis, adest musicus!

(Intrat musicus)

(Exeunt scholares cum mappis, trahentes
hospitam, filiam et ancillam;
saltant NICHADES cum ANNA,
DOULERUS cum IOANNA,
PHILOPINUS cum SUSANNA.
Pastor agit tympanistam)

ACT 3. SCENE 7.

(Enter PIGEON, followed by a shepherd)

PIGEON: An, shep'erd, shep'erd, I were goin' to call 'e to come an' play. 'Tis a good thing that you 'as your pipe an' tabor wi' you, fur the feast be lifeless because there ain't no wine, an' silent because there ain't no music. Already them scholars of ours, whom I wants to treat wi' ev'ry kind o' pleasure, be seated at table. Let 'em laugh till they cries, let 'em sport, let 'em dance, let 'em drink, let 'em be masters in this 'ouse, let 'em say an' think that we be fools, fur students 'as a foolishness o' their own. They shan't go unpunished, but they shall return 'ome wi' empty purses, past the penniless bench! Ho! Sirs, if you wants to dance, 'ere be a musician!

(He enters)

(Exeunt the students, with their table-napkins, and drawing the hostess, her daughter and the maid after them: NICHADES dances with ANNA, DOULERUS with JOANNA, PHILOPINUS with SUSANNA; the shepherd accompanies them on the tabor.)

ACTUS 4. SCENA I.
ANNA. SUSANNA.

ANNA: Susanna, expergefacias filiam, si dormiat,
Iubeasque induere novas vestes, ut ornatior
Appareat generosis. Tu interea ientaculum pares.

SUSANNA: Curabitur sedulo.

(Exeunt)
(Intrant academici)
(Buttoning, trussing, putting on their cuffes)

DOULEHUS: Iam Aurora punicantibus labris arridet nostris iocis.
Hesterna nocte, quam hilares fuimus inter caenandum!
O quantos ludos fecit Ioanna! Dum prae modestia
Cibum negligebat, manusque et oculos nesciebat
                       gerere,
Et pene concrepuit gaudio, dum adaperto capite,
Aliisque nugis curialibus, ad eius salutem bibimus. IO
Hoh! Ancilla! Proma, conda, allam afferas cito,
Cum pane tosto, et cum muscata nuce!

(Intrat SUSANNA)

Salve, Susanna, des veniam, non potui venire ut
                       promiseram.

ACT 4. SCENE I.

ANNA. SUSANNA.

ANNA: Susanna, wake me daughter, if 'er's still a-sleepin', an' bid 'er put on 'er new clothes, so 's 'er may appear smarter to the young gen'lemen. Meanwhile, prepare the breakfast.

SUSANNA: I'll do 't at once.

(Exeunt)

(Enter the students, buttoning, trussing, putting on their cuffs.)

DOULERUS: Now rosy-lipped Dawn smiles upon our jests! Yesterday evening how merry we were at supper! Oh, what great amusement Joanna gave us! When, on account of her shyness, she would n't touch even a morsel of food, and did n't know how to occupy her hands and eyes; and she very near clapped for joy, whilst, doffing our caps and performing other courtly gestures, we drank her health! Ho! Wench! Draw forth - , bring -, fetch - some ale quickly, and some toast with nutmeg.

(Enter SUSANNA)

Good day to you, Susanna, pray forgive me, but I could n't come as I promised.

PHILOPINUS:	Nec ego.
NICHADES:	Nec ego.
DOULERUS:	Num omnibus consenserat?

     Num de faeminis tenet maxima: quo communius, eo melius?

SUSANNA:	Detis veniam, locuta sum tantum ioco.
DOULERUS:	At sic ex virgine fieres mater ioco.

     Sed erubescit, non penitus fronte periit pudor.
     Hunc nigrum cyathum exhauriam.

       (Bibit)

         Vetus est dictum:

     Quisquis ad annos Nestoris cupit vivere,   20
     Ad lacrimas usque, mane debet bibere.

PHILOPINUS: Mihi videtur, quod potus sic distribuatur die,

     Alla mane, cervisia lupulata meridie,
     Vinumque vesperi; sed cur cesso bibere?

       (Bibunt)

PHILOPINUS: Nor I.

MICHADES: Nor I.

DOULERUS: Surely she did'nt say "yes" to all of us? Surely the maxim : "The more, the merrier" does n't hold good with regard to womankind!

SUSANNA: Get along with 'e! I were only jokin' !

DOULERUS: Ah, but that way you might have changed from a maiden into a mother - only jokin'! Still, she blushes: modesty has n't faded altogether upon her brow. I'll drain this dark ladle dry.

(He drinks)

There 's an old saying:

"He that wishes to live to Nestor's years,
Must drink each morning until he sheds tears!"

PHILOPINUS: I think that liquor ought to be evenly distributed throughout the day, like this:

Ale at the start of the day, and beer in the
middle of the day;
wine at the end of the day: but why my drinking
do I delay?

(They drink)

(Intrat PIGEON; fidicen ludit intus,
The hunt is up)

PIGEON: Boh! Quis est iste fidicen? Cur? Unde? Accersente quo?
Habitat in proxima villa, et generosos adesse audiens,
Offert suam artem si placet.

DOULERUS: Quod sponte offertur
vilescit.
Plectrum reponat, capsula condat fides;
Nec aerem verberet amplius.

(Intrat fidicen)

Nisi desinas, nos non faciemus concentum bonum. 30
FIDICEN: Detis veniam, obsecro.

(Ludit)

DOULERUS: Nisi desinas, plusquam δὶς διὰ πασῶν discordes
erimus.
FIDICEN: Detis veniam, quaeso.

(Ludit)

PHILOPINUS: Si pergat ludere, volumus eum deludere.

(Enter PIGEON. Within a minstrel is heard playing
              "The hunt is up")

        Ho! who 's that lute-player? Why 's he here? Where's he come from? Who told him to come?

PIGEON: 'E lives in the next village, an' 'earin' that you gen'lemen was 'ere, offers 'is services, if you wish it.

DOULERUS: (That which is offered of its own accord, is worthless.) Let him lay down his plectrum, put his lute away in its case, and no longer lash the air.

        (Enter the lute-player)

        Unless you stop playing, we shan't provide good harmony.

LUTE-PLAYER: Forgive me, I beseech you.

        (He plays)

DOULERUS: Unless you stop playing, we shall prove more discordant than discordant chords!

LUTE-PLAYER: Forgive me, I pray you.

        (He plays)

PHILOGINUS: If he goes on playing, we shall have to play *him* false!

FIDICEN: Audite, quaeso, paululum musicae.

(Ludit)

PHILOPINUS: Hic surdus est, est ille longe te peritior,
Ego non amo musicam; ne radas aures amplius,
Iniussus numquam desistet.
DOULERUS: Imo nec iussus quidem.
Quodnam genus modulaminis possis ludere?
Num Coranto, aut Spanilette?
FIDICEN: Minime. 40
DOULERUS: Num Lavinianium aut Canarias?
FIDICEN: Minime.
DOULERUS: Nihilne? Num tu solus obambulas, utque raucus cuculus
Eandem semper canis cantilenam? Abi in malam crucem!
Abi hinc! Abi Hinckay!
PIGNON: Domini, sinatis obsecro:
Musica tempore matutino recreat animum.

LUTE-PLAYER: 'Arken, I pray you, to a little o' my music.

(He plays)

PHILOPINUS: This man's stone-deaf, that fellow's far more skilled than you, and I, for my own part, don't like music, nor any sound that grates upon the ears. "When no one asks him to play, he never stops"!

DOULERUS: Nay, when he's asked to play, he does n't even stop! What kind of tunes do you know? The Coranto, or the Spagnoletto?

LUTE-PLAYER: No, neither.

DOULERUS: The Lavinian, then, or the Canary?

LUTE-PLAYER: No, neither.

DOULERUS: None of them? Why, surely you don't walk up and down all by yourself, and keep on singing the same old song, over and over again like a cuckoo with the croup? Go hang! Be off with you! Begone from Hinksey!

PIGEON: Sirs, be forbearin', I beseech you, for music early in the mornin' revives the spirit.

DOULERUS: Si velit non tam nobis, quam ut sibi perplaceat,
Nec solum ludat, sed etiam cantet simul,
Ut viva vox coniungatur cum ligni sono.

FIDICEN: (Cantat et ludit)

    Non hinc diebus undecim   (Bonny Nell)
    Lutetia excepit principem,   50
    Et peperit murem denuo,
    Parturientes decennio,
    Trivitque quinque ferias
    Per ludos et res serias.

DOULERUS: Credidit hoc maxime placere nobis Oxoniensibus,
Sed, st, st; ex ungue leonem. Satis apparet quam
                              pessime canis.

FIDICEN: Si placet, audietis canticum novum et lepidum;

    Vapores Phaebus bibit,   (The Bedlam)
    Suae lucernae oleum;
    Quaerunt humidos plantae fluvios,   60
    Ut sibi constet folium.

DOULERUS: If he does n't so much want to give pleasure to us, as he does to himself, let him not merely play, but sing, too, so that the live voice may blend with the sound of the lute!

LUTE-PLAYER: (He sings and plays)

    Scarcely eleven days ago   (To the tune
    Paris to the prince did welcome show,   of
    An' after ten years o' labour's pain,   "Bonny Nell")
    Brought she forth — a mouse! again,
    An' five festive days wore out did she
    'Twixt serious matters an' revelry.

DOULERUS: He thought we'd greatly appreciate that — being Oxford men, but — tut, tut — "a lion is known by his claw." It's quite clear how badly you sing.

LUTE-PLAYER: If you'll permit me, you shall now 'ear a new an' charmin' song:

    The sun it draws up vapours,   (To the tune
    The oil fur its own lamp: of
    A ' the plants they know fur their   "The Bedlam")
        leaves to grow,
    They must seek rivers damp.

Vapores luna sorbet,
Dum turget succo facies,
Quum imbrium plus, hilaris tellus
Et agros linquit macies.

Dum cantito, procul hinc, procul ite,
Ite procul ite:
Queis cerebrum est aridum,
Et guttur raucum siti.

Culmum producit seges,   70
Cum pluit aut cum ningit,
Et arridet flos, quando cadit ros
Guttisque caulem tingit.

Aqua, a qua sunt cuncta,
Orbem connectit totum.
Quaenam ergo mens sensu indigens
Mihi negare potum?

Dum cantito, procul hinc, procul ite, &c.

The moon it sucks in vapours,
Its face full wi' sap makes:
When the rain pours down, earth loses 'er frown,
An' drought the fields forsakes.

Whilst I sing, "Get you 'ence, far away,
Go away, go away far,"
To those 'ose brains must be as dry as dust,
An' 'ose throats 'oarse wi' thirst are.

The corn puts forth its blades,
After snow or shower,
An' when falls the dew, an' stalks doth imbue
Wi' drops, smiles the flower.

Water, from which all things come,
The 'ole wide world doth link:
So, therefore, what brain, albeit insane,
Can forbid me to drink?

Whilst I sing, "Get you 'ence, far away,
Go away, go away far,"
To those 'ose brains must be as dry as dust,
An' 'ose throats 'oarse wi' thirst are!

DOULERUS:	Hoc est vetus et cauponarium: satis est musicae.
	Non dabimus enim ei trigesimam secundam partem
	denarii. 80
PICMON:	Illud esset vobis pudori. Detis aliquid, obsecro.
DOULERUS:	Hem, accipe. Dabo instrumento non tibi.

(Inserit aheneum calculum instrumento)

FIDICEN:	Hic est calculus non nummus.
DOULERUS:	Hoc potes calculare nummum. Abi, nimis es molestus.
FIDICEN:	Nihilne valet musica?
DOULERUS:	Oh, iam dabimus.
	Hospes, accommodes mihi solidum. Nonne iam sperns
	mercedem certam?
FIDICEN:	Etiam.
DOULERUS:	Sicut igitur tu nos lactasti inani voluptate, sic
	nos lactabimus te inani spe: iam sumus ergo pares.
	Afferentur
	Duae patinae.

(Patinis includitur solidus)

DOULERUS: Why, that's an old drinking-song! Enough music! We shan't even give him one thirty-second of a penny!

PIGEON: Shame on 'e! Give 'im somethin', I beseech you.

DOULERUS: Hm, take that, — I'll give it to your instrument, not to you.

(He places a bronze counter between the strings of the lute)

LUTE-PLAYER: But this be a counter, not a coin.

DOULERUS: Then you can count your coins with it, can't you? Be off! You're too much of a nuisance!

LUTE-PLAYER: Ain't my music worth anythin' at all?

DOULERUS: Oh, well, we'll give you something. Landlord, lend me a shilling, would you! Now you're expecting definite payment, are n't you?

LUTE-PLAYER: Of course.

DOULERUS: Well, then, just as you deceived us with vain pleasure, so shall we deceive you with vain hope: so now we're even! Fetch me two dishes!

(The shilling is placed inside the two dishes)

DOULEHUS: Nonne iam animus tuus est in patinis? Quod si neges,
Probabo facile, ubi nummus, ibi est animus; at nummus est in patinis, 90
Ergo animus est in patinis. Quam suaviter tinnit hoc argentum et
Musico tenore delectat aures, animumque recreat.
FIDICEN: Quaeso, habeam, non audiam.
DOULEHUS: Nequaquam, habes sonum pro sono,
Argenti sonum pro sono instrumenti; iam sumus ergo pares.
Sed ne postquam cecinisti, lugeas; tene hunc solidum.
Abi domum!

(Exeunt)

DOULERUS: Now your "heart lies in the dishes", does it not? But if you deny it, then I'll easily prove that where the money lies, <u>there</u> lies your heart: but the money lies in the dishes, so consequently your "heart lies in the dishes"! What a sweet tinkling sound the silver makes! How its musical strains delight the ear and revive the spirit!

LUTE-PLAYER: Let me 'ave it, I pray you. I won't listen to any more!

DOULERUS: Oh, no! You have sound in return for sound, - the sound of silver in return for the sound of the lute! So now we're even! But don't grieve after you've sung. Here, take this shilling, and get off home!

(Exeunt)

ACTUS 4. SCENA 2.

(Manet solus PHILOPINUS,
et obambulat Oxonium contemplans)

PHILOPINUS: O dulce nomen Oxonii, te videre me quantum iuvat;
Tuumque multa turre pinnatum caput,
Ubi tot alumni Musarum student
Sedulique horas computant libris, nec umbra gnomonis
Velocius procedit, quam umbra recedit ignorantiae.   100
Vos occidentis Phoebi, et resurgentis iterum,
Vidistis radios penetrantes foramina
Angusta vestras cellae: vos bibliothecis conditi
Ingenia seculorum omnium contemplamini typo.
Nos autem rusticantes inter risum et pocula,
Conterimus tempus, otio languentes et gaudio.
Date veniam, tutores tetrici, quique Atheniensibus
satis Areopagitae: tot domi studentium greges
Socordiam nostram redimant, et nobis etiam fersitan
Sapientior placebit conditio, cum inanis impetus   110
Reliquerit animos, cum iuvenilis deferbuerit calor.
Sed iam necesse est nobis per innocuos sales
Viam aperire, ut quiete redeamus domum.

ACT 4. SCENE 2.

(PHILOCINUS remains alone;
he walks up and down, gazing at Oxford)

PHILOCINUS: O Oxford! Sweet name! What great joy it gives me to behold thee, and thy head crowned with many a tower! Where so many of the Muses' children study, and untiringly reckon the hours by their books: the shadow on the sun-dial does not advance more quickly than the shadow of ignorance falls back! You that dwell on the west side, where the sun sets, and you on the east, where the sun rises, have once more seen its rays filtering through the narrow windows of your cell; whilst you, in the seclusion of the library, meditate upon the great thoughts of all past ages, set out in print before you. But we, down in the country, wile away our time amidst laughter and drink, languishing in idleness and mirth. Pray forgive us, stern tutors, and you who are the City-fathers of that second Athens: may the many droves of students who have remained at home, atone for our folly; perhaps a more prudent way of life will be acceptable to us, too, when vain impetuosity has forsaken our hearts, and our youthful ardour has cooled. But now through harmless sport we must open up the way for ourselves to return sedately home.

ACTUS 4. SCENA 3.
(DOULERUS amplexans IOANNAM. NICHADES)

DOULERUS: O clara Veneris stella, quae solem sequens
Hesperus vocaris, eiusque praeveniens iubar,
Eadem vocaris Lucifer, quam laetus nitor
Refulget oculis, exisque a Tethyos sinu,
Ornatior multo quam cum subibas lacum.
IOANNA: Mi Doulere, clam surripui hoc aureum poculum.
DOULERUS: O charissima Ioanna, cuius amore torqueor, 120
Iam fidelitatem tuam praecepi, sed mortalium nemini
Hoc dicas, donec serio proficiantur nuptiae.
IOANNA: Ego dicam? Citius mihi linguam auferent quam fatear.
DOULERUS: Te amo, te diligo, te amplector, te interdiu cogito,
Te nocte somnians video; tu semper observaris animo,
Amorem quomodo patefacerem meum, et pectoris
Affectus referarem? Num placet gustare haec suavia?

(Dat ei hypotrimmata purgativa,
et pulverem crepacem)

ACT 4. SCENE 3.

(DOULERUS embracing JOANNA;
NICHADES.   )

DOULERUS: O bright star of Venus, who art called Hesperus when you follow the sun, and likewise Lucifer when you come before its radiance: what a joyous light shines within your eyes, and you leave Tethys' bosom far more beautiful than when you sank beneath the waves!

JOANNA: My sweet Doulerus, I 'ave secretly stole this golden drinkin'-bowl.

DOULERUS: O my dearest Joanna, I am tortured with love of you, and I have now received in advance a token of your constancy, — but don't tell a living soul about this, until our marriage is performed in earnest.

JOANNA: Me? Blab? They'd sooner cut out me tongue than I confess to 't!

DOULERUS: I love you, I respect you, I embrace you; in the daytime I think of you, at night I dream of you: you're always uppermost in my mind. How can I show my love for you? How can I tell you what I feel in my heart? Would n't you like to sample these sweetmeats?

(He gives her some opening medicine and some powder to induce the breaking of wind)

Quorum tamen suavitatem longe superat amoris suavitas.
Hic est pulvis Veneris, et haec sunt Cupidinis
                              hypotrismata,
Quae ambo conglutinant amorem et lites auferunt: 130
Et hoc recipe praescribitur ab Ovidio in libris
De arte amandi.

IOANNA: O me faelicem quae generosum amo!
Ego posthac superciliose rusticos adolescentes despiciam,
Et illorum nuces et poma et alia munera reiiciam;
Sed paulisper abeundum est mihi.

                (Exit IOANNA)

DOCLERUS: Illae cupediae saccharo conditae ventrem solvunt illico;
Et ille pulvis strepitum et crepitum parit;
Iamque abiit ad latrinam scio, operantur enim medicamina.

                (Intrat PIGEON cum urinario
                 aqua rosacea referto)

But love's sweetness far surpasses the sweetness of these. Here's some of Venus' powder, and some of Cupid's potion: both these help bind love together and put an end to quarrels. Indeed, this recipe 's set down by Ovid in his book on the art of loving.

JOANNA: Oh, 'ow fortunate I be to love such a gen'leman as this! 'Enceforth I will look 'aughtily down on they country lads, an' I will 'ave nought to do wi' them nuts an' fruit an' t'other things which they offers me as gifts. But excuse me, I've got to go.

(Exit JOANNA)

DULLENUS: Those 'delicacies', hidden beneath their coating of sugar, open the bowels straightaway; and that powder causes rumbling in the stomach, and the breaking of wind! And she has, I know, already gone off to the privy, for the medicine even now is beginning to take effect!

(Enter PIGEON carrying a chamber-pot filled with rose-water)

- 177 -

PIGMON: O domini, repentino quodam malo laborat filia!
Ventrem, ventrem inclamat, quasi possessa fuerat a
                                    spiritu,   140
Aut quod magis metuo, virginitatem corruperat.
Quaeso, aspicite urinam, et remedium dicite.

(Aspicit urinam)

PHILOPINUS: Est quid$\widehat{e}^m$ ut dicis spiritus, qui vexat
                                    filiam,
Non a Plutone, sed immissus ab Aeolo,
Qui ventos congessit in ventris eius sacculum
Quasi iterum Ulysses navigaret in Ithaca.
Causas sic habeto: crudus et flatuosus cibus
Ebullitione quadam distendit mesenterium
Unde quaerit exitum: et si loquamur apodictice,
Quod ructus est a priori, crepitus est a
                                    posteriori.   150

PIGEON: O sirs, me daughter 'as suddenly been struck down wi' some dread disease! 'Er complains loudly o' pains in the stomach, as if 'er was possessed by a spirit, or what I be more afraid of, - 'ad done 'er virginity a mischief! 'Ave a look at 'er water, I pray you, an' prescribe a cure.

(PHILOPINUS looks at the water)

PHILOPINUS: There is indeed something wrong, and, as you say, it's a spirit which troubles your daughter. However, it's a spirit sent into her <u>not</u> by Pluto, but by Aeolus, who, - just as though Ulysses were sailing to Ithaca again! - has gathered all the winds together - in that little sack which forms her stomach. You have the cause here: indigestible and flatulent food makes the mesentery swell up with a certain gas, and then the gas seeks a way out of there; to put it demonstratively: wind is belched forth from one end, and given off from the other!

Triplex autem est crepandi genus, vel mutum
Quod fertur in vehiculo viscosioris materiae:
Vel liquidum, in quo magis timendum est de vestibus
Quam de salute: vel denique vocale, quod proprie
Nominatur crepitus. Sub hoc membro sunt aliae species,
Edit enim sonum vel parem vel imparem, vel impariter
               parem,
Vel pariter imparem. Adde quod diiudicantur eius
              differentiae
Ab organo duplici: vel ab aure, utrum sonat
Acute vel grave, utrum altum aut bassum,
Aut contratenorem, vel a naso, utrum odor   160
Sit acerbus vel amarus, vel septicus.
Certe Tongilianus genus alimenti deprehenderet
Ex odore crepitus. Sed adveniat filia,
Ne imprudens violaret edictum Claudii
Et sic in morbum incideret. Advenire facias illico,

    (Exit PIGEON)

Ut scilicet rideamus. Nos medici saepenumero
Destinamur sordidis officiis, sed bonus odor lucri.
Tu, Doulere, sponsam cures, ego non appropinquabo.

For there are three kinds of fart: there is the silent
type, which is carried in the medium of stickier matter;
there is the wet sort, in which case one has to fear more
for the safety of one's clothes than one's health; and
finally there is the noisy kind, which is properly
called fart. Other types fall into this category, for
either an equal or unequal sound can be produced, either
an unequally equal sound or an equally unequal sound.
Moreover, the differences can be discerned by two of the
sense organs: either by the ear, as to whether it sounds
high or low, treble or bass, or counter-tenor; or by the
nose, as to whether it smells sharp or pungent, or
poisonous. Indeed, Tongilianus could guess the sort of
food which has been eaten, from the smell of the fart!
But let your daughter come here, lest quite unawares she
breaks the rule laid down by Claudius, and so falls ill!
send your daughter to us at once

   (Exit PIGEON)

          so that we can,- not to
put too fine a point on it,- have some fun just now! We
physicians are often appointed to do dirty work, but the
smell of the money is good! You, Doulerus, can look after
your betrothed, - I'll not go near her!

(Spargit urinam)

Hoc est lac virginis, ne formidetis!

(Redit IOANNA. Foh,
rident inter se)

DOULERUS: Quaeso, fruamur dulcissimo tuo consortio 170
Nec aversis radiis, et eclipsim et noctem et hiemem
inferas:
Praesente te floreo, sed te absente morior.
IOANNA: Ego non amplius inter ancillas rusticas
Certabo cursu, aut pila palmaria, aut osculabor
aliquem:
Sed statim redeo.

(Exit IOANNA)

NICHADES: Suavissimam habes sponsam, Doulere: iterum ad cloacam
abiit;
Vult, credo, totam priorem rusticitatem expurgare,
Ut inducatur nova et sincera generositas.

(Redit IOANNA. Crepat:
foh, nasos claudunt)

(He sprinkles the water about)

This is only aqua mercurialis, so don't be afraid!

(JOANNA returns. She breaks wind:
they laugh amongst themselves)

DOULERUS: Let's enjoy your most charming company, I pray you, and don't, my little sunbeam, turn your rays away from me, and so bring about an eclipse, or cause night and winter to draw on. For when you're near, I bloom, but when you go away, I die!

JOANNA: I shall no longer run races wi' t'other country lasses, nor play them at tennis, nor kiss nobody neither. But I'll be back presently.

(Exit JOANNA)

NICHADES: You have a very sweet betrothèd, Doulerus, — she's just gone off to the privy again! I believe she means to rid herself of all her old country ways, so that she can don a fresh and clean gentility!

(JOANNA returns. She breaks wind;
they hold their noses)

IOANNA: Si quis colonus posthac me tentabit osculari,
Impingam ei colaphum et me reservabo tibi. 130
DOULERUS: Cur me relinquis, qui sine te sum miserrimus?
Non abibis iterum.
IOANNA: Necesse est, ne teneas.

(Crepat et foetet)

DOULERUS: Feh! Non potes avelli; simul hinc, simul ibimus.
Num te cœpit fastidium mei?
IOANNA: Absit, imo aliud est.

(Pugnat abire)

Quaeso, ne teneas.
DOULERUS: Quid aliud est? Num bene est tibi?
IOANNA: Non optime.

(Crepat)

DOULERUS: Nec erubescas, nec timeas:
Res est ventosi plena fragoris amor.
Haec est vis Cupidinis, cum laxat arcum,
Alvumque solvit, plusquam succus aloes.

JOANNA: 'Enceforth if any one o' they village lads tries to kiss me, I'll slap 'is face fur 'im, an' save meself fur you!

DOCLERUS: Why do you keep on forsaking me? I'm very miserable without you. You shall not go away again.

JOANNA: I must. Let me go!

(She breaks wind, and turns the air foul)

DOCLERUS: Pooh! You can't be taken from me, — we shall leave here together. Surely you're not beginning to tire of me already?

JOANNA: 'Eaven forbid! Nay, 'tis somethin' else.

(She struggles to get free)

Let me go, I pray you!

DOCLERUS: What's the matter? Is all well with you?

JOANNA: No, not very.

(She breaks wind)

DOCLERUS: Ah, don't blush, don't be afraid, for love is full of wind and din! This is the force of Cupid when he slackens his bow, and opens the bowels faster than oil of aloes!

(Taset)

   O mea fragrantissima Rosamunda,   190
    Non redoles, sed oles quae redolere soles.

NICHADES: Poh! Quam gravis odor nares infecit meas!
    Partem aliquam a vento, et ad vestras referant.
    Intumulant nares quod peperere nates.

(He restrains her)

O my most sweet-scented Rosamunda:

Smell of anything you don't,
Save what to smell of you are wont!

NICHADES: Pooh! what a strong smell has reached my nose! May some of it be wafted on the breeze to your nostrils! what the rump gives out, is buried in the snout!

ACTUS 4. SCENA 4.
PIGEON. CULLIE.

CULLIE: Ubi sunt isti generosi generosissimi? Num venabuntur hodie?

NICHADES: Non, sed redituri sumus domum; volumus autem prius,
Si vos consentiatis, ludificare agricolam,
Eumque arte magica reddere invisibilem,
Ut optabat heri.

CULLIE: Erit lepidissimum,
Si nihil mali faciatis, et ludatis sine iniuria: 200
Et nos erimus in secundis, ut promoveatur iocus;
Dignus est haberi ludibrio, quum sit adeo fatuus.

(Intrat DAWSON)

DAWSON: Venit ad me nescio quis, et in aurem susurrat nescio quid,
Quod uxor mea nescio cui dixerat aliquid.

PHILOPINUS: Hoc aliquid nihil est. Salve, quomodo se uxor habuit?

DAWSON: Valde laboravit stomacho, dumque antrorsum vomit,
Gemit retrorsum: salva reverentia, aegrare aegre tulit.

Deus vortat bene.

ACT 4. SCENE 4.

PIGEON. CULLIE.

CULLIE: Where be they most genteel gen'lemen? Surely they'll not be goin' 'untin' today?

NICHAIES: No; but we are just about to set off for home: first, however, if you're agreeable, we mean to have some sport with the farmer, and by the aid of our magic powers make him invisible, as he wished us to do yesterday.

CULLIE: That'll be a fine jest, providin' you does nothin' evil, an' sports with 'im without doin' no 'arm; an' we'll give you our support so's the trick can succeed. 'E deserves to be made a laughin'-stock, 'cos 'e's such a fool!

(Enter DAWSON)

DAWSON: Somebody comes up to me, an' whispers somethin' in me ear, — that the missus 'ad said somethin' to somebody...

PHILOXINUS: This something is nothing! Good day to you, how fared your wife?

DAWSON: 'Er was greatly troubled with 'er stomach: while 'er 'eaved fro'ards, 'er strained back'ards! Savin' your reverence, 'er took bein' ill very ill! May the Lord moike 'er better!

PHILOPINUS:	Necesse est mutarier
	Statum corporis, antequam evadat prolifica;
	Scio quod pharmaci salsa qualitas sit ingrata
	stomacho, 210
	Nec profuturum ventriculo, sed ventri dixeram.
DAWSON:	Deus vortat olli bene.
PHILOPINUS:	Vortat olli?

(Ridet)

	Quam barbare loqueris et rustice! Sed ne dubites,
	Veniet stato tempore filia, quae te vocabit patrem.
DAWSON:	Vix credo vera quae iactastis de vestris artibus,
	Vos posse visum decipere et alia.
PHILOPINUS:	Odi compotorem
	memorem!
	Sed, Nichades, habesne tecum annulum et instrumenta
	caetera?
NICHADES:	Etiam facile experietur, si cupiat agricola
	Vim artis magicae. Sed hac conditione:
	Ut interim nihil mali faciat, et ad pristinum habitum
	redeat cito. 220

PHILOPINUS: But the condition of the body has to be changed before she can become fruitful. I'm well aware that the salty nature of the medicine would irritate the stomach, and that it would n't do the belly any good either, but I had intended it for the womb.

DAWSON: May the Lord moike 'er better!

PHILOPINUS: Moike 'er?

(He laughs)

What barbarous and countrified English you do talk! But never fear, a daughter will arrive at the appointed time to call you father.

DAWSON: I can scarcely believe that the things which you boasts that you can do with your skills, - such as deceivin' the eye an' t'other things - be true.

PHILOPINUS: I hate a drinking-companion with a good memory! But, Nichades, have you the ring and the other trappings with you?

NICHADES: The force of our magic powers can easily be demonstrated, if the farmer so wishes, but on this condition: that in the meantime, he does no harm, and quickly returns to his former shape.

DAWSON: Nihil inest periculi?
NICHADES: Nihil omnino.
Sed pluribus utendum est ceremoniis:
Non fit opus tam arduum et grande sine ceremoniis.
Primo calcem sinistram dextra tenens manu,
Iam in hac cathedra sedeas, et surges asinus.
DAWSON: Num me facies asinum?
NICHADES: Nequaquam.
Asinus nascitur non fit. His gestibus
Alliciendus est spiritus invisibilis
Cuius eris similis. Iam capias hunc annulum.
DAWSON: An iterum uxorem ducam? Quam sit plus satis
       duxisse semel?   230
NICHADES: Imponatur naso tuo per aliquod temporis spatium,
Nam sic fieri oportet.
DAWSON: An nasum rostrum porcinum
        putas?
Hic est tantum vulgaris annulus.
NICHADES: Ita videtur tibi,
Sed virtute est consecratus mystica, et ter aut novies
Repetitis verbis. Fateor si characteribus
Signatus esset hierogliphicis, plus efficaciae daret;
Sed hic aeque proderit.

DAWSON: It ain't dangerous, is it?

NICHADES: No, not at all, but several rites have to be performed, for a task so difficult and remarkable as this, cannot be accomplished without ritual. First, you must take your left shoe in your right hand; now sit down in this chair, and you'll get up an ass.

DAWSON: You ain't turnin' me into an ass, are you?

NICHADES: Of course not: an ass "is born **not** made!" but the **invisible spirit** to which you will be similar has to be called forth by these actions. Now, take hold of this ring.

DAWSON: Am I to marry again, then, when to 'ave bin married once be once too often?

NICHADES: Stick the ring on the end of your nose for a little while, since this is how it must be done.

DAWSON: Think you that me nose be a pig's snout? Why, this be just an ordinary ring!

NICHADES: It may appear so to you, but it has in fact been made sacred by mystical powers and by having words chanted over it three, or nine times. I admit that had it been engraved with hieroglyphic letters, it might be more efficacious: but this one will do equally well.

　　　　　　　　　　Iam indatur annulus.
　　　　　　Articulo secundo pollicis, ut solebat Gyges.
　　　　　　Paulatim magis et magis rarescas, ut tandem
　　　　　　　　　　　　　　evanescas penitus.
　　　　　　Nunc induatur capiti reticulum, quo non minus
　　　　　　　　　　　　　　tegeris　　　　　　　　240
　　　　　　Quam olim Aeneas opaca matris nebula.
　　　　　　Obscurior incipis videri, quasi procul esses.
　　　　　　An tu, Roberte Dawson, cupis omnia videre?

DAWSON:　　　　　　　　　　　　　　　　　Cupio.
NICHADES:　　　　　　　　　　　　　　　Fiat.

　　　　　　An tu cupis a nullo videri?

DAWSON:　　　　　　　　　　Cupio.
NICHADES:　　　　　　　　　Fiat.

　　　　　　　　　　Farbus, Bumbo, Dolon,
　　　　　　　　　　Bumbo, Dolon, Farbus,
　　　　　　　　　　Dolon, Farbus, Bumbo.

　　　　　　　　　　　　　　　　(Ter circuit)

　　　　　　Ecce, mirum! Abiit! Evanuit! Inanis relinquitur
　　　　　　　　　　　　　cathedra!

DAWSON:　　Bonne me videtis?

Now place the ring on your middle finger, like Gyges used to. You will gradually become thinner and thinner, until finally you will vanish altogether. But this net over your head, so that you're every bit as well hidden as Aeneas once was in his mother's shadowy cloud! Already you're beginning to look less distinct, as though you were far away. Do you Robert Dawson desire to see all things?

DAWSON: I does.

ALCBIADES: It shall be done. And do you desire to be seen by no one?

DAWSON: I does.

ALCBIADES: It shall be done:

Farbus, Bumbo, Dolon,
Bumbo, Dolon, Farbus,
Dolon, Farbus, Bumbo.

(He walks round him three times)

Lo, a miracle! He's gone! Vanished! The chair's empty!

DAWSON: Come, surely you can see me?

NICHADES: Ubi es? Te quidem audio non video.
Quaeso, aliquid loquere, ut te videam.

DAWSON: Nonne me vides, faber? 250

CULLIE: Ubi es? Vocem quidem audio. O artis prodigium!
Iam posset uxores corrumpere, suffurari et admittere
Quodvis facinus impune.

(DAWSON vellit aurem fabri)

Oh! Quid vellit meas auriculas?

(DAWSON cathedram elevat)

PHILOPINUS: O naturae prodigium! Movetur cathedra, a nullo movente!
Iam contigit forsan terrae motus quem vult Copernicus.

(Intrat CAECILIA)

MICHADES: Where are you? Indeed, I can hear you, but I can't see you. Say something, I pray you, so that I may see where you are.

DAWSON: Surely <u>you</u> can see me, Master Blacksmith?

CULLIE: Where be you? I 'ears your voice. Oh, what marvellous skill! How 'e can seduce other men's wives, steal, an' commit any other sort o' crime 'e likes without gettin' punished fur 't.

(He tweaks the blacksmith's ear)

O-o-Oh! what's tweaking me ear?

(DAWSON lifts up the chair)

PHILOTINUS: Oh, wonders of nature! The chair's moving - all by itself! Perhaps this is what Copernicus meant when he said the earth moves!

(Enter CECILIA)

CAECILIA: Mirum est si possit abesse vel semihorulam ab hoc
                                                    loco.
Ubi est Robertus? Quo abiit? O tu medicorum pessime,
Me nocte tota fecisti aegrotam et vigilem.

PHILOPINUS: Sis bono animo, post aegritudinem veniet salus,
Et post dolores partus, gaudebis quod medicina
                    operata sit fortiter.   260

(DAWSON se furtim subducit)

CAECILIA: Quo te proripis, otiose nebulo?
DAWSON: Audit me, non videt.
CAECILIA: Ego fustibus te abigam ex hoc loco!
DAWSON: Nihil videt.
Sed forsan audit sonitum ambulantis.

(Verberat DAWSONEM CAECILIA)

CAECILIA: Quis te ornavit ut moriones? Quis grossum caput
Inclusit reti?

CAECILIA: 'T would be a miracle if 'e could spend even 'alf an 'our away from 'ere! Where be Robert? Where's 'e gone? O you worst of physicians, on account of you I were ill all night long an' did n't get a wink o' sleep!

PHILOPINUS: Cheer up, for after illness will come health, and when the pains of labour are over, you'll be glad the medicine had such a powerful effect.

(DAWSON begins to steal away in secret)

CAECILIA: An' where d you think you be 'urryin' off to, you lazy, good-for-nothin' scoundrel?

DAWSON: 'Er can 'ear me, but 'er can't see me.

CAECILIA: I'll take me stick to you, an' beat you out o' this place!

DAWSON: 'Er can't see nothin', but most like 'er can 'ear me walkin' about.

(She beats him)

CAECILIA: Who's dressed you up to look like a fool, an' stuck your great fat 'ead in a net?

NICHADES: Dawson charissime,
Si sis in hoc loco, et salvus esse cupias,
Exuantur annulus et reticulum, et ad propriam formam
Redibis.

(Exuit)

En apparet repente corporeus!
DAWSON: At uxor me sensit, et ego illius sensi verbera:
Quod si res bene successerat, ego in aulas principum   270
Me insinuarem, inter heroicos luderem,
Secretiora consilia nullo vidente cognoscerem:
Erratum est in aliquo.
NICHADES: Etiam proculdubio,
Aut uxoris oculi possunt per incantamentum penetrare.
CAECILIA: Cur garris? Abi domum! Nihil nisi te ludificant.
DAWSON: Valete, generosi optimi.
CULLIE: Abeundum est etiam mihi.
Vobis habeo maximas gratias. Vale, domini.

NICHADES: Dawson, my dear fellow, if you're still in this place, and wish to be saved, take off the ring and the net, and you'll return to your own shape.

(DAWSON takes off the ring and the net)

See! he's suddenly appeared again in the flesh!

DAWSON: But the missus could feel me presence, an' I cud feel 'er blows! If the experiment 'ad bin successful, I wud 'ave bin able to creep into the courts o' princes, an' sport among 'eroes, an' get to know the most secret o' plans, without anyone seein' me. Somethin' went wrong somewhere.

NICHADES: Undoubtedly it did, — either that, or your wife's eyes can see through magic spells!

CAECILIA: Why be you a-prattlin'? Get you 'ome, — they be doin' nothin' but makin' sport o' you!

DAWSON: Fare you well, noble gen'lemen.

CULLIN: I must be off, too. A thousand thanks! Sirs, farewell.

(Exeunt CAECILIA, DAWSON et CULLIE)
(Rident scholares)

NICHADES: Crudelis Caecilia turbavit omnes dolos,
Et comaediam infaeliciter mutavit in tragaediam.
Sed deliberemus intus, quo res transigantur modo. 280

(Exeunt)

(Exeunt CAECILIA, DAWSON and CULLIE;
the students laugh)

MICHADIS: Cruel Caecilia has spoiled our jest, and unhappily has turned this comedy into a tragedy! But let's go in, and decide how the matter is to be resolved.

(Exeunt)

ACTUS 4. SCENA 5.
IOANNA.

IOANNA: Quam turpiter fortuna ludit in mediis bonis:
Cum placere maxime cupiebam generoso meo,
Pudore me confundit et exposuit ludibrio:
Scio quod farta sunt in causa; sed nihil est, non curo.
Et dominae et reginae non possunt non pedere.
Iam autem excipiam generosum vultu benignissimo
Oculisque blandissimis, ut eius recuperem benevolentiam.

(Intrant academici)

DOULERUS: Dilecta sponsa, gaudeo te videre incolumem.
Poh! Omnia cum fecit, Thaida Thais olet.
IOANNA: Quidam repentinus morbus invasit meum stomachum 290
Ut magno dolore coacta sim vos relinquere.
DOULERUS: Condonabo totum, modo firmior sit posthac amor.

(Intrat PICEON. Exit IOANNA)

PHILOPINUS: Quid est solvendum? In toto pro victu et aliis?

ACT 4. SCENE 5.
JOANNA.

JOANNA: What shameful tricks fortune do play, - jest when all be goin' well! Fur when I desired to please me gen'leman very much, 'e caused me great embarrassment an' turned me into a laughin'-stock! That were the reason, I know, fur me fartin', but 'tis o' no importance, I does n't mind, - even ladies an' queens be entitled to fart! But now I shall welcome me gen'leman wi' a most pleasant countenance, an' wi' the most bewitchin' eyes, - so's I may win back 'is good-will!

(Enter the students)

DOULEROS: My darling betrothed, how glad I am to see you safe and sound! Pooh!, "Thais, when she's done everything, still smells of Thais!"

JOANNA: Some sudden disorder attacked me stomach, so's I was, regretfully, obliged to leave you.

DOULEROS: I shall forgive you everything, - only in future see that your love for me is stronger.

(Enter PIGEON. Exit JOANNA)

PHILOCLAUS: What do we owe you altogether - for our food and other items?

PIGEON: Si placet, quindecim solidi et quatuor denarii.
PHILOPINUS: Tantumne?
            Mi hospes, non est nobis pecunia, sed reddemus Oxonii.
PIGEON: Siccine? Oh! Non est pecunia? Siccine luditis?
            Necesse est mihi habere pecuniam, aut ego pileum,
            Et togam, et bombardam retinebo pignora.
            Siccine nos pauperes decipitis verbis magnificis?
DOULERUS: Toga mihi est singularis numeri, non possum
                                            dimittere;   300
            Ut unicum togatum corpus, sic unica sufficit toga.
            Nec non statuta iubent habere pileum;
            Nec audeo mutare quadrata rotundis, pileum
            In argentum vertere. Sed serio totum reddetur Oxonii.
PIGEON: Egone vobis crederem? Forsitan agitis mecum mutuatis
                                            nominibus?
            Sed ego vos deducam ad iusticiarium academiae,
            Qui vos omnes compinget in numellas suas.
NICHADES: Nos te deferemus (triobolaris homuncio) pro latrone
                                            et lenone!

PIGEON: Fifteen shillin's an' fourpence, please.

PHILOPINUS: As much as that? Landlord, my dear fellow, we have no money with us, but we will pay you back at Oxford.

PIGEON: So that's it, is it? Oh, there's no money, ain't there? That's 'ow you sports wi' me, is it? Well, I must 'ave some money, or else I shall confiscate your caps, gowns an' fowlin'-piece, an' keep 'em as security! This is 'ow you deceives us penniless countryfolk wi' your 'igh-flown talk, is it?

DOULERUS: My gown occurs only in the singular – I can't afford to lose it: as I've only one body to gown, so one gown is enough. Moreover, it says in the rules that we must wear a cap – I don't dare to change that square into the round by turning my cap into money! But, I speak in earnest, the whole sum will be paid to you at Oxford.

PIGEON: Am I to believe you? Per'aps you be a-dealin' wi' me under false names. Still, I shall 'aul you up before the Judge of the University, who will clap the lot o' you in irons!

NICHADES: And we shall denounce you, you twopenny-ha'penny scoundrel, for a thief and a pimp!

PIGEON: Bona verba. Ubi tuus iam familiaris spiritus?
Cur non gazas et thesauros affert ab Indis aut
Guiana? 310

(Intrat ANNA)

ANNA: O coniux, nullibi possumus invenire crateres!
PIGEON: Quo malum abiit? Quis obseratum potuit tollere?
IOANNA: Invenimus quidem cistam clausam et tuta reliqua.
Quis tolleret clausa cista? Malum supervenit malo.
Ingrediamur et omnem scrutemur angulum.

(Exeunt)

NICHADES: Bene se res habet. Ego prior redibo domum cum
cratere:
Nostis cubiculum meum humile in infima regione?
Hoc erit theatrum, ubi segnior diabolus deludet
hospitem.
Omnia parabo sicut inter nos est conclusum.

(Exit)

PIGEON: Well said! But where be your familiar now? Why don't 'e bring riches an' treasures from the Indies or Guiana?

(Enter ANNA)

ANNA: Oh, 'usband, 'usband, we can't find the punchbowl anywhere!

PIGEON: Where can the damn thing 'ave gone? Who cud possibly 'ave stole it when it were kept under lock an' key?

JOANNA: Indeed,... er ... we...we... er ... found the chest still closed an' ev'rythin' safe. Who... er ... who... er ... cud 'ave stole it while the chest were locked? One misfortune follows another! Let's go in an' search ev'ry corner!

(Exeunt)

NICHADES: All's well! I shall return home first with the punchbowl; you know my humble chamber in the lower regions, don't you? Well, that will be the stage upon which a senior devil will have some sport with the innkeeper! I shall prepare everything just as we agreed.

(Exit)

ACTUS 4. SCENA 6.
ANNA.

ANNA: Negat filia, negat ancilla, negant omnes. O infaelix
dies! 320
Illud domus ornamentum, et decus supellectilis,
Coruscus ille, crater abiit!

PHILOPINUS: Sorte venit, sorte abiit.

ANNA: Hunc destinabam filiae, hunc ostentabam hospitibus:
Hic, vae mihi! Repente dilabitur!

PHILOPINUS: Male parta male
dilabuntur.

ANNA: O utinam potui furem deprehendere, aut saltem
cognoscere,
Ut post haec caverem!

PHILOPINUS: Qui non ante cavet, post dolebit.

(Intrat PIGEON)

PIGEON: Legem ponite! Pecunia numeretur, o scholastici!

ACT 4. SCENE 6.

ANNA.

ANNA: Our daughter says 'er knows nothin' about it, so does the maid, so does ev'ryun! O un'appy day! The 'ouse'old's pride an' joy, our most treasured ornament, that glitterin' punchbowl - 'as gone!

PHILOFINUS: Ah, well, easy come, easy go!

ANNA: I was savin' it fur me daughter; I used to show it to all our guests. But now, - woe is me! - it's suddenly vanished!

PHILOFINUS: Indeed, ill-gotten gains are soon forfeited!

ANNA: Would that I might catch the thief, or at least know who 'e was, so's 'enceforth I might take more care!

PHILOFINUS: Yes, better to be safe than sorry!

(Enter PIGEON)

PIGEON: Forget about the law! Jest count out the money, you scholars!

PHILOPINUS: Etiamsi non vis credere pecuniam, credas tamen de
                             pecunia
             Quod scilicet non simus solvendo, sed nobiscum eas
                             Oxonium,
             Et habebis in numerato.
PIGEON: Tum aliquid addetis insuper. 330
             Me maxime ringit crater, adibo aliquem necromanticum.
DOULEHUS: Nos quasi imperitos spernis? At si condones omnia,
             Addasque coronatum Gallicum, videbis quid Nichades
                             efficiet,
             Qui prior abiit negotiis avocatus ad horam undecimam.
PIGEON: Me facturum sancte recipio, si scilicet arte magica
             Recuperetur poculum. Cur non properamus?

             (Intrat IOANNA)

DOULEHUS: Cordis mei custos, et cogitationum domina,
             Quam misere divellor! O vos praecipites aquae,
             Parcite dum venio, mergite dum redeo!

PHILOPINUS: Even if you don't wish to give us credit, at least credit that we cannot, - frankly - pay what we owe! But come with us to Oxford, and you shall have the money in cash.

PIGEON: Then you must give me somethin' else besides. This business of losing the punchbowl vexes me greatly; I shall seek the 'elp of some magician.

DOULERUS: And are you going to pass us by, as though we were unskilled in that art? If you were to forgive us everything, and in addition were to pay us one French crown, you would see what Michades is capable of accomplishing. He has gone on ahead, for he was called away on business at eleven o'clock.

PIGEON: I vows that I'll be true to me word, if, indeed, the punchbowl be recovered by magic. Why does n't we 'ie us to Oxford?

(Enter JOANNA)

DOULERUS: Guardian of my heart, and mistress of my thoughts, how miserable I am at being torn from your side! O, you rushing waters, spare me as I come, drown me as I return!

	Venientem accellerent, redeuntem impediant aquae! 340
	(Taceas de cratere) abibo tantum, ut redeam ad te
	citius;
	Et nuptias celebrabimus die quinto mensis proximi.
IOANNA:	Imo volo, sed nolo: at iterum nolo: non est
	concedendum
	Primo tempore: sic enim praecepit mater.
	Non ero valde facilis nec valde difficilis: nolo,
	tamen volo.
DOULERUS:	En pudor et timor liliis miscent rosas!
	Subit ille supremus virginitatis amor,
	Primaeque modestia culpae, confundit vultus.
	(Taceas de cratere) interim valeas, dilectissima.
IOANNA:	Vale, mi Doulere. Non possum tenere lachrymas,
	vale. 350
PHILOPINUS:	Vale, hospita. Vale, domina Ioanna.

(Exeunt)

May the waters hasten my arrival, but prevent my turning back! (Don't blab about the punchbowl), I go away only that I may return to you all the more quickly: our marriage will be solemnised on the fifth of next month.

JOANNA: Nay, I be willin', - yet unwillin'; an' again I be unwillin': a girl did n't ought to say yes the first time, - this much 'as mother taught me! I shan't be very yieldin', nor very obstinate neither: I be unwillin', - yet willin'...

DOULERUS: See! Modesty and fear are intermingled, - the roses in her cheeks blend with a lily-white pallor! "That last, lingering love of maidenhood wells up inside her, and the shame of first guilt spreads o'er her countenance." (Don't blab about the punchbowl), in the meantime, fare you well, my beloved.

JOANNA: Farewell, my dear Doulerus, I cannot 'old back me tears. Farewell.

PHILOFINUS: Farewell, hostess. Farewell, Mistress Joanna.

(Exeunt)

ACTUS 5. SCENA I.
NICHADES.

NICHADES: Iam omnia parata sunt ad coniurationem necessariam.
Primo sciatur quod sub hoc meo cubiculo,
Porrigatur cella vetus et inanis quae ignoratur a
                                                plurimis.
Dissertis itaque tabulatis fabricatum est occultum
                                                iter,
Quo facile ascendatur ex cella subterranea.
Deinde puer mihi serviens, qui est ingeniosus carnifex,
Accepit apparatum et vestes ab illis mutuo,
Qui terrore magno, dum aguntur comoediae,
Et lampade et fuste, recentes a feribus fugant.
Ille optime aget diabolum, et ego ero Doctor Forman, 10
Illumque coniurabo, per terminos categorematicos, et
                                                syncategorematicos,
Per sensum analogicum, et tropologicum et similia.
Propterea tres pueros comparavi qui saltare possunt
                                                ludicrum,
Qui vestibus ridiculis induti ad meum imperium aderunt,
Ut arti maior adsit fiducia. Haec omnia et reliqua
In promptu sunt, quae vel prudentem, et scientem
                                                fallerent.
Sed miror quod nondum advenerint socii cum hospite.

ACT 5. SCENE 1.

NICHALES.

RICHADES: Now, everything is ready for the magic ceremony we need! Firstly, let it be known that beneath this, my cell, there lies an old, empty chamber, - of the existence of which most people are quite unaware. So, when the floor-boards are taken away, a secret passage is formed, by means of which one can easily come up from the underground room. Secondly, my serving-lad, an ingenious little wretch, has borrowed some clothing and equipment from those who, causing great terror, drive freshmen away from the door with torches and cudgels, during the performance of comedies! he'll play the part of the devil very well, and $\underline{I}$ shall be Doctor Forman! I shall call him up with categorical and syncategorical words, with analogical and figurative language, and the like! Moreover, I've secured the help of three boys, who can leap up and down in a playful fashion, and who, dressed in comical attire, will come at my bidding, to lend my skill greater authenticity. All these things, and more besides, are ready at hand, - things which would trick even a wise and intelligent man! But I'm surprised that my companions have n't ~~yet~~ arrived yet with the innkeeper...

ACTUS 5. SCENA 2.
PICEON. DOULERUS. PHILOPINUS.

NICHADES: Faeliciter advenistis, nunc hilares simus Oxonii.
PICEON: Non possum remanere: quaeso, numeretur pecunia.
NICHADES: Ut loculus erat inanis apud Hinckey;   20
           Sic arca est nobis inanis Oxonii;
           Oportet evocari daemonem, si reddatur pecunia.
PICEON: Quid phantasticis verbis et terriculamentis me adhuc deluditis?
           Si placeat, evocate daemonem, ut mihi crateram afferat,
           Et omnia condonabo et praeterea dabo 6 solidos ut pepegistis.
PHILOPINUS: Fiet, (tibi constes) fiet, mi hospes, si non me fallit Nichades.
NICHADES: Vos egrediamini cubiculo, ut soli colloquamur.

(Tacite)

Videte ut omnia recte subserviant in cella subterranea.

(Exeunt DOULERUS et PHILOPINUS)

ACT 5. SCENE 2.

PIGEON. DOULERUS. PHILOFINUS.

NICHADES: Now that you are safely come, let's be merry here at Oxford!

PIGEON: I can't tarry. Count out the money, I pray you.

NICHADES: Just as our purses were empty at Hinksey, so our coffers are empty at Oxford! The devil will have to be conjured up, if the money's to be paid.

PIGEON: What? Is you still a-tryin' to make sport o' me — wi' your fanciful talk an' frightenin' stories? If you wish, call forth the devil, so's 'e can bring me back the punchbowl! Then I shall forgive you ev'rythin', an' I shell, moreover, pay you six shillin's, just as you requested!

PHILOFINUS: It shall be done, (rest assured), it shall be done, innkeeper, my dear fellow, — that is, unless Nichades fails me!

NICHADES: Leave the room, so that we can talk alone.

(In a low voice)

See that they're doing everything right in the underground chamber.

(Exeunt DOULERUS and PHILOFINUS)

Falsissimum est quod vulgo dicitur, posse neminem
Excitare diabolum, nisi sponte et ex pacto velit.   30
Fateor quidem quod plurimi serviunt diabolo,
Paucissimi imperant, quod inter paucos mihi contigit
                                                   tamen.
Ritibus et verbis etenim constringitur daemonis potentia
Ut a peritis in bonum dirigatur eius malitia,
Frendensque frendensque faciat, quod necromanticus velit,
Seu morbidos sanare, seu res ablatas reportare iusserit.
Haec autem didici ex manuscripto codice veteris monachi.

PIGEON: Pulchre fabulam narras.
NICHADES: Loquetur ipsa res me verum loqui. Sed iurabis
            Inprimis te non vulgaturum hanc artem meam,   40
            Nec mihi periculum creaturum, nec aliquid alicui
                                                        dicturum.
PIGEON: Nolo ne timeas, non faciam ut vicini me rideant.
NICHADES: Dic vero qualis apparebit, num muris aut bufonis
                                                        specie?
            Aut masculosi felis, quae omnium est teterrima?

What most people say about no one being able to call forth the devil, unless he, himself, agrees to it, is quite untrue. Indeed, I must own that there are very many who serve the devil, and very few who have command over him, but I, however, am one of the privileged few. For the devil's power can be held in check by words and ritual, so that his evil forces can - by the skilled - be directed towards Good, and so that, with much gnashing of teeth, he has to do what the magician wishes, whether he bids him heal the sick or recover stolen property. I learned these things from a manuscript which belonged to an old monk.

PIGEON: You can tell a fine tale!

NICHADES: The deed, itself, will prove that I'm speaking the truth. But above all, you must swear not to make known this skill of mine, nor to put me in any danger, nor to say anything to anyone.

PIGEON: I shan't, don't worry, I does n't want to make all the neighbours laugh at me!

NICHADES: Then say, truly, in what form he is to appear, whether in the shape of a mouse or a toad, or a spotted cat? - which is the most hideous of all.

PIGION:	Non felis, obsecro; hunc plus abominor quam spiritum taum.
NICHADES:	Bene apparebit itaque eodem modo, quo pingi solet:
	Niger et deformis, virgata cauda, ungulis
	Scissis et bisulcis, et cornibus longioribus quam tua sunt.
PIGION:	Erit pullatus quia nigrior est academicis.
NICHADES:	Unguibus erit aduncis quia rapacior est hospitibus. 50
PIGION:	Habebit togam et cucullum, quia novit literas.
NICHADES:	Te osculabitur quia perdite caupones amat.
	Accingam me ipsum huic operi; primo ducendus est circulus.

(Induit pileum, capillum, carbone circulum describit)

PIGION:	Agis circulatorem optime.
NICHADES:	Iam disponantur planetarum domus et penaeria.

(Ducit characteres)

PIGEON: Not in the form of a cat, I begs you. I loathes that more than your familiar!

NICHADES: Very well, he shall appear, therefore, in the same way as he's usually painted, - that is, black and ugly, with a forked tail, cloven hoofs, and horns even longer than yours are!

PIGEON: 'E'll be dressed in black because 'e be blacker than students!

NICHADES: He'll have hooked claws because he's more grasping than innkeepers!

PIGEON: 'E'll 'ave a gown an' an 'ood because 'e can read an' write!

NICHADES: And he will embrace <u>you</u> because he loves innkeepers to distraction! I shall prepare myself for this task: first, a circle must be drawn:

(He puts on his cap and his hood, and draws a circle with a piece of charcoal)

PIGEON: You plays the part o' mountebank very well!

NICHADES: Now the houses of the planets and their limits must be arranged in order:

(He draws some magical signs)

PIGEON: Num me credis Dawsonem alterum, ut persuadear
Videre et non videre prout vobis placeat?

      (Ter pede terram concutit, candida
       candida virga capita munit)

NICHADES: En ululant canes, ventusque murmurans crepat!
PIGEON: Obtusior est mihi auditus, ego nihil audio.
NICHADES: Irata tellus fremit, et faetet aer quid sulphureum.   60
PIGEON: Nasus est mihi mucosus, ego nihil quidem olfacio.
NICHADES: En nocte caeca bubo feralis gemit
Latratque trino tartari canis sono!
Horrenda Ditis monstra cum Furiis tribus
Quatiunt catenas; territus latet polus,
Et nube spissa Phaebus abscondit caput.
Umbrae silentes, Stygiae paludis incolae,
Reserate claustra, fas sit ignotum chaos
Aperire caelo, et regis inferni domos.

PIGEON: You ain't thinkin' I'm another Dawson, am you, – to be persuaded to see an' not to see, just as the fancy takes you?

(He stamps on the ground three times, and waves a wand over their heads to purify them)

NICHADES: Hark! the dogs are howling, and the wind sighs and moans!

PIGEON: I be 'arder of 'earin' than you, – can't 'ear nothin'.

NICHADES: The angry earth roars, and the air smells of brimstone!

PIGEON: I've got a cold in the nose, – I can't smell nothin' at all!

NICHADES: Listen! In the darkness of the night, the ill-boding owl gives a mournful cry, and the hound of hell bays with three-fold voice; the dreadful monsters of Hades, along with the three Furies, rattle their chains; the terrified heavens lie hidden, and Phoebus buries his head in a dense cloud. O, you silent shades, you inhabitants of the Stygian marsh, throw open the gates: let it be lawful to reveal to the sky unknown chaos, and the king of the underworld's abode!

PIGEON: Non audiunt, eloquere; vox tua vix penetrat   70
 Ad purgatorium, nedum ad infernum!

(Quasi legit NICHADES
 in nigro codice)

NICHADES: Mos, flos, ros, et Tros, mus, dens, mons, pons,
 simul et fons.
 Barbara, Celarent, Darii, Ferio, Baralipten,
 Te adiuro Belimoth, per illa duodecim monstra,
 quae
 Vocantur Aries, Taurus, Gemini, Cancer, Leo, cum
 sodalibus;
 Per caelestem heptarchiam virorum quinque et duarum
 Faeminarum, per piel et puel, per hiphil et hophil,
 Et trigonum et tetragono; Graspas, exurgas.
 Suspicias in hoc vitro triangulo. Iam adest enim
 spiritus.
PIGEON: Faciam, ut quorsum haec evadant sciam.   80
NICHADES: Volvola brachin hoai la volvola drame pagloni,
 Sinto pavar boni, dragatante falombo feloni,
 Exurgas.

(Fit sonitus, aperitur claustrum,
 excitatur flamma)

PIGEON: Speak up, man, they can't 'ear you: your voice
scarce reaches as far as purgatory, never mind 'ell!

    (NICHADES pretends to be reading from
    a black book)

NICHADES: Our forefathers' dower: a blossoming flower;
    one dewy shower; the seat of Priam's power;
What the cat chases; teeth with no braces;
A hill, and a rill, and a bridge standing still!
Barbara, Celarent, Darii, Ferio, Baralipton! I adjure
you, Belimoth, by those twelve signs, which are called
the Ram, the Bull, the Twins, the Crab, the Lion, -
together with their companions; by the heavenly
heptarchy of five men and two women; by piel and puḁgl;
by hiphil and hophḁil; by triangle and quadrangle:
Grampas, rise up! Look into this three-sided glass
vessel, for already the spirit is present.

PIGEON: I'll do't, fur
I'd very much like to know 'ow all this will turn out.

NICHADES: Volvola braehin homi la volvola drame pagloni
Sinto pavar boni, dragatante falombo feloni:
Rise up!

    (There is a crash, the floor opens and
    flames shoot up)

PIGRON: Deus bone! Non audeo manere, mortuus sum!
Nec urinam possum continere nec rem alteram!
NICHADES: (Tenet fugientem)
Extra circulum nihil est periculi.
Foh! Nonne iam oderaris aerem faetidum?
Si craterem cupias, maneas, et facias imperium meum.

Iterum coniuro te,
Per nigros colubros
Capite pendulos,   90
Per limum barathri,
Per imum dolii,
Quod implent filiae
Danai miserrimae,
Perque breve, breve crus,
Madidique rostri pus,
Per sordes unguium,
Per colles dumium,
Surge, surge, quasi ros,
Rape, rape hoc in os,   100
Per humum labe
Horridam sordido,

Erumpe, erumpe.

PIGEON: Good lord! I dare n't stay, — I be done for! I can't 'old me water, nor t'other thing neither!

NICHADES: (restraining him as he tries to run away)

There's no danger outside the circle. Pooh! Surely you can smell how foul the air is, now, can't you? If you want your punchbowl back, remain here, and do as I say.

    Once again I thee conjure:
    By those black snakes that dangle
    From your head, — at an angle;
    By the slimy pit of hell;
    By the bottom of each vess-el,
    Which every poor Danaid daughter
    Does her best to fill with water;
    By your lack of height 'twixt knee and toes;
    By your dripping, runny nose;
    By your claws, all filled with dirt:
    O'er the hills, with brambles girt,
    Rise up, rise up, like the dew!
    Seize this in your mouth askew!
    For I totter 'cross the ground,
    Which, rough, in foulness doth abound!
Come forth, come forth!

ACTUS 5. SCENA 3.

(Exurgit Daemon ho, ho, ho!)

PIGMON: An vigilans somnio? Ubi sum? Num apud inferos?
An me fallunt oculi? Deus bone, miserere mei!
DAEMON: Opaca linquens Ditis inferni loca,
Adsum profundo Tartari emissus specu,
Ubi colla nigris Cerberus iactat iubis;
Ubi stultus agilem patitur Ixion rotam;
Ubi pensiles fructus ore ieiuno videt,
Et inter undas Tantalus perit situ; 110
Ubi toties luso Sysipho redit lapis;
Ubi rodit aquila saevus accrescens iecur;
Quid est agendum? Quorsum me ex imo vocas?
NICMADES: Spiritus maligne, dic, sine omni mendacio,
Ubi crater aureus hospitis nostri latet?
DAEMON: Ancilla suffurata est.

ACT 5. SCENE 3.

(The devil appears, bellowing)

PIGEON: Be I awake an' dreamin'? Where be I? Not in 'ell, surely? Or does me eyes deceive me? Good lord, 'ave pity on me!

THE DEVIL: "Forsaking the shadowy regions of the infernal king, I am present, sent forth from the deep pit of hell": where Cerberus tosses his shaggy black necks; where foolish Ixion suffers on the swiftly spinning wheel; where Tantalus with ravenous mouth gazes at the overhanging fruit, and though amid the waves, dies of thirst; where the boulder rolls back to Sisyphus, so often tricked; where the cruel eagle gnaws at the ever-growing liver. What do you want of me? Why have you called me forth from the depths?

NICHADES: O evil spirit, say truthfully where the golden punchbowl, belonging to this innkeeper, lies hidden?

THE DEVIL: The maid stole it.

NICHADES: Mentiris Belimoth.
Ambagibus itaque et mendaciis remotis omnibus,
Volo, iubeo, impero, ut craterem afferas velociter,
Sive post tabulata, sive sit in puteo, sive abscondatur
Inter vestes, sive defodiatur sub limine, sive   120
                                         iaceat
In cella; ubicumque sit, afferas, et redeas cito!

(Exit Daemon et redit)

Iam videas, hospes, quam celerem habeo nuntium.
Cur tremis et palles? Ecce craterem tuum!
PIGEON: Ipsissimus est! Deus bone! Horror me occupat,
Eriguntur comae, pectus tremit, caligant oculi!
NICHADES: Numquid aliud vis scire quod conducat tibi?
PIGEON: Nihil occurrit memoriae, nisi utrum filia sit virgo?
NICHADES: Impure cacodaemon, an Ioanna Pigeon solvit
Virgineam zonam?

NICHADES: You're lying, Belimoth. So, away with all digression and falsehood, I wish you, I bid you, nay, — I command you, to fetch the punchbowl quickly, — whether it's hidden under the floor-boards, down the well, or amongst the clothes; whether it's buried beneath the threshold, or whether it lies in the cell; wherever it is, fetch it, and return immediately.

(Exit the devil. He comes back again)

Now you see, innkeeper, what a speedy errand-boy I have! But why are you trembling and turning pale? See, here's your punchbowl!

PIGEON: Why, 'tis...'tis...'tis the very one! Good lord! I be overcome wi' fright, — me 'air be a-standin' on end, me 'eart be a-poundin', an' me eyes be a-swimmin'!

NICHADES: Is there anything else you'd like to know which might be to your advantage?

PIGEON: Nothin' comes to mind, — save whether me daughter still be a virgin?

NICHADES: Unclean Cacodemon, has Joanna Pigeon loosed Chastity's belt yet?

DAEMON: Ho, ho, ho!

> Esse se si nescit, 130
> Non esset si esset;
> Sciat se non esse,
> Tum esse non necesse.

PIGEON: Quid ait? Ego nihil memini, nisi nescit et esset.
NICHADES: Semper solet diabolus in ambiguis aequivocare,
A quo didicerunt Iesuitae artem suam veteratoriam.
Sed antequam descendat, necesse est ut des iusiurandum.
Primo stabis promissis, nec ulteriorem facies molestiam.
PIGEON: Nolo.
NICHADES: Scholares recentes non decipies
Semiplenis poculis aut semiputri caseo. 140
PIGEON: Nolo.
NICHADES: Ancillas non prostitues
Ut magno pretio famem peccantes redimant.
PIGEON: Nolo.

THE DEVIL: Ho! Ho! Ho!

If she does n't know she is,
She would not be if she could be:
Let her know that not she is,
Then 't ain't necessary to be!

PIGEON: What's 'e say? I does n't remember anythin' save "she does n't know", an' "she could be".

NICHADES: The devil is always wont to talk in riddles: it was from him that the Jesuits learned their cunning art! But before he departs, you must swear an oath: first, that you will keep your promise, and not cause any more mischief.

PIGEON: I won't!

NICHADES: That you will not cheat freshmen by giving them half measure, or mouldy cheese.

PIGEON: I won't!

NICHADES: That you will not prostitute your serving-wenches, so that those who fall into sin, have to buy back their good name at a very high price.

PIGEON: I won't!

NICHADES:	Haec omnia te observaturum iurabis,
	Et ad maiorem fidem osculaberis ipsum podicem
	cacodaemonis.
PIGMON:	Absit num adorabo diabolum? Nunquam faciam.
NICHADES:	Aut facias, aut illico mittam hunc malum angelum
	Ut diruat domum tuosque incendat lares.
PIGMON:	O dolor! Si necesse sit, faciam.

(Osculatur)

NICHADES: Iam sufficit. Satur Ammior, Aylitef, Belimoth,
            Abeas, redeas, descendas!   150

(Descendit Daemon)

Visne ulterius, hospes, in pecuniae tuae solatium
Videre luculentius artis meae testimonium,
Aliosque spiritus subterraneos aspicere?

NICHADES: You are to swear that you will carry out all these things, and to make your oath more binding, you must kiss the Devil's bare buttocks.

PIGEON: 'Eaven forbid! Surely I ain't to worship the devil? I'll never do 't!

NICHADES: You will do it, else straightaway I shall send this bad angel to destroy your house, and set your home on fire!

PIGEON: Oh, woe is me! If 't be necessary, I'll do 't.

(He kisses the devil)

NICHADES: Now, that's enough. You've had your fill, Azmior, Aylitef, Belemoth: be gone, return, go down!

(The devil departs)

Innkeeper, do you wish to see even finer evidence of my skill, as further compensation for the money you've lost, and to look on other sprites from under the ground?

PICEON: Nequaquam, si me ames. Satis est, nondum sum apud me.
NICHADES: Ne timeas, evocabo diabolos minorum gentium,
            Qui tantum possunt ludere, non possunt laedere,
            Qui ridiculo habitu et mimicis gestibus,
            Excutient tibi risum, non incutient timorem;
            Imitabuntur autem antiquos Panes et Satyros,
            Quos familiariter cum mortalibus versatos refert
                                            antiquitas.   160
            Iam autem rarius apparent haec poetarum numina,
            Nisi precibus alliciantur. O vos Fayries, et Mammets,
            Bugges, Apesfaces et Hobgoblins inferioris ordinis;
            Verecundi Dandiprats, Hop et eius progenies,
            Seu Panes, aut Manes, seu satyri vel fityri,
            Seu lares aut lemures aut Penates vocamini;
            Qui dormientum brachia comprimitis unguibus,
            Virgines et puellas lividis signantes notis,
            Qui iunctis manibus quercus annosas cingitis,
            Saltitantes circulo, tritumque gramen pedibus   170
            Nigricans arescit, qui media de nocte luditis
            Cum infantibus ad focum, puram diligentes aquam,
            Ignemque vivum; respondete iam votis meis,
            Nec timidi nimis ora mortalium fugite.
            Adeste tripudiantes cum musica quemadmodum
            Fecistis olim, quum Oberon reginam duxerat.

PIGEON: No, indeed, as you loves me! That be quite enough! I ain't myself again yet!

NICIADES: Don't be afraid, I shall call up devils of a smaller variety, who can only charm, – not harm! Who, with their comical clothes and farcical antics, will excite laughter in you, – not incite fear! For they will imitate the Pans and satyrs of old, who, antiquity tells us, lived on friendly terms with mortals. But nowadays these poets' gods are seldom seen, save when they are summoned forth by prayers: o you Fairies, and Mannets, Pugs, Apesfaces, and Hobgoblins of the lower order: shy Dandiprats, Mop and her brood; whether you are called Pans or Manes, satyrs or fityrs, lares or ghosts or Penates; you who pinch black and blue the arms of sleeping maids and girls; you who, joining hands, make a circle round the agèd oak, dancing in a ring, while the grass, worn by your feet, grows brown and dry; you who at midnight sport with infants before the hearth, loving the fresh water, and the lively fire: answer now my prayers, and be not so timid as to shun the sight of mortals. Draw nigh, and dance to the music in the same way as you did long, long ago, when Oberon had wed his queen.

Vestros colonus sic neutiquam turbet choros,
Nec nauseam vobis sordida supellex creet,
Vestrosque liberos lautior pascat cibus,
Nec aqua consecrata, nec superstitio crucis   130
Abigat timentes. Apparete faelici omine!

If this be done, may no farmer disturb your rout, nor slovenly households provoke disgust in you, and may your children feed upon more sumptuous fare, and may neither holy water nor the belief in the cross drive you fearful away. Appear with favourable omen!

ACTUS 5. SCENA 4.

(Exeunt 3 pueri, antiquos imitantes, et saltant)

PIGEON: Ha, ha, he!

(Diffugiunt lamiae)

Quam lepidos ludos video!
De his narrare solebat avia prolixas fabulas,
Gestiebat igitur hos puppos et lamias cernere.

(Intrat PHILOPINUS et DOULERUS)

PHILOPINUS: Num rediit caelo facies, et inferno spiritus?
Facinusque tenebrarum discussum reddidit diem?
Olet adhuc locus tetrius, quam Avernus, aut barathrum.

PIGEON: Generosi, non exprimit saepe lingua, quod imprimunt
oculi.
Vidi, vidi archidiabolum mugientem et rugientem;
Vidi tres pusiones seu pigmeos seu nescio quas
lamias   190
Gesticulantes, rectumque deducentes miris modis.

ACT 5. SCENE 4.

(Exeunt three boys, imitating the satyrs of old, and dancing)

PIGEON: Ha, ha, he!

(The 'boggarts' run off)

What delightful sport 'ave I seen! Many's the tale me old grandam was wont to tell about these. 'Er longed, therefore, to see them elves an' boggarts!

(Enter PHILOPINUS and DOULEUS)

PHILOPINUS: Has the face of heaven returned, and the spirit gone back to the lower world? Has the deed of darkness restored the scattered daylight? For the place still smells more foul than either Avernus, or hell!

PIGEON: Gen'lemen, oftimes the tongue can't express what the eyes impress. I...I...I 'ave seen the arch-fiend a-rumblin' an' a-roarin'; I 'ave seen three little lads, - whether they was dwarfs, or boggarts, I could n't tell, - a-caperin', an' a-walkin' upright in a remarkable fashion.

PHILOPINUS: Adhuc cogitans tremo. Ecce craterem redditum!
Ὦ παντοκράτορα Nichedae! Mihi crede, huic servit
diabolus,
Et quasi famulus domesticus semper est presto ad
manum,
Saepe sternit eius, saepe candelam accendit tenebris.
PIGEON: An est possibile? Est itaque eius familiaris spiritus.
PHILOPINUS: Rectissime. Tullius non magis est familiaris Lentulo;
Sed iam reddatur coronatus Gallicus ut pepegisti.
PIGEON: Faciam; interim tamen afficior damno non levi, 200
Et perdidi plus quam duos bonos angelos.
PHILOPINUS: Interea vidisti plus quam tres malos angelos,
Et cum Vespasiano facile resarcias damnum ex lotio.
PIGEON: Quid intelligis per illud?
PHILOPINUS: Nempe ex cervisia,
Quae per bibones currens vertitur in lotium.
PIGEON: Verissime dicis; apud nos enim nihil nisi bibunt et
mingunt.

(Intrat pauper scholaris cum cervisia
et pane scisso)

PHILOPINUS: I tremble even to think of it! Lo and behold! The punchbowl's been recovered! O almighty Nichades! Believe me, the devil is this man's slave, and, like a domestic servant, he is always close at hand: he often blows out his candle, and often lights it for him in the dark!

PIGEON: Be it possible? 'E must be 'is familiar, then?

PHILOPINUS: Of course: Tully is not more a familiar to Lentulus! But now pay us the French crown you promised us.

PIGEON: I will, but the damage I've suffered in the meantime ain't slight, an' I've lost more than two good angels!

PHILOPINUS: Ah, but meanwhile you've seen more than three bad angels, and, like Vespasian, you'll easily make good your loss - from piss!

PIGEON: What does you mean by that?

PHILOPINUS: Well, from ale, - surely - which passing through tipplers, turns into piss!

PIGEON: Ay, what you says, be very certain true, fur at our 'ouse they does nothin' but tipple an' piddle!

(Enter the poor student, with a jug of ale and a slice of bread)

DOULEBUS:	Cratere tuo bibemus. Propino tibi et fabro,	
	Et agricolae et uxori tuae, nec oblitus sum Caeciliae,	
	Sed praecipue dominae Ioannae, cui a me impertias	
	Multam salutem. Sed nihil audeo statuere	
	Parentibus non consultis de nostro connubio.	210
PIGEON:	Respondebo promptissime, omnibusque dico	
	gratissimum vale.	
DOULEBUS:	Hoc unicum a te obnixe peto, ut postquam redieris	
	domum,	
	Convocatis vicinis tuis nostrisque familiaribus,	
	Hoc canticum cantare velis in medio choro.	

(Dat chartam)

PIGEON: Faciam libenter sed prius tentabo.

     Scholares hic fuere,
     Et epulas habuere,

OMNES: Nec obolum reddidere.
     O hilaris iocus, iocus!

DOULERUS: We shall drink from your punchbowl. I drink a toast to you and to the blacksmith, to the farmer and to your wife, and I have n't forgotten Caecilia either, but above all I drink a toast to Mistress Joanna, - please give her my best wishes. However...I dare n't make any arrangements about our marriage, without first seeking my parents' approval.

PIGEON: I shall agree most readily! I bids you all a fond farewell!

DOULERUS: I ask of you this one favour - and I won't take no for an answer, - that after you return home, you call together all your neighbours and our friends, so that while you sing the verses of this song, they may sing the chorus.

(He hands him a sheet of paper)

PIGEON: I'll do 't gladly, but I'll try it out fust:

There were some scholars 'ere today,
An' to supper they did stay,

ALL: But not a penny did they pay,
O what a jest! What a merry jest!

PIGEON: Et allam potavere,   220
              Et musicam audivere,

OMNES: Nec obolum reddidere.
                O hilaris iocus, iocus!

PIGEON: Et oscula dedere,
              Et oscula sumpsere,

OMNES: Nec obolum reddidere.
                O hilaris iocus, iocus!

PIGEON: Agricolam lusere,
              Uxorem purgavere,

OMNES: Nec obolum reddidere.
                O hilaris iocus, iocus!

PIGEON: Et domum me duxere,
              Et Daemonem ostendere,   230

OMNES: Nec obolum reddidere.
                O hilaris iocus, iocus!

PIGEON: An' wi' my ale thirst did allay,
An' listened to the music play,

ALL: But not a penny did they pay,
O what a jest! What a merry jest!

PIGEON: An' kisses did they give away,
An' pretty lips they did waylay,

ALL: But not a penny did they pay,
O what a jest! What a merry jest!

PIGEON: The farmer in sport did lead astray,
'is wife's impurities purged away,

ALL: But not a penny did they pay,
O what a jest! What a merry jest!

PIGEON: An' to their 'ome showed me the way,
An' put the devil on display,

ALL: But not a penny did they pay,
O what a jest! What a merry jest!

PIGEON: Ha, ha, he! Iterum, domini, dico vobis valete, et si
                                                      redeatis
         Ad nostram villam, erimus multo hilariores, quam
                                                      prius.

                        (Exit PIGEON)

                         (Rident)

PIGEON: Ha, ha, he! Once again, sirs, I bids you farewell, an'
            if you ever comes back to our village, we shall be far
            merrier than before!

                    (Exit)

                (They laugh.

ACTUS 5. SCENA 5.
(Manent academici)

NICHADES: Ad exitum laetum iam producitur noster iocus,
Fuimusque hilares gratis, victumque et musicam
Habuimus gratis, moresque hominum varios
Perspeximus gratis: hos autem iuveniles dolos
Iuvabit olim meminisse senili cathedra.
PHILOPINUS: Omnia iam redigamus in ordinem, et depositis
Fictis nominibus, veros agamus academicos. 240
Laxatus animus alacrius multo studet.
DOULERUS: Nunc studia repetat, quisque revolvat libros,
Nativitatis festum semel in anno ridet:
Et qui semel in anno ridet, non peccat grave.

ACT 5. SCENE 5.

(The students remain)

NICHADES: Now has our jesting been brought to a successful conclusion! We've been merry free of cost; we've had our share of both food and music free of cost; and we've observed the various manners of men free of cost. But one day, when we're old and seated in our arm-chairs, it will be a joy to reflect upon how we sported in our youth!

PHILOPINUS: Let's now put everything back in order again, and, laying aside our false names, behave like true students. The mind, when refreshed, applies itself all the more keenly to learning.

DOULERUS: Let every one who turns the pages of books, now resume his studies: he laughs but once in a year, - at Christmas, and he who laughs but once in a year, does not greatly err!

GENIUS ACADEMIAE, vice Epilogi.

Querela vetus academicam turbam arguit
Ebrietatis, lasciviae, necromantiae;
Vidistis autem quod simulata plerumque vitia,
Nugae dolosae, hilares imberbium ioci
Ab invidis obiiciantur, quasi vera crimina,
Totis Athenis; pura sic vas acidum
Corrumpet, et flos araneo venenum dabit;
Non leviter expiandum scelus, nec iniuria levis
Academiae, mihique; irato sed vivant Apolline,
Miseraeque vitae sit haeres infamia.   10
Quod si aliquibus apud vos tetricis censoribus,
Prudentibusque, canis displiceant haec ludicra,
Revocetur in memoriam quam iniqua postulant
Qui mutatis ipsis cuncta mutare volunt,
Mundumque delirare. Inconstans hominum genus
Spernit quod olim petiit, nec satis memor suas
Confundit aetates. Non illico nascuntur senes,
Non una nocte canescunt iuvenes nisi prodigio;
At vos benignae, animae candidissimae
Date veniam, paulisper indulgete genio,   20
Animoque facili dignemini, et oculo propitio
Hos innocentes ludos, qui non agebantur prius;
Quos ad theatrum, non ad tribunal voco.

(The GENIUS OF THE UNIVERSITY, in
place of the Epilogue)

For centuries now the scholarly band have been accused of
drunkenness, licentiousness, and the practice of black magic. But you
have seen that these vices are, for the most part, feigned: let the
envious throughout the whole of this city of learning condemn the
cunning jokes and merry sport of the young, as if they were real
crimes, - in this way will clean water sully the vessel that is
already sour, and the flower give poison to the spider! An evil deed
such as this, must not be atoned for easily, nor is the wrong done to
the University and myself, slight; but may the live under Apollo's
wrath, and may slander be heir to a life of misery. However, if this
sport displeases any of the stern, wise, white-haired critics amongst
you, remember what unfair demands are made by those who, having changed
themselves, wish to change everything else and to turn the world mad.
Fickle mankind despises what once it sought, and, forgetful, confuses
its own ages. Old men are not born instantly, nor do young men grow old
over-night, save by a miracle: but you, kind and honest souls be
favourable, indulge our talent for a little while, and deem this harmless
play, - which has not been performed before - worthy of a willing heart
and an eager eye: I summon you to the theatre, <u>not</u> to the judgement seat.

Et sic recedens dico iam cunctis, vale,
Huic academiae fausta comprecatus omnia:
Vigeat et crescat in octavum miraculum,
Verisque studiis floreat, et moribus bonis:
Oculusque unicus Europae Polyphemicae
Habeatur a Chinensibus; nec orbis latius
Aut diutius extendatur, quam eius decus; 30
His precibus meis quisquis academiae favet
Consentiat clare manibus incussis sono.

    Sine venia nullum placuit ingenium.

And so now, as I depart, I bid you all farewell, having prayed that this University may enjoy every good fortune: may it thrive, and grow to be the eighth wonder of the world; and may it flourish with a zeal for true study, and with sound customs; may it be considered by the Chinese to be the one and only eye of polypheric Europe; and may its glory reach to the four corners of the earth, and endure as long as the world, itself! Let every one who is the University's champion, accord with these, my wishes, by loudly clapping his hands!

Without favour, no talent was ever pleasing.

NOTES

NOTES

1. **Mercurius Rusticans:** In classical Latin, the name 'Mercurius' refers specifically to Mercury, the messenger of the gods, the patron of traders and thieves, and the conductor of the souls of the dead to the Lower World. However, in mediaeval and renaissance Latin, the word begins to have a much wider application. It is often used in a general sense to denote any kind of messenger: for instance, during the period of the Civil War, the name 'Mercurius' appears in the title of many weekly papers, both Royalist and Parliamentary, e.g. **Mercurius Aulicus**, **Mercurius Britannicus**, and **Mercurius Academicus**; and, indeed, some modern newspapers have retained the name. Since a messenger, or herald, must possess a certain degree of eloquence, 'Mercurius' can also mean one skilled in the art of rhetoric, a disciple of Mercury, or a student. Hence, 'student' is the meaning given to the word in the title of this particular play.

2. **Scena: Hynckaey vel Hincksie:**

    "In the two Hinkseys nothing keeps the same;"

    (Matthew Arnold, *Thyrsis*)

    Most, though not all, of the action of **Mercurius Rusticans** takes place in the village of Hinksey, but, unfortunately, there is no definite indication as to whether this is North Hinksey (sometimes called Ferry Hinksey), or South Hinksey. However, there are two small clues in the play which seem to point to the fact that the setting is very probably North Hinksey. For example, in Act I, 1.100, a reference is made to what appears to be a passage across a stream. The village of North Hinksey is situated on the right bank of a river (a branch of the Isis), which is here crossed by a ferry, known to have been in existence at least as early as 1467, if not before. Also, in the fourth act of the play (stage direction at Sc. 2), one of the three students is described as "walking up and down, looking at Oxford". In the western part of the parish of North Hinksey, the ground rises from the banks of the river to a height of about 380 ft. The view that can be had from this hill of the city of Oxford, was in the past a very great favourite with artists (see below, note to Act 4, ll. 96 - 113). It seems more than likely, therefore, that this is the spot from where Philopinus is looking down on Oxford in Act 4, and that North Hinksey is the location for the play.

North Hinksey, itself, is a small Berkshire parish, comprising some 797 acres, and is first mentioned as being a separate village from South Hinksey in 1316. Both the Hinkseys, and the surrounding countryside, have been immortalised in the Oxford poems of Matthew Arnold.

(For further information about North Hinksey, see V.H.C.Berkshire, IV, 405 - 10, and Henry W. Taunt's most interesting and well illustrated account of the village and its neighbourhood, in his edition of The Oxford Poems of Matthew Arnold (Oxford, 1929)).

3. Pigeon..Robertus Dawson...Richardus Cullie: The names Pigeon, Dawson and Cullie were quite common in the Oxford and Berkshire areas during the sixteenth and seventeenth centuries, and one is tempted to wonder whether the characters who appear in the play are based on real people with whom the author was, himself, acquainted.

It was not at all unusual for students and college men to mix with the countryfolk from around Oxford. Not only did scholars spend many of their leisure hours in the country, but also the villages and hamlets that lay close to the city frequently had very close associations with the various colleges, since it often came about that the clergy in their particular parish were Fellows and Chaplains of the University. Moreover, at a later date, many country people were, in fact, married in college chapels (see G. Lambrick, 'Oxford Colleges and Some Country Parishes round Oxford in the Early 18th. Century', Oxoniensia, 25 (1960), 109-120).

Unfortunately, however, the parish records (births, marriages and deaths, etc.) for North Hinksey date back only as far as the year 1703, making it impossible to ascertain if anyone of the name

Pigeon, Dawson or Cullie, was living in the village at about the time the play is thought to have been written. Nevertheless, the villagers of Hinksey, as they are portrayed in the play, - whether they are modelled on people whom the author knew personally, or no - are very typical, especially in their attitude towards University students, of the countryfolk with whom he might have come into contact.

4. Puer: In the list of Dramatis Personae, the word 'puer' occurs twice, but in the play itself, 'a boy' appears only once, at Act I, ll. 182-186.

5. lamiae: In classical mythology, a 'lamia' is represented as a child-stealing witch. The very first 'lamia' is thought to have been the daughter of Belus and Libya, whose children were put to death by Hera because Zeus was her lover, whereupon she became mad with grief (see O.C.D., s.v. Lamia (1). The poet, John Keats, also has this conception of a 'lamia' in his work of the same name.

However, Thomas Cooper, in his T.L.R.B. describes a 'lamia' as "a beast that hath a womans face, and feete of an horse", making no mention of the fact that this creature is greatly to be feared because it snatches babes from their cradles; whilst here, the word seems to be synonymous with satyr, and can perhaps best be translated as 'boggart', or 'bogey'.

PROLOGUE

The prologue to <u>Mercurius Rusticans</u> is spoken by the Genius Academigae, a character who does not actually take part in the play, itself. In Roman comedy, it was quite common for the play to be introduced by a god, or a character outside the main action, e.g. in Plautus' <u>Trinummus</u>, where Luxury appears as the Prologue, and in the <u>Rudens</u>, where Arcturus fills this rôle. The prologue to <u>Mercurius Rusticans</u> also follows the conventions laid down by Roman comedy in its function, (see, too, note to Act I, 1.19), which is, above all, to gain the audience's attention and secure a favourable hearing for the play. It can be divided into three main sections: (i) ll. 1-10, in which the Genius Academigae introduces himself; (ii) ll. 10-20, in which he explains the reason for his coming, and hints briefly at the circumstances in which the action of the play originates; and (iii) ll. 21-30, the 'captatio benevolentiae', which is virtually a confidential address to the audience to put them in a good humour, and a plea to give the play their undivided attention.

6. <u>Genius Academigae</u>: The tutelary deity of the University. Here, the Genius is also represented as a quasi-mythological figure, personifying the University as an institution: cf. Milton's use of the word 'genius' in <u>Il Penseroso</u>, l. 154,

"the unseen Genius of the wood".

(In my quotations from Milton, I use the standard Globe edition).

7. <u>armis academiae scuto depictis</u>: The shield which the Genius carried, probably displayed the coat-of-arms of Oxford University as a whole, rather than those of any particular college, since throughout the prologue he speaks of the University in general terms. A full heraldic description of these arms is given in F.P. Barnard and T. Shepard <u>Arms and Blasons of the Colleges of Oxford</u>, (London, 1929), frontispiece, and pp. 29-30:

"Asure, upon a book open proper, leathered gules, garnished or, having on the dexter side seven seals of the last, the words DOMINUS ILLUMINATIO MEA, (N.B. the motto engraved here has varied down the centuries), all between three open crowns, two and one, gold".

These arms are thought to have been in use since the middle of the fifteenth century, and to have been based on a fictitious coat invented for the Anglo-Saxon king and martyr, St. Edmund, - asure, three open crowns, two and one, or, - as can be seen, for example, on the tomb of Edmund, Duke of York (d.1402), at King's Langley. The book was added to these arms. They are represented for the first time in a window of the old library, at Balliol College, which dates from c. 1412-17. They can also be seen among the armorial decorations in the Canterbury Cloisters, and in the roof of the Divinity School at Oxford, which was built about the same time.

The motto, written on the book, has differed greatly from age to age, according to custom and tradition. Of the four, which are on record, probably the oldest is "In principio erat verbum, et verbum erat apud Deum" (Vulgate, Joan. I,I). The present motto, "Dominus illuminatio mea" (Vulgate, Ps.XXVI,I), is believed to have first appeared about 1540-50. A third motto, "Bonitas regnabit, Veritas liberavit" (partly from Vulgate, Joan.VIII,32) dates from 1517-1756. Finally, the words "Sapientia et Felicitate", are found for the first time in print, in Joseph Barnes' engraved University Arms: Barnes was the earliest printer to the University. This motto is very likely compounded from "perfectam sapientiae felicitatem" (St. Augustine, De Civitate Dei, XIII, 17); and "deus non vincit sapientem felicitate" (Seneca, Epistulae Morales, LXXIII,13).

2. mater alma: In Roman times, this was a title given to several of the goddesses, especially Ceres, Cybele and Venus. Later, however, the term was transferred in English to schools and universities, which were looked upon as being 'foster-mothers' to their pupils, or 'alumni'.

3-5. Est alius urbis...non satis aliquando convenit: A reference to the great rivalry which existed between the University and the City of Oxford, during the Middle Ages and the sixteenth and seventeenth centuries. Students and townspeople often came into conflict with one another: the Oxford clerks, many of whom were high-spirited and rebellious, used to brawl in the streets and cause riots, while the townsmen, for their part, would raise food prices and the rent for lodgings which they let to students. Frequently, the Sovereign was called upon to settle these disputes, but through fear of falling foul of the Church and risking excommunication, the Crown usually took the side of the clerks against the laymen of Oxford, granting extra privileges to the University, and imposing fines and imprisonment upon the townspeople. Many of the students abused the privileges which they were thus given, and the laymen grew more and more angry as they lost one right after another, and the power of the University became stronger and stronger. The two communities vied with one another in importance for several centuries.

(A full discussion of the jealousy that raged between Town and Gown can be found in Mallet, A History of the University of Oxford, vols. I and II.).

6-7. qunm primum Alfredus domum Musis sacravit: An allusion to the legend, readily accepted by some historians in the mediaeval period, which stated that King Alfred had founded University College, Oxford, in A.D. 873.

7. Athenas novas: In the ancient world, Athens was a great centre for

learning. Plato had taught philosophy at the Academy there, during the fourth century B.C., and later, one of his ex-pupils, the great philosopher, Aristotle, founded his own school of philosophy in the city. Amongst the many celebrated Romans who visited Athens hundreds of years later to pursue their studies, may be noted Cicero, Octavian and Horace. Just as Athens, through the ages, had attracted scholars from all over the then known world, so students flocked to Oxford in large numbers during the Middle Ages and the sixteenth and seventeenth centuries. Hence, the University is here referred to as a 'new', or 'second' Athens.

8-9. <u>bis quater centum...Annis...usque ad hodiernum diem</u>: If the date of the legendary founding of the University is taken as being A.D. 873, then the play, itself, according to the prologue, must have been written eight hundred years later, about 1673. (See Introduction, section II, for the date of play's composition.)

14. <u>aetatis lubricae</u>: The Roman historian, Tacitus, uses a similar phrase to this, when describing the stormy adolescence of the young Nero. In <u>Annals</u>, XIII, 2, Tacitus speaks of the

        "lubricam principis aetates".

(In my quotations from classical authors, I use the standard Loeb editions, unless otherwise stated.)

17. **quasi speculo:** An allusion to the theory that comedy is 'the mirror of life'. Aristophanes the Grammarian praised Menander, the most famous writer of Greek New Comedy, for the way in which his plays closely reflected life: "O Menander and Life, which of you imitated the other?" (ὦ Μένανδρε καὶ βίε, πότερος ἄρ' ὑμῶν πότερον ἀπεμιμήσατο;).

This view of comedy is also endorsed by Donatus. In <u>De Comoedia</u>, V, I, he says,

> "comoediam esse Cicero ait (in a work no longer extant) imitationem vitae, speculum consuetudinis, imaginem veritatis".

and in V, 5, he adds,

> "aitque (i.e. Cicero, in a work no longer extant) esse comoediam cotidianae vitae speculum, nec iniuria. nam ut intenti speculo veritatis liniamenta facile per imaginem colligimus, ita lectione comoediae imitationem vitae consuetudinisque non aegerrime animadvertimus."

(For Donatus and Evanthius (mentioned below) see Teubner edition).

18. **Non facta, sed ficta:** See below, note to 1.19.

19. **leges comicae**: The classical examples and precepts for the writing of comedy, as laid down by Evanthius and Donatus, and for which renaissance dramatists had great respect, and were desirous of obeying. These rules were concerned mainly with the structure of comedy. Evanthius, (<u>De Fabula</u>, IV, 5) states that comedy is divided into four parts: prologue, protasis, epitasis and catastrophe. The Prologue is described as the preface to the play proper, in which the audience is told something about the plot, the author, or the actors taking part. The protasis is the first act and the beginning of the play; whilst in the epitasis, the plot is developed further, complications set in, and a climax is reached. Finally, there is the catastrophe, or dénouement, where the plot is unravelled in such a way that a happy ending is brought about.

Moreover, Evanthius declares that the characters appearing in comedy are to be ordinary men, and not the kings and great heroes of tragedy, and that the events of comedy are to be imaginary, and not real — the "non facta, sed ficta," of l.18.

20. <u>metrici verborum modi</u>: See Introduction, section VIII.

21. <u>Viri ter venerabiles et egregii</u>: The members of the audience.

24. **Saturnalia:** Originally, the festival of Saturn, celebrated on 17th. December. It was one of the merriest feasts in the Roman calendar: slaves were temporarily allowed to do as they pleased, and gifts were exchanged (see O.C.D., s.v. Saturnus.) Here, however, the word is synonymous with our Christmas. The author is quick to seize the opportunity of playing on the meaning of 'Saturnalia' and 'saturnii', for although the festival of Saturn was, itself, a period for great rejoicing and riotous merriment, those born under the influence of the planet Saturn are by nature considered to be dull and gloomy. Thus, the juxtaposition of these two words provides a humorous contrast.

27. **Linguis, animisque favete:** A Roman religious formula, which was spoken by the priest at sacrifices. It was really a request for silence, so that no words of ill-omen would be uttered by those present. The phrase occurs frequently in Roman literature, where the poet, assuming the 'persona' of priest, asks his readers to listen attentively to what he has to say: cf. Horace, *Odes* III, I, 1.2,

"favete linguis".

and Ovid, *Fasti* I, 1.71,

"linguis animisque favete!"

In this particular prologue, of course, the term is used merely as a plea to the audience to give the play that is to follow, a favourable hearing.

27. <u>rectis oculis</u>: Literally, 'with riveted gaze'. The adjective 'rectus' is seldom used in classical Latin with 'oculi'. The only parallels which appear to exist occur in Seneca, <u>Epistulae Morales</u>, <u>LXXVI</u>, 33, and <u>CIV</u>, 24.

28. <u>porrectis frontibus</u>: cf. Plautus, <u>Casina</u>, 1. 281.

    LYSIDAMUS: Primum ego te porrectiore fronte
                  volo mecum loqui;

29. <u>Pro gratia vestra rependam gratias</u>: a play on words. The author has here taken advantage of the fact that in Latin, 'favour' and 'thanks' can be rendered by the same word. There is no exact equivalent in English.

30. <u>Facilem lienem</u>: The spleen was once supposed to be the cause of laughter. For instance, in Shakespeare's <u>Twelfth Night</u>, Maria says to Sir Toby Belch, III, ii, ll. 63-4,

    "If you desire the spleen, and will laugh yourselves
    into stitches, follow me."

(In my quotations from Shakespeare, I use the standard Alexander text.)

So to wish a person 'facilem lienem' is another way of hoping that they will indulge in hearty laughter.

ACT I

<u>togatus</u>: "dressed in a toga". The 'toga' became the modern academic gown. It was a robe or tunic, worn by almost anyone, and in the early days of the University, could be any colour the wearer might choose. However, in the sixteenth century, more sombre colours were insisted upon, and eventually black took precedence. (See Mallet, I, pp. 145, and 147).

<u>pileatus</u>: "wearing a pileum". This was the cap which completed the academic dress, and which was usually worn by Masters rather than Bachelors. Mallet (I, p.146) states that 'according to high authority,' the Almighty, Himself, presented it to those who were Doctors of the Mosaic Law.

1. <u>Duri parentes, matre sed durior pater</u>: The verb 'esse' is understood here. The whole sentence smacks of an exercise in the use of the comparative adjective in a student's Latin grammar!

4. **Iudicor...hyliuo:** A clever pun, facilitated by the very great resemblance between the genitive plural of 'litum', and that of 'liber'. It is impossible, in English, to reproduce exactly the word-play here.

6. **Pili...feriis:** It was permissible for students to spend as many as twenty days in the year away from Oxford. (See Ward, The Statutes of Corpus Christi College, c.30.)

10. **Alea, pictaeque chartae:** Games forbidden by the College Statutes. (See Ward, c. 29).

12. **Diebus...infestis:** The adjectives 'festus' and 'infestus', although very similar in appearance, are almost opposites in meaning, — a fact of which the author makes ready use, in order to add yet another humorous touch to Doulerus' soliloquy.

13–14. **expertus sum...inferias:** Once again, words similar in sound, but totally different in meaning, — 'feriae' and 'inferiae' — are used side by side for comic effect.

16–17. **Nec oppidani...vade:** There were many money-lenders in Oxford, who, the evidence shows, often took advantage of penniless scholars.

Quite early in the University's history (1248) a Royal Charter was granted to the students, one of the results of which was that Jewish usurers were checked in their charges. (See Mallet, I, 39).

18-19. cum hirundine...dormire: It was formerly believed that swallows did not migrate, but that they hibernated. (See Gilbert White, *The Natural History and Antiquities of Selborne*, (London, 1789) Letter 18.).

cane Gallico: Probably a beagle, since later in the play it becomes clear that the dog referred to here, is one used specifically for hunting hares. The name 'beagle' is thought to be derived from the French 'bayer', to gape, and 'gueule', throat. Thus, beagle is Latinized as 'canis Gallicus'. Students were not supposed to keep hunting-dogs. (See Ward, c. 29).

bombarda: Philopinus, too, is breaking the rules, for in the statutes of Corpus Christi College, which date from the beginning of the sixteenth century, it is laid down that the only weapons which a student may carry, are a bow and arrow. (See Ward, c. 28).

27. <u>Ornatus et oneratus</u>: A play on words, to heighten the humour in Nichades' account of his dream.

31. <u>Stans pede in uno</u>: This is a direct quotation from Horace, <u>Satires</u>, I, 4, 1.10.

33. <u>atrae bilis</u>: In former ages, it was thought that the human body was influenced and controlled by four 'humours', each of which was equivalent to the four elements: Air, Fire, Earth and Water. These four 'humours', or moistures, are (i) Sanguis, or blood, into the composition of which Air enters; (ii) Cholera, or yellow bile (sometimes called red), which contains a great deal of Fire; (iii) Melancholia, or black bile, in which the Earthy element exists, and (iv) Pituita, or phlegm, in which water is predominant.

It was not believed that the human body was occupied exclusively by one of these humours, but rather that the body contained a mixture of all four, - the predominant one determining the person's temperament. Philopinus considers that Nichades must have an excess of black bile (Melancholia) to have dreamt what he did, for melancholic persons were said to be especially prone to nightmares. This is alluded to in an old Latin poem, <u>Regimen Sanitatis Salerni</u>, (London, 1634), p. 173,

"Hi (i.e. melancholic persons) vigilant studiis,
nec mens est dedita somno."

and a medical writer of the thirteenth century, Gilbertus Anglicus, also says (<u>Compendium Medicinae</u>, Lyons, 1510), that melancholic persons see before their eyes black and terrible forms, such as monks, black men trying to kill them, and demons.

37. <u>gradatio</u>: A rhetorical term, meaning a climax in speaking. There is a description of this particular figure in Cicero, <u>Rhetorica ad C. Herennium</u>, IV, 25, 34,

"Gradatio est in qua non ante ad consequens verbum descenditur quam ad superius ascensum est, hoc modo: 'Nam quae reliqua spes manet libertatis, si illis et quod libet licet, et quod licet possunt, et quod possunt audent, et quod audent faciunt, et quod faciunt vobis molestum non est?' "

38-39. <u>Nil habet ulterius,...Posteritas</u>: These lines are obviously taken from Juvenal, <u>Satires,</u> I, 11.147-8, despite the fact that the second word in the sentence here reads 'habet', whereas all standard texts for Juvenal give 'erit':

"Nil erit ulterius quod nostris moribus addat/posteritas,..."

40-41. **cur sic ambulas melancholicus?...phlegmaticum**: See above, note to 1.33.

45. **mercatorum mercurius**: Mercury was the god of merchants and traders.

46. **quam comprimunt clanculum**: A pun on two different meanings of 'comprimo', which here are (i) to check, or hold back; and (ii) to force, or violate. A similar play on words occurs in Plautus, Amphitruo, 1.348 and also in Rudens, 1.1073f., Truculentus, 1.262, and Asinaria, 1.2;2.

46. **dum faenus ut faetus editur**: The author avails himself of the great resemblance between the appearance and sound of 'faenus' and 'faetus', and of the difference in their meanings, to add to the humour of this passage.

48-49. **malo virum...pecuniam viro**: A direct quotation from Valerius Maximus, VII, 2, ext.9.
(For Valerius Maximus see Teubner edition).

50. **Paupertas Musarum comes est**: It was a common conceit amongst both Hellenistic and Roman poets, that poverty went hand in hand with

poetry and the Arts. The figure of the 'poor poet' recurs quite often in the epigrams of Callimachus and in the works of the Latin love-elegists, such as Tibullus. The spirit of materialism was considered foreign to the Muses. Frequently, in Roman literature, there are lengthy and elaborate comparisons between poetry and material possessions, between the simple life and the life of luxury.

51. <u>Divitem et Ditem Plutum et Plutonem nihili</u>: Dives is, of course, the rich man, mentioned in the Gospel of Luke (c.16); and Plutus, in classical mythology, is the god of wealth. Dis and Pluto are the Roman and Greek names respectively for the ruler of the infernal regions. What Philopimus is saying here, is that he considers a life lived in wealth and luxury to be equal to a life spent in hell!

52. <u>satrapam</u>: (khshatrapavan) A title given to a Persian provincial ruler. The satrap had widespread powers within his own province, but he was ultimately responsible to the Great King. (For further information, see O.C.D., s.v. Satrap.).

56. <u>coronidem</u>: Literally, a flourish, formed with a pen, which writers were accustomed to make at the end of a book, - in other words, 'the finishing touch'.

62-64. **Linguam sinamus...criticus auscultator:** Undoubtedly, a reference to the fact that students at Oxford were required by the college statutes to talk solely in Latin or Greek, whilst they were in the University buildings, or precincts. Scholars heard speaking English, and so disobeying this law, were sometimes given corporal punishment. (See T. Fowler, The History of Corpus Christi College, pp. 53-4.).

65. **senes bis pueros:** cf. Hamlet, II, ii, 1.381, "an old man is twice a child."

65. **Semel insanivimus omnes:** These words are taken directly from the First Eclogue (1.118) of Baptista Mantuanus (1448-1516). His poems, though now, for the most part, relegated to obscurity, had very great influence upon the English literature of the sixteenth and seventeenth centuries. This can be clearly seen from the large number of quotations from Mantuanus that appear in the works of the most important writers of the period. The line 'semel insanivimus omnes', alone, occurs in Greene, 'Epistle to the Gentlemen Schollers of both Universities', prefixed to his Mourning Garment; in Nashe, Summer's Last Will and Testament, Prologue, and Have with you to Saffron-Walden; and in Bishop Hall, Satires; it is also quoted in The Return from Parnassus, and

three times in Burton, Anatomy of Melancholy. There is, moreover, a particularly interesting passage in Boswell's Life of Johnson, concerning this quotation,

> "When I once talked to him of some of the sayings which every body repeats, but nobody knows where to find,... he told me that he was once offered ten guineas to point out from whence 'Semel insanivimus omnes' was taken. He could not do it; but many years afterwards met with it by chance in Johannes Baptista Mantuanus."

(I quote from Boswell's Life of Johnson, edited by George Birbeck Hill, revised by L.F.Powell, 6 vols. (Oxford, 1934), IV, 181-2).

67. **Nec ad senectam nuces et nugas reiicit:** cf. Persius, Satires, I, 11.9-11,

> "tunc cum ad canitiem et nostrum istud vivere
> triste/aspexi ac nucibus facimus quaecumque
> relictis,/cum sapimus patruos;"

68. **philosopharis:** MS. reads 'philisopharis'.

68. **tertius Cato:** cf. Juvenal, Satires, II, 1.40,

> "tertius e caelo cecidit Cato."

70. **Laelaps**: The name given by Ovid to one of Actaeon's hounds in *Metamorphoses*, III, 1.211,

> "inde ruunt alii rapida velocius aura,
> Pamphagos et Dorceus et Oribasus, Arcades omnes,
> Nebrophonusque valens et trux cum Laelape Theron".

72. **Ibo, quamvis haud satis paratus**: Now that Doulerus has agreed to accompany his friends, Nichades and Philopinus, to Hinksey, the scholars are acting in accordance with the college statute which decreed that students were not to go out in groups of less than three. (See Ward, c. 28).

72. **Lepidum caput te amo**: cf. Terence, *Eunuchus*, 1.531,

> "o capitulum lepidissumum!"

74. **Bacon, Scoggin, et reliqui boni socii**: The persons referred to here are Roger Bacon, the Franciscan friar and famous philosopher and inventor, and John Scoggin (sometimes spelt Scogan), a rather obscure figure, who lived in the latter half of the fifteenth century. Scoggin is thought to have gained an M.A. at Oriel College, Oxford, and later to have become the fool

at King Edward IV's court, whence he was temporarily banished to France. All that is known of Scoggin is contained in a book, which is alleged to include his original jests, - a work compiled in the sixteenth century by Dr. Andrew Boorde, 'a witty physician who died in 1549'. However, there is reason to suspect that the whole is a work of fiction, and Scoggin merely an imaginary character.

The earliest extant edition of Scoggin's Jests is dated 1626, and the full title reads as follows, The First and Best Part of Scoggin's Jests. Full of Witty Mirth and Pleasant Shifts, done by him in France and other places: being a Preservative against Melancholy. Gathered by Andrew Boord, Doctor of Physicke, London. Printed by Francis Williams, 1626.

There are numerous references to Scoggin's Jests in sixteenth and seventeenth-century English literature. For example, in 1575, the work was in the library of Captain Cox, and, together with The Hundred Merry Tales, was listed as a handbook of popular witticisms in the epilogue to Wily Beguil'd (1606). In the year 1607, another collection of jests appeared, called Dobson's Drie Bobbes, son and heire to Scoggin. Moreover, Scoggin's Jests is named as a widely read book of the day, by John Taylor, the water-poet, in his Motto (1622), and in both Harry White his Humour (1640?) and the comedy, entitled London Chaunticleers (1659). (For further information, see D.N.B., s.v. Scogan, John.)

76. **monachi, et iocosi fraterculi**: Throughout the Middle Ages, and in later centuries, too, many monks and members of other religious orders had a reputation for wickedness and deceit. Some monks are said to have lived in wealth and idleness, and the friars to have travelled around the countryside shamelessly begging, and exacting money from those they met, by trickery, - the 'facetiae' and 'strategemata' of l.75. Chaucer paints a very vivid picture of the merits and defects of mediaeval monks and friars, in his prologue to the <u>Canterbury Tales</u>.

81. <u>Pileum tu pilam facis</u>: A skilful play on words. The author makes use of the great resemblance in appearance and sound between the accusative cases of 'pileum' and 'pila', to introduce a joke about making the square round, or squaring the circle. It is practically impossible to produce exactly the same effect in English.

83. <u>quadraturam circuli</u>: Apuleius mentions the 'squaring of the circle' in <u>LIBER ΠΕΡΙ ΕΡΜΗΝΕΙΑΣ</u>, IX, 5f.,

> "ex hisce igitur in prima formula modis
> novem primi quattuor indemonstrabiles
> nominantur,...sicut circuli quadratura,
> ...impertiant."

(For Apuleius see Teubner edition).

84. **ut curas iugulemus**: cf. Martial, *Epigrams*, VIII, 51, 1.2., "ut iugulem curas,"

86. **Ego habeo solidum, ille sex denarios**: Cooper, in his T.L.R.B., states that a 'solidus' is equal to a shilling, and a 'denarius' to a penny.

93. **Primus, Secundus, Tertius**: This line is probably intended as a parody of Lily's *Latin Grammar*, where 'primus, secundus, tertius' are often quoted as examples of ordinal numbers (p.73), or nouns of number requiring the genitive case (p.46).

95. **Nichades**: A combination of 'Old Nick', meaning 'the devil' and Hades, 'the underworld', or 'hell'. Hence, 'Old Nick of Hades' becomes Nichades. 'Old Nick' is a name commonly given to the devil in the North of England. It is thought to be Danish in origin, from the title of an evil genius among the ancient Danes. (See J. Brand, *Popular Antiquities*, 3 vols. (London, 1849) II, 519, n.3).

96. **Doulerus**: A compound of 'doulos' (δοῦλος), 'a slave', and Eros ("Ἔρως), 'Love'. Doulerus, therefore, means 'Love's slave'.

97. **Philopinus**: A mock Greek name, formed from 'philo' (φιλέω), 'to be fond of', and the verb 'pino' (πίνω), 'to drink'.

100. **Vultisne cum domino per vadum ferri?**: A reference to the Hinksey ferry. This was established in 1467, or possibly earlier, since the causeway leading from the opposite bank of the river into the Botley Road is the most direct route from Hinksey to Oxford.

   At the start of the sixteenth century, the ferry and land at Hinksey belonged to William Bulcombe and his wife, Maud. In 1539, they passed to John Croke, and remained in the possession of the Croke family for some seventy years, up until 1604. A short while afterwards, William Fynmore, – and later, his son – became owner of the land and the 'passage over the Isis'. Eventually, the estate was handed over to Brasenose College, and it is still in the College's keeping today. (See **V.H.C.B.** IV, 406-7).

105. <u>Bene...rem</u>: Dawson takes up Pigeon's words, and twists their sense: he pretends to misunderstand what the innkeeper has said to him and interprets 'res' as meaning 'wife'.

116. <u>Et sedulo...incumbunt studiis</u>: The phrase "sedulo studiis incumbere" occurs very frequently in the Registers of Punishments for Corpus Christi College, the entries of which were made in the offenders' own handwriting. T. Fowler, <u>The History of Corpus Christi College</u>, pp.359-36, quotes several extracts from the Registers of Punishments: two of which read as follows:

    1641. April 22. "Ego Iohannes Tooke privatus sum convictu per septimanam, quod deprehensus fuerim vix sobrius satis; et punitus etiam ut in bibliotheca per unum mensem a precibus matutinis ad vespertinas usque <u>sedulo studiis incumbam</u>".

    1653. Term. 3°. "Ego Nicolaus Page privatus sum convictu per unum mensem, eo quod deprehensus fui a Procuratore minus sobrius, et punitus etiam ut in Bibliotheca per unum mensem <u>sedulo studiis incumbam</u>."

"Sedulo studiis incumbere" was, it seems, almost a set formula, known no doubt to the majority of students — particularly those who were all too familiar with the Punishments book! By putting the phrase into Cullie's mouth, the author is parodying the entire formula.

118. **Alii sectantur forum...diligo**: The sentiments expressed in this song are very similar to those found in the works of many Roman writers. In Augustan literature particularly, a life of peace and simplicity is greatly preferred to the dangers which constantly threaten those who are always in the public eye, soldiers going into battle, and traders sailing the high seas.

125. **quamvis sit profundum**: The song lists the various qualities of the drinking-cup.

134. **corculum**: cf. Plautus, Casina, ll.835-7,

>   LYSIDAMUS: suax,
>   nunc pol demum ego sum liber.
>   meum corculum, melculum, verculum.

135. Burde, blennue: cf. Plautus, Bacchides, ll.1085-6,

>   NICOBULUS: Quicumque ubi ubi sunt, qui fuerunt
>   quique futuri sunt posthac/stulti,
>   stolidi, fatui, fungi, bardi,
>   blenni, buccones,

149. trunco aut stipiti: Cicero uses this phrase in the
In Pisonem, IX, 19,

>   "...sed qui tamquam truncus atque stipes, si
>   stetisset modo, posset sustinere tamen titulum consulatus."

152. miserrima: MS. reads 'miserima'.

162-163. Nam vos Actaeonios...possumus facere: In classical mythology, Actaeon was the grandson of Cadmus. One day, whilst out hunting, he surprised Diana bathing with her nymphs in a stream. The goddess, angry at being seen thus naked by a man, immediately turned him into a stag. He was later chased and torn to pieces by his own hounds. The episode is related by Ovid in Metamorphoses, III, 1.138f. (See also O.C.D., s.v. Actaeon.)

164. **lemures nigri**: cf. Persius, *Satires*, V, 1.185,

> "tum nigri lemures ovoque pericula rupto,
> ....
> incussere deos inflantis corpora, "

165. **Alecto huius oppidi**: Alecto was one of the three Furies.

166. **patibulo**: MS. reads 'patibubo'.

167. **hoddy doddy**: A common expression: cf. *Nobody and Somebody*, (in *The School of Shakespere*, edited by R. Simpson, 2 vols. (New York, 1878), I), 1.376, "a very hoddy doddy, all breech."

168. **a wispe, et cucking stoole**: Both these were forms of punishment meted out to scolds. According to Nares' Glossary, "a wisp, or small twist, of straw or hay, was often applied as a mark of opprobrium to an immodest woman, a scold, or similar offenders; even, therefore, the showing it to a woman was therefore, considered as a grievous affront". There is an amusing reference to it in Gabriel Harvey's *Pierces Supererogation*, (London, 1593) p.146,

> "why, thou errant Butter-whore, thou Cotqueane and scrattop of scolds, wilt thou never leave afflicting a dead carcasse, continually read the Rethorique Lecture of Rammally?

A wisp, a wisp, a wisp, ripp, ripp, ripp, you kitchen-stuffe wrangler."

It is interesting to note that Horace, in *Satires*, I, 4, 1.34, also refers to the custom of attaching a wisp of straw to a person or creature that is to be feared for their vicious temper or vindictive nature. Men, he tells us, avoid the satirist as they would a ferocious ox, saying,

"faenum habet in cornu: longe fuge!"

The cucking-stool (less correctly called a ducking-stool) mentioned here, is, of course, the traditional punishment given to a scold. The word appears in James Scudamore, *Homer à la Mode*, (Oxford, 1664), p.43,

" As with her father she was diving,
And catching craw-fish for her living,
(For she belong'd to Billingsgate,
And often times had rid in state,
And sate i' th' bottom of a poole
Inthroned in a cucking-stoole;)"

172–173: **te cogerem Saltitare nudam**: cf. Marlowe, <u>The Tragical History of Doctor Faustus</u>, <u>II</u>, iii A$, ll. 4-6,

> "Now will I make all the maidens in our parish dance at
> at my pleasure stark naked before me, and so by that means
> I shall see more than ere I felt or saw yet."

(In my quotations from Marlowe, <u>Doctor Faustus</u>, I use the edition by F.S.Boas (London, 1932).).

176. **meretrices...vehi**: MS. reads 'meritrices'. This practice of carting whores through the streets for the people to hurl abuse at them, is referred to by John Rainolds, in <u>The Overthrowe of Stage-Playes</u>, (Middleburg, 1599), p.116,

> "As with us when theeves are hanged or hoores carted,
> we shew them to our children, to breede a detestation of
> theft and hoordome in them."

179. **Et morietur...vincitur**: Pliny, in his <u>Natural History</u>, X, 43, states that nightingales compete with one another in song, the loser dying,

> "certant (i.e. lusciniae) inter se, palamque animosa
> contentio est; victa morte finit saepe vitam, spiritu prius
> deficiente quam cantu."

ACT 2

6. **Utinam valeret ut valediceret:** A play on words. The author here takes advantage of the fact that 'valeo', to be healthy, and 'valedico', to say good-bye, look very similar, but have quite different meanings: cf. the English verbs 'to fare well', and 'to bid farewell'.

7. **linguam garrulam:** A chattering tongue brought about Tantalus' downfall. In *Amores*, II, 2, ll. 43-4, Ovid says,

> "quaerit aquas in aquis et poma fugacia captat
> Tantalus; - hoc illi garrula lingua dedit."

8-10. **Facile superat omnes rhetores,...perturbantur omnia:** Dawson's wife seems to be the epitome of all the feminine faults, as they are listed by Juvenal in his famous satire against women: she talks too much, she quarrels with her husband, she is cruel to her servants, and so lacking in self-control that when angry, she beats dumb animals: cf. Juvenal, *Satires*, VI, ll. 438-442,

> "cedunt grammatici, vincuntur rhetores, omnis
> turba tacet, nec causidicus nec praeco loquetur,
> altera nec mulier; verborum tanta cadit vis,
> tot pariter pelves ac tintinnabula dicas
> pulsari..."

cf. ibid., 11.268-269,

> "Semper habet lites alternaque iurgia lectus
> in quo nupta iacet; minimum dormitur in illo."

cf. ibid., 11.456-493,

> "Praefectura domus Sicula non mitior aula;
> nam si constituit solitoque decentius optat
> ornari et properat iamque expectatur in hortis
> aut apud Isiacae potius sacraria lenae,
> disponit crinem laceratis ipsa capillis
> nuda umeros Psecas infelix nudisque mamillis.
> 'altior hic quare cincinnus?' taurea punit
> continuo flexi crimen facinusque capilli."

and cf. ibid., 11.415-418,

> "   nam si latratibus alti
> rumpuntur somni, "fustes huc ocius," inquit,
> "adferte" atque illis dominum iubet ante feriri,
> deinde canem..."

15. <u>supernaculum</u>: According to Nares' Glossary, a kind of mock-Latin term, meaning 'upon the nail', and often used among drinkers. The derivation of the word is described in Nashe, <u>Pierce Penilesse</u>, p.205, note to l.7,

"Drinking 'super nagulum', a devise of drinking new come out of Fraunce: which is, after a man hath turned up the bottom of the cup, to drop it on his naile, and make a pearle with that is left; which if it slide, and he cannot make it stand on, by reason ther's too much, he must drinke again for his penance."

(In my quotations from Nashe, I use <u>The Works of Thomas Nashe</u>, edited by R.B.McKerrow, second edition, revised by F.P.Wilson, 5 vols. (London, 1958).).

21. <u>O laetam paupertatem...redimendam</u>: Accusative of exclamation.

31. <u>Est enim mea occupatio, cuppatio...bibere</u>: The whole of this
34. passage depends for its humour on the successful use of word-play and alliteration. It is practically impossible to gain the same effect when translating the lines into English.

36. **nefastum buxi signum**: i.e. the inn-sign.

43. **in potu enim veracitas**: cf. Pliny, *Natural History*, XIV, 141, "vulgoque veritas iam attributa vino est".

44. **triumviri**: Three men holding office together. The two famous triumvirates in Roman history were those formed by Caesar, Pompey and Crassus, in 60 B.C., and by Octavian, Mark Antony and Lepidus, in 43 B.C.. Shakespeare, in *Antony and Cleopatra*, II, vii, 1.69, refers to the members of the latter as,

    "These three world-sharers,"

49-50. **Nos tres sumus...hilares simul**: Odd numbers, and especially multiples of three and nine, were considered lucky. Philopinus takes the fact that there are **three** villagers and **three** students present, as an indication that there will be much pleasant and amusing conversation between them, for the Graces, the patron goddesses of wit, were three in number. (See also note to Act 4, 1.234). **tria sunt omnia** was a well-known proverb.

54-55. **Id est columbus...quasi lumbos colens**: Philopinus translates 'Pigeon' as 'columbus', and with the bawdy sense of humour so typical of much of the play, tries to make out that the word is a compound of 'lumbus' and 'olens'.

56. <u>Et Cypriae dicat Veneri</u>: Doves were, of course, sacred to Venus, so this is why Philopinus speaks of a 'columba' as being able to commune with the goddess.

Venus is described as 'Cyprian' because it was just off the shore of the island of Cyprus, that, according to legend, she rose out of the sea. In ancient times, the shrines of the goddess at Paphos and Amathus on the island, were especially renowned.

57. <u>Monedulae filius</u>: Philopinus takes the name 'Dawson' as meaning 'the son of a daw', and translates it into Latin literally.

62. <u>Cullie...i, unum valet</u>: Philopinus treats the letters that go to make up the name 'Cullie', as Roman numerals, and attempts to find their sum total. In the sixteenth century, this process of adding up the numbers which the letters in a person's name signified, was used as a form of divination. Scot, <u>The Discoverie of Witchcraft</u>, p.175, writes,

"There is a lot also called Pythagoras lot, which (some saie) Aristotle beleeved: and that is, where the characters of letters have certeine proper numbers; whereby they divine

(through the proper names of men) so as the numbers of each
letters being gathered into a summe, and put together, give
victorie to them whose summe is the greater: whether the
question be of warre, life, matrimonie, victorie, &c: even as
the unequall number of vowels in proper names portendeth lacke
of sight, halting, &c: which the godfathers and godmothers
might easilie prevent, if the case stood so."

63-64. *Si ad numerum literarum...Bataviios*: The Dutch had a
reputation for being notable drinkers. In Shakespeare's
Othello, II, iii, l.71f., they are referred to as some of the
world's greatest topers,

    IAGO: I learn'd it (i.e. a drinking-song) in England,
where indeed they are most potent in potting:
your Dane, your German, and your swag-bellied
Hollander, - Drink, ho! - are nothing to your
English.

66. *Faber ferrarius...Italus es*: A pun facilitated by the very great
similarity in sound and appearance between 'ferrarius', the
adjective formed from 'ferrum', and Ferrara, the name of a city
in northern Italy.

69. <u>An agrum colere potes...non potes?</u>: The verb 'colo' is used here in the sense 'to make fertile'.

70. <u>non omnis...tellus</u>: cf. Vergil, <u>Georgics</u>, II, 1.109.

"Nec vero terrae ferre omnes omnia possunt."

74. <u>exiccavi hunc calicem</u>: MS. reads 'exiocabii'.

77. <u>Vulcane...domi</u>: Vulcan as the god of fire, was the tutelary deity of blacksmiths and forges. In classical mythology, his wife is usually Venus, so that craftsmanship is joined, as it were, to beauty. (For further information about Vulcan, see O.C.D., s.v. Volcanus.)

Doulerus addresses Cullie as Vulcan, because he is a smith, and assumes that, like Vulcan, he, too, must have a beautiful wife.

78. <u>Sed non videbitur...deditis</u>: Mars, god of war, was once Venus' lover. The story of how they used to meet secretly, and were finally trapped in a net which Vulcan had forged for them, is related by Ovid in <u>Ars Amatoria</u>, II, 1.561f..

Cullie is afraid to let his wife be seen by 'those who are devoted to warfare', lest they seduce her, as Mars did Venus. The humour of these lines is heightened by the assonance of 'Marti' and 'Arti'.

75. **nos Minervam...colimus**: Minerva was the Roman goddess of wisdom and patroness of the Arts: hence the students' reverence for her.

81. **Literatus...odor**: An allusion to the close proximity of Hinksey to the city of Oxford.

84-85. **Michades...facile**: A pun on the two meanings of 'coniuratio': (i) conspiracy, and (ii) conjuration. The 'coniuratio Catilinae' referred to here, is obviously the account of the Catilinarian conspiracy given by the Roman historian, Sallust, in his monograph, the Bellum Catilinae.

95. **Tibi deus tutelaris Vulcanus faveat**: See above, note to 1.77.

96. **Tibi Alma Ceres arrideat**: Ceres was the Roman goddess of corn and agriculture, and, therefore, the patroness of farmers.

97-100. **Sed tibi...Comus:** Bacchus was god of wine, but Pigeon serves chiefly beer and ale, so consequently, another tutelary deity must be found for him. Philopinus suggests Comus. Comus (Κῶμος) is found in late antiquity as the god of festivity and joy. Therefore, Philopinus thinks he would be an appropriate patron for ale-drinkers, since they are usually full of mirth. Comus was generally represented as a wingèd youth, and Philostratus, in **Eikones** I, 2, gives a description of the god as he was depicted in a certain painting: he is seen in a drunken stupor, having just partaken of a large feast; his head is lolling on his breast, and he sleeps in a standing position, with his legs crossed. (See **D.G.R.B.M.**, s.v. Comus).

Comus, of course, is also the name of the main character in Milton's famous masque, performed at Ludlow Castle, in 1634.

104. **nihil meum non habebitis:** MS. reads 'habibetis'.

109-III. **Talis enim...haec eadem est:** Doulerus' portrait of Joanna Pigeon follows very closely the rules laid down for describing feminine beauty in mediaeval text-books on the art of writing poetry.

In the Middle Ages, poets vied with one another in giving full-length portraits of female grace and loveliness, and there were handbooks to aid and offer advise to would-be poets, in compiling this kind of description. One of the most celebrated text-books of the day was the Poetria Nova of Geoffrey de Vinsauf, (fl.1200).

It is interesting to note that the parts of Joanna's physiognomy commented on by Doulerus, are described in almost the same way as that advocated by Geoffrey de Vinsauf, Poetria Nova, ll.565-70, and ll. 574-5,

"   Vaccinia nigra coaequet
Forma supercilii; geminos intersecet arcus
Lactae forma viae; castiget regula nasi
Ductum, ne citra sistat vel transeat aequum;
Excubiae frontis, radient utrimque gemelli
Luce smaragdina vel sideris instar ocelli;
- - - - - - - - - - - - - -
- - - - tanquam praegnantia labra tumore
Surgant, sed modico rutilent, ignita, sed igne
Mansueto - - - "

(I quote from the text of the poem as printed in E. Faral, Les Arts Poétiques du XIIe et du XIIIe siècle,(Paris,1962), pp. 194-262).

It is more than likely, therefore, that the author of
Mercurius Rusticans was conversant with the mediaeval arts
of poetry.

These lines (109-11) are also reminiscent of a passage in
Seneca, *Troades*, 11.464-9, where Andromache compares the
appearance of her little son, Astyanax, to that of his father,
Hector,

> "   hos vultus meus
> habebat Hector, talis incessu fuit
> habituque talis, sic tulit fortes manus,
> sic celsus umeris, fronte sic torva minax
> cervice fusam dissipans iacta comam."

It is in much the same way that Doulerus describes the
great resemblance between Joanna Pigeon and the girl whom, he
alleges, he saw in his dream.

114. **habent et suos eventus somnia:** Dreams were thought to presage
what was to happen in the future. (See Macrobius, *Commentary on
the Dream of Scipio*, translated by William H. Stahl, (Columbia
University Press, New York and London, 1966), pp. 87-92).

120. **Eduxi nuper e sortilegio**: The ancient Egyptians used to practise sortilege, or divination by lot. (See Scot, p.174).
121. Centumque libras:'a hundred pounds'. According to Cooper, T.L.R.E., a 'libra' is equal to one pound.
122. **Vino...hedera**: 'Good wine needs no bush', an old proverb, quoted by Shakespeare in <u>As You Like It</u>, Epilogue, 1.3 f., where Rosalind says,

"If it be true that good wine needs no bush, 'tis true that a good play needs no epilogue."

It refers to the practise of hanging up a bunch of twigs or a wisp of hay at a roadside inn, as an indication to passers-by that drink may be had inside. The custom is thought to have been derived from the Romans, who used a bunch of ivy (ivy being a plant sacred to Bacchus) as a sign of a wine shop. 'Vendible wine needs no ivy hung up' was a common expression amongst them.

This tradition is often alluded to by English writers in the sixteenth and seventeenth centuries. For example, in Nashe, <u>Summer's Last Will and Testament</u>, 1.485,

"Greene Iuy-bushes at the Vintners¹ doores".

and also in Hausted, <u>Rival Friends</u>, edited by Lauren J. Mills

(Bloomington, 1951), p. 55,

" 'Tis like the ivy bush unto a tavern."

123. **Virtus est dos optima**: cf. Horace, <u>Odes</u>, III, 24, 11.21-2,

"dos est magna parentium

virtus..."

125. **Sed...hilarescitis?**: Anna should exit after this line, since by l.196 she is off-stage, calling to Joanna. However, no stage direction is given in MS.

126-
128. **O quam te memorem virgo...An nympharum sanguinis una?**: These lines are taken directly from Vergil, <u>Aeneid</u>, I, 11.327-329.

130-
132. **Chara deum soboles...Saturnia regna**: Each of these three lines is a direct quotation from Vergil, <u>Eclogues</u>, IV: (i) 1.49, (ii) 1.7, and (iii) 1.6.

134-
135. **O crudelis Alexi,...Mori me denique cogis?**: This passage is taken word for word from Vergil, <u>Eclogues</u>, II, 11.6-7.

137-
138. **Galatea?...hedera formosior alba**: A direct quotation from Vergil, <u>Eclogues</u>, VII, 11.37-38.

140. *Credimus?...somnia fingunt?*: This line is borrowed from Vergil, *Eclogues*, VIII, 1.108.

142. *Infandum, regina,...dolorem*: These words are taken directly from Vergil, *Aeneid*, II, 1.3.

144- *Non Thomas te,...admorunt ubera tygres*: This passage is very
145. closely modelled on Vergil, *Aeneid*, IV, 11.365-367. The last line is, in fact, a direct quotation.

149. *regina lemurum saltantium*: i.e. Proserpine.

153- *Caelibi Diana lare...Continens par iuvenile*: See Introduction,
164. section V.

165. *O luscinias,..sphaerarum cytharas*: The nightingale has, of course, always been renowned for its sweet song, but the common swan, though noble in appearance, can hardly be said to produce a melodious sound. However, there is a somewhat romantic theory, dating from very ancient times, that the swan sings sweetly just before it dies. There are several allusions to this belief in the plays of Shakespeare. For example, in the *Merchant of Venice*, III, ii, 11.44-5, Portia remarks,

"   he makes a swan-like end,
Fading in music."

This idea is thought to be derived from the fact that the swan is sometimes identified with Orpheus. Sir Thomas Browne, Pseudodoxia Epidemica, says that "after his death, Orpheus the Musician became a Swan. Thus was it the bird of Apollo, the god of Musick by the Greeks."

(I quote from The Works of Sir Thomas Browne, edited by G. Keynes, second edition, 4 vols.(London, 1964), III, 254).

Although this assertion that the swan sings before its death, has been revived countless times throughout the ages as a poetic fiction, it has found no place in the works of natural history. Pliny, for one, disbelieved the theory. (See Natural History, X, 32).

syrenas: In classical mythology, the Sirens were creatures, half women and half bird, endowed with enchanting voices. They dwelt on an island close to Scylla and Charybdis, and are said to have lured sailors to their death with their bewitching songs. (See O.C.D., s.v. Sirenes).

sphaerarum cytharas: The ancients believed that the movement of the celestial spheres created a beautiful and harmonious music, inaudible to the human ear. Pythagoras was the first to expound this theory, and Plato, in *Republic*, X, 617B, describes how a siren sits on each planet, singing sweetly in time with the motion of her own particular sphere, yet also harmonizing with the other seven. Cicero, too, explains how heavenly music is produced by the movement of the planets in *De Republica*, VI, 18-19.

The music of the spheres is also referred to in much English literature of the sixteenth and seventeenth centuries. For instance, in Shakespeare's *Merchant of Venice*, V, i, 11.60-2, where Lorenzo says,

> "There's not the smallest orb which thou behold'st
> But in his motion like an angel sings,
> Still quiring to the young-ey'd cherubins;"

and Milton, in *Arcades*, 11.63-4, tells of

> "   the celestial Sirens' harmony,
> That sit upon the nine infolded spheres,"

167- *Quid diutius impedit...vel mihi redde meum*: In the thirty or so
198. lines that follow, Joanna and Doulerus plight their troth. The
ancient ceremony of betrothing was still, it appears, in full
use in the sixteenth and seventeenth centuries. Joanna and
Doulerus become espoused in the presence of two witnesses,
Philopinus and Nichades, and such betrothals, performed before
witnesses, were considered as constituting a valid marriage, if
the vows then made were solemnized by the Church shortly
afterwards.

In the betrothal ceremony the couple usually joined hands
(1.170), made vows to be loving and faithful to one another
forever, exchanged kisses (1.167), and gave each other tokens of
their affection (ll.174-175). Normally rings were interchanged,
but in this case a crystal glass and a punchbowl are substituted!

Many allusions to the various customs accompanying courtship
and marriage in sixteenth and seventeenth-century England can be
found in the plays of Shakespeare. For instance, in both
The Winter's Tale, IV, iv, ll.352-83, and The Taming of the Shrew,
II, i, ll.306-316, there is a very good example of how the
betrothal ceremony was performed.

170. *Lucina*: The Roman goddess of birth, so called because she was
thought to make the child see the light of day. (For further
information, see *O.C.D.*, s.v. Juno).

171. Hymen, o hymenaeo Hymen: In ancient Greece, it was the custom at weddings to cry " Ὑμὴν Ὑμέναι᾽ " or " ὦ Ὑμὴν Ὑμέναιε." This was taken as being an invocation to some god or other, whose name was Hymen. Various legends grew up around him, telling how Hymen was a very handsome young man, who was either happily married, or had met with some disaster on his wedding-day. (See O.C.D., s.v. Hymenaeus, and also Catullus, LXI, 1.4, and LXII, 1.5).

174. Confirmetur: MS. reads 'Corfirmetur'.

176. Eques aureae periscelidis: i.e. a Knight of the Garter. According to Froissart, this - the highest order of English knighthood - was instituted by Edward III, in the year 1344. Tradition has it that the garter was originally that of the Countess of Salisbury, which fell off as she was dancing with the King; whereupon the King picked it up and put it round his own leg, saying to the on-lookers, "Honi soit qui mal y pense"!

The Garter, itself, which is the badge of the Order, is a ribbon of dark-blue velvet, edged with gold, and fastened by a gold buckle. The words which the King is alleged to have uttered, are embroidered on the ribbon in gold letters. The garter is worn below the left knee; hence Joanna would resemble a knight of this order, by wearing a garter on one leg only. (See O.L.D., for further information).

178- **hoc vitrum crystallinum...dolos**: A glass was one of the most
180.
important tools in the sorcerer or magician's trade. Both
Prospero, in the *Tempest*, and Comus, in Milton's masque, have
their charming-rods and glasses. Fortune-tellers, too, in the
sixteenth and seventeenth centuries, used a beryl, or a glass,
when pretending to foretell what was to happen in the future.
In a passage from the *Penal Laws against Witches*, it is
stated that "they do answer either by voice, or else set
before their eyes in glasses, chrystal stones, etc., the
pictures or images of the persons or things sought for."

Angelo, in Shakespeare's *Measure for Measure*, (II,ii),
refers to this practice, when, in ll.94-6, he describes how the
law

"   like a prophet,
Looks in a glass that shows what future evils -
Either now or by remissness new conceiv'd," &c.

Similarly, Macbeth, (IV, i, ll.118-120), after "a show
of eight kings" has been set before him, declares, on seeing the
seventh,

"   I'll see no more.
And yet the eighth appears, who bears a glass
Which shows me many more;"

Moreover, at an earlier date, Spenser (<u>Faerie Queene</u>, III, 2) tells of the glass that Merlin fashioned for King Ryence; while a very similar kind of mirror was given to Cambinskan, in the story told by the Squire, in Chaucer, <u>Canterbury Tales</u>, and in Boaistau, <u>Theatrum Mundi</u>, translated by John Alday, (London, 1566?), p.255, the reader is told how "A certaine Philosopher did the like to Pompey, the which shewed him in a glass the order of his enemies ready to march in battell."

181. <u>Pluris quam quatuor minis</u>: Cooper, in his <u>T.L.R.B.</u>, states that ten 'minae' are equivalent to twenty pounds; therefore, four 'minae' would equal eight pounds.

186. <u>O campos Elysios</u>: The Elysian fields, the abode of the blest in the Lower World. (See <u>O.C.D.</u>, s.v. After-Life).

188. <u>nepenthes</u>: A plant said to drive away sadness, and which, when mixed with wine, made all who drank it, deliriously happy. Pliny, in <u>Natural History</u>, XXI, 159, says,

" nepenthes illud praedicatum ab Homero, quo tristitia omnis aboleretur".

192. *arte chymica*: i.e. by alchemy, the pretended art of making gold and silver, or of turning the base metals into the noble ones.

193. *uxor Midae*: Midas was a legendary Phrygian king. Many stories have been told about him, perhaps the most famous being that which describes how Midas showed great hospitality to a Silenus, whom his subjects had found in a drunken stupor and had taken prisoner. Dionysus, the god of wine, eager to reward Midas for his kindness, told him that he might have anything he wishes for: Midas asked that everything he touched might turn into gold. He soon discovered, however, that even his food and his wife became solid gold, and prayed that this power might be taken from him. On the advice of the wine-god, he bathed in the river Pactolus, the sands of which have remained gold ever since. (See O.C.D., s.v. Midas, and also Ovid, Metamorphoses, XI, 1.85f.).

195. __tiara Gallica:__ Probably a French hood, a pretty head-dress, sometimes called a Paris-hede. Continental, but more especially French, fashions had a great influence upon English dress at this time. Phillip Stubbes, (_Anatomy of the Abuses in England in Shakespere's Youth A.D.1583_, edited by F.J.Furnival, The New Shakespeare Society, (London, 1877-9), p.69) writes thus of women's millinery in the sixteenth century,

"on toppes of these stately turrets (I meane their goodly heads wherin is more vanitie than true Philosophie now and than) stand their other capitall ornaments, as french hood, hat, cappe, kercher, and such like: wherof some be of velvet, some of taffatie, some (but few) of woll, some of this fashion, some of that, and some of this color, some of that, according to the variable fantasies of their serpentine minds. And to such excess is it growen, as every artificers wyfe (almost) wil not stick to goe in her hat of velvet everye day, every marchants wyfe and meane Gentlewoman in her french-hood, and everye poore Cottagers Daughter in her taffatie hat, or els of woll at least, wel lined with silk, velvet or taffatie."

198. **basium**: MS. reads 'bastium'.

205. **Fugientem...fugit**: cf. Erasmus, *Adagia*, II, 562 B,

"Fugit amantem, insequitur fugientem".

(I quote from Erasmus, *Opera Omnia*, 10 vols. (Leyden, 1703-1706), $\overline{II}$)

219. **Nempe signum amoris vitrei**: MS. reads 'vitrii'. Susanna implies that just as glass is brittle and soon broken, so Doulerus' love for her mistress will not endure for long.

230-232. **in aure enim ponuntur incus et malleus...longe subtilior**: MS. reads 'sublilior'. In anatomy, 'incus' and 'malleus' are the names given to two small bones situated within the middle ear, on the inner side of the tympanum, or ear-drum. The bones are so called because they resemble a tiny anvil and hammer in shape. When sound waves strike the tympanum, the incus and malleus oscillate, causing parts of the inner ear to vibrate, so that eventually the impulses reach the brain.

233. **Habesne...soleas?**: Cullie, not having had a university education, quite naturally misunderstands what Doulerus says, and takes his words literally.

235-238. **in cerebro habeo et totum equum...representative Distinctionem repete**: An argument based on some form of syllogism, such as the following:

>   PREMISE 1:   Man is an animal.
>   PREMISE 2:   A horse is an animal.
>   CONCLUSION: Man is a horse.

The important distinction between Man and horse, however, lies in the fact that in logical terms Man is a _rational_ animal, whereas the horse is a _sensitive_ animal. (See below, note to $\overline{\text{III}}$, l.69.)

239. **Tractent fabrilia fabri**: MS. reads 'frabrilia'. If the mood of 'tractent' (present subjunctive) is ignored, this line is a direct quotation from Horace, _Epistles_, $\overline{\text{II}}$, I, l.116.

243. **Molossum**: In classical Latin, 'Molossus' meant a specific type of dog, — a Molossian hound. (I translate as 'Alsatian'). The adjective 'Molossus' is derived from the Molossi, a people that dwelt in the eastern part of Epirus.

252. <u>lex talionis</u>: In juridical language, a form of retaliationary law, whereby the offender is given a punishment similar and equal to the injury which he inflicted upon his victim. Many of the laws in the Code of Hammurabi, - the sixth king of the Amoritic or West Semitic dynasty of Babylonia, who reigned from 2067-2025 B.C. - prescribed, as punishment, retribution in kind, such as 'an eye for an eye'. To modern thought they seem rather cruel and barbaric, but in Hammurabi's day they were an advance in legal theory.

It is also interesting to note that it is by a kind of retaliationary law that Aegeon in Shakespeare's <u>Comedy of Errors</u> is seemingly doomed to die. The Duke of Ephesus, I, i, ll.13-20, declares,

> "It hath in solemn synods been decreed,
> Both by the Syracusians and ourselves,
> To admit no traffic to our adverse towns;
> Nay, more: if any born at Ephesus
> Be seen at any Syracusian marts and fairs;
> Again, if any Syracusian born
> Come to the bay of Ephesus - he dies,"

260. **geometrice**: Pertaining, or according to, the laws of geometry. In geometry a problem may often be solved by proving that a particular set of measurements, or angles, are *equal*. Hence, -----Doulerus is here attempting to settle the dispute between Dawson and Cullie, - 'geometrically', i.e. by proving that both have suffered an *equal* loss: Dawson has lost his grain, and Cullie's pig has had its ear bitten off, a fitting punishment for the crime it has committed. However, although Doulerus' reasoning might seem quite satisfactory to a student of logic, it is doubtful whether Dawson and Cullie share the same view!

265. **Primus haustus...ebrietatis**: cf. Shakespeare, *Twelfth Night*, I, v, ll.122-5,

>OLIVIA: What's a drunken man like, fool?
>
>CLOWN: Like a drown'd man, a fool, and a madman: one draught above heat makes him a fool; the second mads him; and the third drowns him."

266- **haec est vita fullonis robae,...haustam revomere**: An allusion to
267.   the process of fulling, used in ancient Rome to clean and bleach

dirty clothes - particularly togas. First, the garment was
immersed in a vat or tub of water, to which a kind of potash,
called lye, was added. Then, the 'fullo', bare-footed and
bare-legged, climbed into the vat and treaded the garment with
his feet, in much the same way as Scottish peasant women used
to wash their blankets. When it had been completely and
thoroughly washed in this way, the garment was allowed to dry
in the open air, and was then brushed and carded in order to
bring up the pile of the wool. Finally, it was laid over a
framework or cage, and some sulphur was burned underneath, the
fumes of which acted as a bleaching agent. Hence, as Doulerus points
out, a drunken man, steeped in alcohol, to the point where his
stomach can take no more drink and he is obliged to vomit
forth what he has just imbibed, - does resemble a garment soaking
up water in the fuller's tub and then being treaded in order to
remove the water once again, plus the dirt and grime that has
been washed out.

270- *Lunae iugales sistere...luridum promant iubar*: cf. Ovid's
275.
description of Medea's magic powers in Heroides, VI, 11.85-88,

"illa reluctantem cursu deducere lunam
nititur et tenebris abdere solis equos;
illa refrenat aquas obliquaque flumina sistit;
illa loco silvas vivaque saxa movet."

276. **quaevis Thessala venefica**: In the ancient world, Thessaly was a region notorious for witches and the practice of black magic. It is referred to countless times in classical literature as an evil place, where poisonous herbs grow in abundance. An elaborate, though somewhat fanciful, account of Thessaly and its witches can be found in Lucan's <u>De Bello Civili</u>, VI,1.43$_{\wedge}^{4}$f..

277. **deae**: Probably Diana, Minerva and Proserpine.

277. **Faustus**: i.e. Doctor Faustus, a sixteenth-century necromancer, who became identified with the man that, in mediaeval legend, sold his soul to the devil. This fable appeared in the <u>Volksbuch</u>, which was published at Frankfurt, in 1587, and it was translated into English under the title <u>The History of the Damnable Life and Death of Dr. John Faustus</u>. Later, Marlowe dramatised the legend in his play, <u>The Tragical History of Doctor Faustus</u> (1588). (See <u>O.C.E.L.</u>, s.v. <u>Doctor Faustus, The tragical history of</u>).

278. *Rogerus Bacon*: See above, note to Act I, l.74.

281-282. *Nam daemon callidus...induit*: It was a common belief in the sixteenth and seventeenth centuries that the devil could at any time assume any colour or shape he liked, in order to further his wicked designs and purposes. This notion is alluded to in Shakespeare's *Timon of Athens*, II, ii, ll.109-15,

> VAR. SERV.: What is a whoremaster, fool?
>
> FOOL: A fool in good clothes, and something like thee. 'Tis a spirit. Sometime 't appears like a lord; sometime like a lawyer; sometime like a philosopher, with two stones moe than's artificial one. He is very often like a knight; and, generally, in all shapes that man goes up and down in from fourscore to thirteen, this spirit walks in.

There is also a reference to it in *Hamlet*, II, ii, ll.594-6,

> "   The spirit that I have seen
> May be a devil; and the devil hath power
> T'assume a pleasing shape;"

282. _polypus_: The polyp, an invertebrate Coelenterate animal, marine or fresh-water. The corals, sea-anenomes, hydra and hydroids all fall into this category. The polyp is noted especially for its ability to change its colour and form to suit its surroundings. Hence, in the English literature of the sixteenth century, the name 'polyp' is often applied to persons who, by nature, are fickle and changeable. For instance, Lodge, <u>Euphues Golden Legacie</u>, p.12, says of women,

> "their passions are as momentarie as the colours of a Polipe, which changeth at the sight of everie obiect".

(I quote from <u>The Complete Works of Thomas Lodge</u>, 4 vols. (New York, 1963), I).

285. <u>Ego nequaquam...nigrior</u>: Cullie, being a blacksmith, practises his own black art!

286-287. <u>transferre possum...machinis</u>: The power to transport buildings from one place to another was, it seems, yet another facet of the magician's many-sided art. It is interesting to recall how

the wicked magician in the story of Aladdin, related by
Scheherazade in The Thousand and One Nights, is said, by
summoning up the Genie of the Lamp, to have transported an
entire palace across the sea, - from the Far East to deepest
Africa!

294. cacodaemone: Another word for 'evil spirit': cf. Shakespeare,
Richard III, I, iii, ll.143-4,

>   "   leave this world,
>   Thou cacodemon:"

295. Non adsunt libri...ambitum: When attempting to call forth the
devil, or some other demon, for a particular purpose, it was
usual for the sorcerer to quote passages out of a book
containing, allegedly, magic spells. These books were, in fact,
the necromancer's chief instruments, without which he was quite
powerless. Caliban, for example, in Shakespeare's Tempest, says,
concerning Prospero, III, ii, ll.87-90,

>   "   Remember
>   First to possess his books; for without them
>   He's but a sot, as I am, nor hath not
>   One spirit to command;"

Nichades makes the fact that he has no books of spells with him, an excuse for not summoning up the devil (which he has no real intention of doing anyway), saying that although he might be able to conjure up some evil spirit, without books he would have no power to constrain it, and it might, therefore, escape and create havoc in the neighbourhood.

299. <u>Praeterea...restituam</u>: Magic was also used to recover stolen property. (See below, note to Act V, 11.29-36).

300. <u>Tibique...imaginem</u>: See above, note to 1.178.

305. <u>Praeterea...cingere</u>: Nichades is mischievously suggesting here that he can walk round gardens and orchards, chanting words of magic to protect them from harm, and to cause the trees and plants to bear fruit in due season. The casting of spells to promote the growth of crops and ensure a good harvest, is inherent in the folk-lore and traditions of all primitive peoples. It is not surprising, therefore, that the practice should have survived into the Middle Ages and later, in the form of black magic and sorcery. Sir James Frazer (<u>The Golden Bough</u>, abridged edition (London, 1949), p.610) describes a ceremony carried out at Pâturages, in France, until comparatively recent

times. The custom was called Scouvion, and its purpose to make the fruit trees yield a good crop that season. Every year, on the first Sunday in Lent, the young people and children, carrying lighted torches, would run through the gardens and orchards, crying at the top of their voices,

> "Bear apples, bear pears, and cherries all black
> To Scouvion!"

On hearing this, the torch-bearer would fling his fiery brand among the branches of the apple-trees, the pear-trees, and the cherry-trees. The following Sunday, the whole process was repeated.

309. **Carfoix**: i.e. Carfax, the centre of Oxford, so called because four roads (quatuor furcae) meet there, and where, in former times, the market was regularly held. Anthony à Wood, *City of Oxford*, I, 60-1, writes of Carfax,

> "As for the beginning and rise of the said streets (viz. (i) The High Street, (ii) Fish Street (now St.Aldate's), (iii) The Great Baylly (now Queen St.) and Castle Street, and (iv) North-gate Street (now Cornmarket Street), are from quatervoys before mentioned or the place which tendeth or

looketh four wayes ('quatuor in ventos ibi se via fundit
eunti'). It is accounted the meditullium of the city and
the heart (head?) of the market and the cheifest place wher
most sorts of merchantdise are exposed to sale. The vulgar
name of it is Carfox, which, though corrupted from quatervois
as most cannot to the contrary but judge soe, yet some there
have bin that have thought it to come or be derived from
'Caerbos' (i.e. the city of Boso who was consul of Oxon in
King Arthur's time, as is before delivered)."

311- Certe...trabi: The author here plays on the words 'aptius'
312. and 'aptant': 'aptius', the comparative adverb, meaning 'in
a more fitting manner', i.e. more suitably, and 'apto', the
verb, 'to fit', in the literal sense.

ACT 3

1. **Lepus...volucres:** This - the opening line of the third act - relies for its effect on the successful use of word-play. The author has taken advantage of the very great similarity in sound and appearance between 'lepus', meaning 'a hare', and 'levipes' - 'fleet of foot', and has also been quick to seize the opportunity of using the word 'volucris' as both a substantive ('bird') and an adjective ('swift'). The pun is difficult to reproduce in English, without altering the sense of the Latin.

4-18. **Lustrate lata Botliae prata...mordet:** See Introduction, section V.

4. **Botliae:** i.e. Botley, formerly a small Berkshire hamlet, situated in the parish of Cumnor, and lying a mile and a half to the west of Oxford. Its only claim to fame is its mill, which is thought to stand on the site of the old mill, that once belonged to the abbots of Abingdon. Today, Botley, now merged with North Hinksey, is a suburb of the city of Oxford. (For further information, see V.H.C., Berkshire, IV, 398).

5. **Cumner:**

> "Or in my boat I lie
>
> Moor'd to the cool bank............
>
> ....
>
> And watched the warm, green-muffled Cumnor
>
> hills,"
>
> (Matthew Arnold, The Scholar-Gipsy)

Cumnor is a village just off the main road that runs from Faringdon into Oxford. The parish of Cumnor comprises about 7,453 acres. It is bounded on the west by the River Isis, and extends eastwards as far as the small parishes of North and South Hinksey. From the eastern and western boundaries, the ground rises by degrees to a height of 520ft. above the ordnance datum - the highest point being reached at Cumnor Hurst. This is why Cumnor is described here as 'altior'.

The village of Cumnor is situated approximately half a mile to the west of this hill and lower down the slope, but even so, a fine view can be gained from here, over the river into Oxfordshire. (See the V.H.C., Berkshire, IV, 398-405).

6. Qua Bagly sylvam iactitat suam:

"In autumn, on the skirts of Bagley Wood – "

(Matthew Arnold, *The Scholar-Gipsy*)

Bagley Wood was originally an area of land, consisting of some 390 acres of woodland on a sloping hill-side, lying three and a quarter miles to the north-east of Abingdon. There is no record of a church, or indeed of any dwellings ever having existed there in the past. In fact, Bagley Wood seems to have been a rather lonely spot, where in the course of the thirteenth century, men were often attacked and even killed. Nevertheless, in later ages, the woods were often visited by the people of Oxford and the villages that lay close by, because of the wild flowers which grew there in abundance during the spring and summer months. Arnold writes of Bagley Wood,

"Some of my most delightful remembrances of Oxford and its neighbourhood are connected with the scenery of the late autumn. Bagley Wood in its golden decline and the green of the meadows reviving for a while under the influence of a Martinmas summer, and then finally fading off into its winter brown."

(Quoted by H. Taunt, p.72).

However, in the nineteenth century Bagley Wood became the favourite haunt of gipsies and other vagrants, and so St. John's College, to whom the land belonged, decided to enclose the area. An Act of Parliament was obtained in 1848. Now, of course, Bagley Wood has been largely swallowed up by the suburbs of Oxford and Abingdon. (See the *V.H.C.*, Berkshire, IV, 393).

19. <u>Cantemus quidem vacui coram latronibus</u>: A line modelled very closely on Juvenal, *Satires*, X, 1.22,

    "cantabit vacuus coram latrone viator."

23-24. <u>cum Keckermanno diligo Dichotomias</u>: A reference to Bartholomew Keckermann, the German theologian and philosopher. Keckermann was born in Danzig (now a city of Poland) in 1571. He received his early education under James Fabricius, who is famous for the zeal with which he fought against the Papists, Anabaptists and other heretics. In 1589, Keckermann entered the University of Württemburg (Tubingen), where he specialized in philosophy and divinity. Two years later he left Württemburg for Leipzig, and pursued his studies at the university there for a further six months, before moving on to Heidelberg in 1592.

It was at Heidelberg University that Keckermann obtained his Master's degree, and having gained for himself a reputation as a great scholar, he was appointed first tutor, and later professor of Hebrew there. In 1597, the senate of Danzig, much impressed by the achievements of their fellow countryman, sent Keckermann a formal invitation to come and undertake part of the management of their own university. At first, Keckermann refused the post, but when a second invitation was extended to him in 1601, and he had by this time been awarded the degree of Doctor of Divinity, he readily accepted.

At Danzig, Keckermann proved a very able teacher. He set out to lead his students through a most intensive training in philosophy by a new and far more compendious method, than had been employed before, so that his pupils might complete the whole course within a period of three years. To aid himself in this enterprise, he prepared a large number of 'systems' and books dealing with all kinds of subjects: logic, rhetoric, economics, ethics, politics, physics, metaphysics, geography and astronomy.

Influenced partly by the teachings of Ramus, and partly by those of Aristotle and Philip of Melanchthon, Keckermann was one of the first to recognize that the notion of 'system' could be successfully applied on a wide scale to philosophical and other types of knowledge. Like Ramus, Keckermann tends to set out his material by definition and by division after division, in other words by dichotomy - dichotomy being the name given in the field of logic to the division of a class, or genus, into lower mutually exclusive classes, or genera. In his works, Keckermann depends very largely upon the familiar dichotomized tables of Ramus, in order to be able to exhibit his discoveries in a convincing manner, and to satisfy his own personal desire for clarity. Along with others of his school, Keckermann succeeded in giving pseudo-scientific organization to the Hebrew alphabet, to history and even to the bubonic plague.

Keckermann died in 1608, at the early age of thirty-seven. His works were published at Geneva in 1614. It was through the writings of such scholars as Keckermann that Ramism came to have its great influence upon Western thought. (For further information, see N.B.U., s.v. Keckermann, Bart.; A.D.B., s.v. Keckermann, Bart., and Ong, pp.298-300).

26. distichon: A couplet of two lines, consisting of a hexameter and a pentameter. Martial, Epigrams, VIII, 29, has this to say on the subject of distichs,

"Disticha qui scribit, puto, vult brevitate placere.
quid prodest brevitas, dic mihi, si liber est?"

27. **si Prisciani caput frangimus:** An allusion to the works of Priscian, the Latin grammarian, who lived in the first half of the sixth century A.D.. He was born at Caesarea, in Mauretania, and taught in Constantinople. His <u>Institutiones Grammaticae</u>, consisting of eighteen books, is easily the longest and most detailed treatise on grammar written b any Latin author. Books I-XVI deal chiefly with the parts of speech, while XVII and XVIII are devoted to points of syntax. Priscian drew upon Greek grammars, and was also well versed in the works of all the more important of his Latin forbears: he quotes frequently from such celebrated authors as Cicero, Vergil and Horace, when wishing to illustrate certain points. The <u>Institutiones Grammaticae</u> was widely read throughout the Middle Ages, and many commentaries were written on it. (See <u>C.C.D</u>., s.v. Priscian).

In the sixteenth and seventeenth centuries, anyone speaking false grammar was accused of 'breaking Priscian's head'. T.R.Nash, in his edition of Butler's <u>Hudibras</u>,(2 vols. (London,1835), I, 305, n.7) writes, "The Quakers, we know, are great sticklers for plainness and simplicity of speech. <u>Thou</u> is the singular, <u>you</u> the plural; consequently, it is breaking Priscian's head,it is false grammar, quoth the quaker, to use <u>you</u> in the singular number: George Fox was another Priscian,witness his Battle-d'or."

30-31. **En atramentum---meis**: cf. Lily, Latin Grammar, p.61,

('Guilielmi Lilii Ad suos

Discipulos Monita Paedagogica; Seu CARMEN de moribus'),

"Scalpellum, calami, atramentum, charta l'belli,

Sint semper studiis arma parata tuis."

(**Scalpunt occiput...versificaturi**): Although only a stage direction, these words are quite clearly based on Horace, Satires, I, IO, 11.70-71,

"...........in versu faciendo

saepe caput scaberet, vivos et roderet unguis."

and on Persius, Satires, I, 1.106,

"nec pluteum caedit nec demorsos sapit unguis."

32. **O faecundi calices**: cf. Horace, Epistles, I, 5, 1.19,

"fecundi calices quem non fecere disertum?"

39. **Nam bona non scribit carmina potor aquae**: It was a common conceit among classical Latin poets that wine aided poetic

inspiration: cf. Horace, Epistles, I, 19, ll.2-3,

"...............nec vivere carmina possunt,
quae scribuntur aquae potoribus."

40. **bona ingenia coincidunt**: cf. the well-known English saying,

"Great minds think alike."

42. **εὕρηκα εὕρηκα**: cf. the words, "Eureka! Eureka!" (εὕρηκα εὕρηκα) "I have found it! I have found it!" alleged to have been uttered by the great mathematician of antiquity, Archimedes, (c.287-212 B.C.) when he discovered, by observing in his bath the water displaced by his body, the means of testing (by specific gravity) whether base metal had been introduced into Hieron's crown. (See O.C.C.L., s.v. Archimedes).

42. **tetrastichon**: A poem consisting of four lines.

47. **O dia poemata**: cf. Persius, Satires, I, ll.30-31,

"................'ecce inter pocula quaerunt
Romulidae saturi quid dia poemata narrent;'"

52-53. <u>Magnae sunt vires...At maius est virus</u>: A play on words.
Doulerus replies to Philopinus' remark in words which soun/d
and look almost the same as those which his friend has just
uttered, and it seems at first as though he is echoing
Philopinus' sentiments. Only as the second syllable of 'virus',
'-us', is spoken, does it become clear that Doulerus is, in
fact, condemning tobacco, and <u>not</u> praising it!

53-57. <u>mini non placet fumus nicotianus...et tobacchus habet
Patronum suum</u>: Doulerus and Philopinus' difference of opinion
regarding tobacco and smoking reflects in a small way the much
more violent battle which raged between the champions and
detractors of the 'herba Indica', in the sixteenth and
seventeenth centuries. Tobacco, it is thought, first reached
England early in the reign of Elizabeth, but its success was
not immediate. There was bitter opposition to smoking, and
tobacco soon became the subject of a fierce pamphlet war, in
which even James I took part with his <u>A Counterblaste to
Tabacco</u> (1604). The first major work opposing the production of
tobacco in England was <u>Opinions of the Late and Best Phisitions
concerning Tobacco</u> (1595). On the cont*i*nent a similar offensive
was launched: in France, Louis XIII forbade anyone to use
tobacco except on doctor's orders; Pope Urban VIII threatened to

excommunicate any member of the clergy found smoking or
taking snuff; while the Swiss added 'Thou shalt not smoke'
to the Ten Commandments. However, despite these prohibitions,
smoking became widespread - in England, particularly - and
references to it occur in many writers of the period, such as
Ben Jonson, Dekker and Spenser. (See C.E., s.v. Tobacco).

55. Phlegethon: A river in the Lower World, which flowed with
fire instead of water.

55. Styx: According to classical mythology, a river in the
infernal regions.

57. Euge poeta: A direct quotation from Persius, Satires, I, l.75.

60-62. Et quidem nihil est fere...dividat: cf. Seneca, Epistulae
Morales, LXXXVIII,43,

"Protagoras ait de omni re in utramque disputari
posse ex aequo, et de hac ipsa, an omnis res in utramque
partem disputabilis sit."

Cicero, too, in <u>De Oratore</u>, III, 36, 145, speaks of the "ancipites vias rationesque et pro omnibus et contra omnia disputandi".

Rhetoric was one of the Seven Liberal Arts studied at University in the sixteenth and seventeenth centuries. Part of the student's training in this subject consisted of learning how to argue for or against any given proposition; occasionally, to better their skills, students would argue first on one side, then on the other. To quote from ancient writers, as Philopinus does in the lines that follow, was always a sure way to settle such an argument.

63. <u>Synesius laudat calvitiem</u>: A reference to Synesius of Cyrene's <u>Calvitii Encomium</u>. Synesius (c. A.D. 370-413) was a Christian Neoplatonist, who studied for a time under Hypatia at Alexandria. However, his real talent lay in writing, rather than philosophy. He has left a collection of nine hymns and one hundred and fifty-six letters, while amongst his most famous rhetorical discourses are one on kingship and another entitled <u>Dion</u>, a vicious attack on the decline of humane culture in his day.

In his *Calvitii Encomium*, Synesius purports to be
answering a eulogy of hair, which he claims was written by
Dio Chrysostom. Synesius says that baldness is a sign of
intelligence and maturity: the more hair a man has, the more
he resembles the animals, and, therefore, the more stupid he
is. Hair, states Synesius, is like the blossom on a tree:
baldness is the fruit, ripening when the blossom dies. He
also believes that bald men are closer to the Divine, since
their heads are as smooth and round as the heavenly spheres,
and the bald are healthier, too, because they have no hair to
harbour germs, or to crowd their eyes and ears.

Synesius was, in many ways, quite an extraordinary
figure: combining the life of a country gentleman with that
of a learned author; Neoplatonist, but eventually becoming
Christian bishop of Ptolemais. (See *O.C.D.*, s.v. Synesius).

64. *Iulianus...prolixam*: i.e. the Roman emperor Julian, who ruled
from A.D.361-3, and who wrote a work called the *Misopogon*, or
Beard-hater. Although the title seems to suggest that Julian did
not favour beards and long hair, it soon becomes abundantly
clear to anyone reading the *Misopogon*, that the whole is a
satire, a clever attack launched against the effeminate and
smooth-shaven Syrians of Antioch, to whom the discourse is

addressed. The obvious pride which Julian takes in stating
that _he_ has a long, shaggy beard, and straggling, unkempt
hair, indicates that he thoroughly approves of this fashion,
and is satirizing himself in order to poke even greater fun
at the people of Antioch. (For further information, see O.C.D.,
s.v. Julianus, Flavius Claudius).

65. Apollo...barbatus: Statues of Apollo always represented the
god as beardless, yet Aesculapius, the patron of the healing
art, and - in classical mythology - the son of Apollo, was
shown as having a beard. Cicero, in De Natura Deorum, III, 34,
83, says that Dionysius the Cynic noted this inconsistency,
when passing by the statue of Aesculapius at Epidaurus,

"neque enim convenire barbatum esse filium (i.e.
Aesculapium) quum in omnibus fanis pater (i.e. Apollo)
inberbis esset."

66. cometa barbatus: The ancients referred to comets as being
'bearded' because it was thought that the long, fiery tail,
which a comet develops on approaching the sun, resembled a
beard. Pliny, Natural History, II, 89, writes,

"namque et in ipso caelo stellae repente nascuntur.
Plura earum genera. Cometas Graeci vocant, nostri crinitas
horrentis crine sanguineo et comarum modo in vertice hispidas.
iidem (i.e. the Greeks) pogonias quibus inferiore ex parte
in speciem barbae longae promittitur iuba."

Comets were once looked upon as evil portents. (See,
for example, Vergil, Georgics, I, 1.488; Shakespeare,
Julius Caesar, II, 2, 11.30-1; Henry VI, (Pt. I), I, I,
11.1-5; The Taming of the Shrew, III, 2, 11. 89-92, and
Henry IV, (Pt.I) III, 2, 11. 46-7.

68. mullus...barbatus: Pliny gives a description of the bearded
mullet in Natural History, IX, 30,

"barba gemina insigniuntur (i.e. mulli)
inferiore labro".

This fish was regarded as a great delicacy by the Romans:
Seneca (Epistulae Morales, XCV, 42) relates how P.Octavius paid
5,000 sesterces (approx. £10 per lb.) for a mullet, weighing
4½ lbs., which Tiberius had sent to the market to be sold.

69. **rationalia**: i.e. 'rational creatures'. In logic, the genus of living creatures, or animals, is subdivided into two classes: (i) rational creatures, and (ii) sensitive creatures. For example, both a man and a bear are the same *generically*, i.e. they both belong to the genus of living creatures, but there is a *specifical* difference, or difference of species, between them: a man possesses reason, a bear does not. Hence, Plato is a *rational*, living creature.

69. **Plato...barbatus**: In ancient Greece, it was customary for men to wear beards: Plato was no exception. There are in existence several busts of the philosopher, which show that he sported a fine growth of beard.   (See P. Friedlander, *Plato: An Introduction*, 3 vols. (London, 1958), I, Frontispiece; A.E.Taylor, *Platonism and Its Influence* (London, 1932), Frontispiece).

70. **contra derident alii...capillos**: St. Paul was amongst those who disapproved of men wearing the hair long. He says (Corinthians, xi, v.14f.),

"Doth not even nature itself teach you, that, if
a man have long hair, it is a dishonour to him? But if a
woman have long hair, it is a glory to her: for her hair
is given her for a covering."

71. **septipedes:** MS. reads 'septupedes'.

74. **caudam, in qua Sertorius...discordiae malum?** An allusion to
the anecdote told about the Roman general, Sertorius, by
Plutarch (The Parallel Lives, Sertorius, XVI) and Valerius
Maximus (VII, 3,6). Both writers relate how, whilst
campaigning in Spain against Pompey and other senatorial
generals, Sertorius became concerned about the disorderly and
impetuous manner in which the barbarians fighting under him,
joined battle. He sought, therefore, a means to demonstrate to
them how much more could be achieved by patience and
perseverance, than by brute force. One day he called all his
soldiers together and ordered two horses to be brought in: the
first was feeble and aged, the second large and strong, with a
beautiful, thick tail. Next to the weak horse stood a tall,
strong man, while beside the more powerful horse, a small,
feeble-looking man. At a given signal, the strong man took
hold of the tail of his horse, and pulled it towards him with

all his might, to try to tear it off. But, in spite of all his
hard efforts, he achieved nothing. The spectators only laughed
at him and he finally gave up the attempt. The weak man, however,
began plucking the hairs out of the strong horse's tail one by
one, and, in no time at all, had stripped his horse's tail of
its hair. Whereupon Sertorius rose and addressed the people,
saying, "Ye see, men of my allies, that perseverance is more
efficacious than violence, and that many things which cannot
be mastered when they stand together yield when one masters
them little by little. For irresistible is the force of continuity,
by virtue of which advancing Time subdues and captures every
power: and Time is a kindly ally for all who judiciously accept
the opportunities which he offers, but a most bitter enemy for
all who urge matters on unseasonably."

76-77. <u>Dromonem barbatum</u>: It is difficult to ascertain the exact
identity of the 'bearded Dromo', referred to here: he may well
be a character in fiction. A slave, called Dromo appears in
three of Terence's plays - <u>Andria</u>, <u>Adelphi</u> and
<u>Heautontimorumenos</u> - but there is no mention of his having a
beard. However, in Nicholas Grimald's <u>Christus Redivivus</u>
(c.1540), one of the Roman soldiers guarding the sepulchre,

bears the name 'Dromo', and he does have a beard ($\overline{II}$,iii).
This might conceivably be a reference to him.

(For the text of Christus Redivivus, by Nicholas Grimald, see
P.M.L.A. ~~of America~~, 14; (1899), 371-444).

80. determinare: MS. reads 'dederminare'.
81. Scotum: i.e. the schoolman, Duns Scotus (1265?-1308?). It is
thought, although there is no evidence to support the claim,
that he was a Fellow of Merton College, Oxford. He is said
to have become Professor of Divinity at Oxford in 1301, and
also to have been 'Regent' of the University of Paris. He died
very probably at Cologne; tradition has it that he was buried
alive.

Duns Scotus wrote several works. Among them may be noted
a philosophic grammar, called De Modis Significandi sive
Grammatica Speculativa, (printed in 1499); the logical
Quaestiones, (edited in 1474); a treatise on metaphysics,
entitled De Rerum Principio, (edited in 1497), and finally, the
Opus Oxoniense, (printed in 1481) which is a commentary on
Peter Lombard's Sententiae.

In the field of logic, Duns Scotus was a conceptualist,
sharing with Ibn Gebriol (fl. 1045) the view of a universal
matter as the common basis of all existences. In theology, he
rejected all possibility of rationalism. (For further
information, see D.N.B.,s.v. Duns, Johannes Scotus).

80. **Buridanum**: i.e. the French philosopher and schoolman, Jean Buridan (1297?-1358?). He was born at Béthune. He studied under Ockham, (see below), and was a philosopher of the nominalist school. In 1327 he became Rector of the University of Paris. Although his own writings offer no proof of this, Buridan is said to be the author of the sophism of the ass, which, both hungry and thirsty, stands between a pile of straw and a bucket of water, but which must die of either starvation or thirst, because if possesses no power of determination to guide itself to one or the other (l'âne de Buridan).

There is a legend, mentioned by Villon in the **Ballade des Dames du temps jadis**, that at the instigation of Jeanne de Bourgogne, wife of Philippe V, Buridan was tied up in a sack and drowned in the Seine. (See O.C.F.L., s.v. Buridan, Jean).

81. **Ockamum**: i.e. William of Ockham (d. 1349?), nicknamed 'Doctor Invincibilis'. He was educated at Oxford University, studying possibly under Duns Scotus, and later became a member of the Franciscan Order. He gained a Bachelor of Divinity degree at Oxford, and from there moved to Paris, where he obtained his Doctorate in divinity, and where he also associated with Marsiglio.

Ockham was a prime mover in the Franciscan controversy concerning poverty, and in 1323 came into conflict with Pope John XXII, who opposed the doctrine of 'evangelical poverty', which had already been recognised by the chapter at Perugia the previous year.

In 1328, Ockham was accused of being a heretic, and was imprisoned at Avignon. He managed to escape, however, and fled to the Emperor at Pisa, whence he accompanied him back to Bavaria in 1330. Here, he stayed in the Franciscan house at Munich, and together with Michael da Cesena, led the 'evangelical poverty' minority group.

Ockham was the author of several works, one of the most famous being the Opus Nonaginta Dierum, written about 1330, where he answers the Pope's treatise against evangelical poverty. In the Compendium errorum papae (c.1338), he accuses the Pope of committing seventy errors and seven heresies; while his Dialogus, now only extant in part, supports Lewis of Bavaria's claim that his election to the Empire is legal without the Pope's confirmation, and embarks upon a general discussion of the principles of imperial and papal authority.

From 1342-49, Ockham was vicar of the Franciscan Order. It is thought that he regained the Pope's favour, after withdrawing some of the more offensive of his doctrines. He died at

Munich, and was buried there.

Ockham is chiefly remembered for his work in the field of logic, philosophy and political science. A second founder of nominalism, he adopted the method of logic, termed 'Byzantine Logic', as his fundamental basis. (See D.N.B., s.v. Ockham, or Occam, William).

81. Gorhamum: i.e. Geoffrey of Gorham (d.1146). He was born in Maine, and taught for a time at Dunstable, where he wrote a miracle play about the life of St. Katharine. For twenty-seven years (1119-46), he was abbot of St. Albans. He was responsible for the building of a guests' hall, and a queen's chamber in the abbey; an infirmary with a chapel, and a shrine to St. Alban. On 2nd. August, 1129, in the presence of Alexander, Bishop of Lincoln, and others, he translated the saint's body.

Gorham was also instrumental in founding the hospital of St. Julian for lepers, on the London Road, and built, or rather, regulated, extended and set aside funds for, a nunnery at Sopwell, not far from St. Albans. (See D.N.B., s.v. Geoffrey of Gorham).

82. alios magistros subtilissimos: Duns Scotus was given the title 'Doctor Subtilis'.

Divum Thomam:
83. ~~alios magistros subtilissimos~~: i.e. Thomas Aquinas
(1225?-1274), the great scholastic philosopher. Born at
the castle of Roccasecca, near Aquino, in the province of
Naples, Thomas received his early education at the abbey
of Monte Cassino. In 1239 he moved on to Naples, where he
studied the seven liberal arts at the university there, and
it was also at Naples, five years later, that he became a
Dominican friar. For three years (1245-48) he pursued his
studies in Paris under Albert the Great (see below, note to
III, 1.83), and when the latter returned to Cologne in 1248,
Thomas accompanied him.

In 1252 Thomas was again in Paris. Here, in the year
1256, after he had written his commentaries on the Bible and
on the Sententiae of Peter Lombard, the degree of Licentiate
in Theology was conferred upon him, and soon afterwards that
of Master in Theology.

The years that followed, Thomas spent chiefly in
teaching, both at Paris and Rome, and in answering attacks
levelled against his Order by William of St. Amour. During the
years 1268-72, he showed opposition to Siger of Brabant, to
the Latin Averroists and also to the Franciscan supporters of
Augustinianism.

In 1272 he was instructed to return to the land of his birth, to teach at Naples. Pope Gregory X summoned him to attend the General Council of Lyons (1274), which had been called to try and settle the differences then existing between the Latin and Greek Churches. However, during the journey to Lyons, Thomas died (March 7th., 1274). He was canonized in 1323 by Pope John XXII.

Thomas was the author of numerous treatises, but the majority of these are only the prelude to his really great work, the Summa Theologica. He first began writing in 1254, when he composed his Commentary on the Sentences of Peter Lombard, which reflects not only the influence of his former teacher, Albert the Great, but also that of the Augustinianism which he later abandoned. Next he wrote discourses on hypothetical theological problems (Quaestiones Disputatae and Quaestiones Quodlibetales), and his commentaries on the Bible. It was about this period, too, that Thomas was preparing his disquisitions on Boethius; on the De Divinis Nominibus of pseudo-Dionysius; on the Liber de Causis; and on the following works of Aristotle: the Physica, Metaphysica, De anima, De sensu, De memoria, Ethics, Politica, Analytica Posteriora, Meteorologica, Peri Hermeneias, De caelo and the De generatione.

However, the two most important of Thomas' works are, undoubtedly, the <u>Summa Contra Gentiles</u> (1259-64), the chief treatise of the Middle Ages on natural theology, and the <u>Summa Theologica</u>, the aim of which was to embrace all known learning. It is divided into three sections: the first is concerned with God, the second with Man, and the third with the God-Man. Parts I and II are entirely the work of Thomas, but in Part III only the first ninety questions are his, the rest of the work was completed - with Thomas' approval - by Reginald of Piperno. Among the many subjects discussed in the book are: the existence, nature and attributes of God; the Trinity; the Creation; Man's will; virtue; sin; the work of Christ; the contemplative life and the sacraments.

No other theologian, with the possible exception of Augustine, has had such a profound influence upon the thought of the Western Church, as Thomas, a fact readily borne out by Pope Leo XIII's Encyclical of August, 1879, in which it is stated that the teaching of St.Thomas Aquinas is to be adopted as the basis of all theology. (For further information, see <u>N.B.U.</u>, s.v. Thomas d'Aquin (Saint)).

83. **Albertum**: i.e. the German philosopher, Albert the Great. He was born at Lauingen, in Suabia, and came of the noble family of the counts of Boddstädt. The exact date of his birth is uncertain: some authorities give the year as 1193, and others as 1205. The surname 'the Great' was very probably a title bestowed on Albert by his contemporaries on account of his astonishing knowledge.

Albert received his early education at Padua, where he surpassed all his fellow students. He continued to make rapid progress, and in 1221, the example of one of his teachers, the famous Dominican friar, Jordanus, made Albert decide to enter the Dominican Order himself. His growing reputation as a scholar having earned him the task of educating the younger members of the Order, Albert went to Paris, where he lectured on Aristotle with great success. It was perhaps Albert who was instrumental in making the Holy See recant a decree, forbidding the teaching of Aristotelian philosophy, which it had issued earlier, and he, himself, was allowed to give lectures in public on the Physica.

Albert's reputation continued to grow, and in 1254, he was appointed provincial of the Dominicans - that is to say, monastic superior in charge of all the religious houses - in Germany. In his official capacity, Albert took up residence at Cologne, a city which, unlike many others, offered at that time great resources to the studious man and the scholar who had a taste and a talent for teaching. Cologne remained Albert's favourite city throughout the whole of his long and laborious life: neither the favours granted to him by Pope Alexander IV, who summoned him to Rome and made him master of the Holy Palace, nor his nomination, in 1260, to the bishopric of Ratisbonne, a post he held for only three years, could keep him away from Cologne for very long.

After paying his own century tribute, by preaching - on the Pope's orders - to the crusade in Germany and Bohemia, and attending the general council, held at Lyons, in 1274, he returned to his retreat at Cologne, where he died in 1280, at the age of eighty-seven, leaving behind more writings than any other philosopher had done before him.

Four hundred years later, Pierre Jammi, himself a Dominican friar, collected a large number of Albert's works together and had them published at Lyons, in 1651. Unfortunately, there is no extant catalogue of <u>all</u> Albert's works: the longest list can be found in the <u>Scriptores Ordinis Praedicatorum</u>, of Quetif and Echard, where it occupies twelve pages (171f.) of vol.I. Many of the writings which go to make up this enormous list are, undoubtedly, works which have been falsely attributed to Albert, or some of his pupils' treatises which have become mixed up with his own; but, setting aside all that which is anonymous, or of doubtful authorship, enough still remains to ensure for Albert the title of the most prolific polygraphist that has ever lived. In the majority of his works, he does little more than comment on Aristotle, and plunder the books of Arab authors. However, his extracts are frequently combined with very shrewd arguments, and his remarks are often extremely judicious. He dealt with all aspects of philosophy, and although he possessed no 'system' that could be called exclusively his own, or that differed essentially from Aristotle, one can glean from his writings a more or less complete body of doctrine.

Of the ancient authors, Albert was, of course, acquainted with Aristotle, and also Denis the Areopagite and Hermes Trismegistus (the author of various Neoplatonic writings), but all these he knew solely in Latin translations. He was conversant with the works of some commentators on Aristotle, such as Themistius and Proclus, and he had read both Cicero and Apuleius; while his knowledge and understanding of Arab and Jewish writers was very great indeed.

In theology, Peter Lombard was Albert's guide and model. One of his chief ambitions was to reconcile the nominalists and the realists through a syncretism of his own invention, but this only served to increase the contradictions and difficulties, which already existed, and to exacerbate further the two schools.

Among Albert's most outstanding works are his explanation of Peter Lombard's **Sententiae**, and his **Commentaries** on Aristotle, which fill the first six volumes of his Collected Works. His **Commentary on the Historia Animalium** has several rather curious additions, which have tempted some scholars to believe that Albert may have had access to Latin translations of some books of Aristotle now lost.

There can be no doubt that the writings of Albert the Great are largely responsible for the tremendous popularity that the works of Aristotle enjoyed during the period of the Renaissance. (See **N.B.U.**, s.v. Albert, le Grand).

83. **Caietanum**: i.e. Thomas de Vio Cajetan, the Italian cardinal and theologian. Cajetan was born in the town of Gaeta, on 20th. February, 1469. At the age of fifteen he entered the Dominican Order, where his natural talents and great knowledge soon earned him a brilliant reputation. In Brescia and Padua he won world-wide acclaim as a teacher of theology, and in 1500, he became procurator-general of his Order, and later general (1508): he was still only thirty-nine years old.

In 1518, Pope Leo X appointed Cajetan his legate in Germany. The main object of this mission was to try and win back Martin Luther to the interests of the Holy See, before he broke away from the Church completely. Cajetan lacked neither the knowledge nor the ability to carry out such a task. He displayed, on the Protestants' own admission, a moderation which did his character credit; but the mere fact that he was a Dominican, attempting to settle a dispute which had arisen out of the rivalry between that Order and the Augustinians, to which Luther belonged, made the chances of success very slim indeed, even from the start. Cajetan, moreover, had an unshakeable belief in the authority of the Pope - in fact, he is considered the first member of the clergy to have ever upheld without question the infallibility of the Pope, a cause which he championed at the Council of Latran. Other obstacles, too, regarding points of etiquette and ceremonial, were thrown in the way of Cajetan and Luther. Both refused to yield, and finally the two parted without having reached any agreement.

In 1519, Cajetan was given the bishopric of Gaeta. He was taken prisoner during the sack of Rome in 1527, and was only able to recover his liberty through a ransom of 5,000 crowns, which afterwards obliged him to live a life of frugality in his diocese, in order to reimburse those who had paid out this sum.

Recalled to Rome in 1530, by Pope Clement VII, he died there on 9th. August, 1534.

Cajetan's extremely busy career did not prevent him from finding time for private study and writing a large number of works. The most important of these are his <u>Commentary on the Bible</u> (Lyons, 1639) to which is attached a life of the author, written by Fonseca; a very short <u>Commentary on the Summa of Saint Thomas</u>, which can be found in the editions of the <u>Summa</u> (Anvers, 1577; Lyons, 1581, and Bergamo, 1590), and in an abridged version in the general edition of his own works, printed in Rome, in 1570, on the orders of Pope Pius V; the <u>Opuscules</u>, which deal with a variety of subjects (Lyons, 1562) the chief of these being a work entitled <u>On the Authority of the Pope</u>, which supports the Holy Father's right to call councils, his supremacy at these great assemblies, and his infallibility, (Cajetan was made a cardinal on the strength of this treatise); <u>Commentaries on the Philosophy of Aristotle</u> and the <u>Tractatus de comparatione papae et concilii</u> (Venice, 1531 and 1562).

Cajetan had a deep understanding of theology, and he exhibits a certain clarity and method when expressing his views, but very often he is doing little more than re-shaping the thoughts of earlier philosophers. He had both zealous supporters and harsh critics: Melancthon paints a shocking picture of him,

but Chamier, on the other hand, praises his integrity, his
candour and his moderation. Bossuet says of him, "C'était
un esprit ardent et impétueux, plus habile dans les
subtilités de la dialectique, que profond dans l'antiquité
ecclésiastique." (For further information, see N.B.U.,
s.v. Cajetan, Thomas de Vio).

84. alios doctores seraphicos: St. Thomas Aquinas was known as
the 'Angelic Doctor'.

87. omnia sunt communia: cf. Terence, Adelphi, V, ll.803-4,

> MICIO: nam vetus verbum hoc quidemst,
> communia esse amicorum inter se omnia.

89. Aetolus aper...agros: An allusion to the boar, which,
according to classical mythology, Diana sent to ravage the
country of King Oeneus, and which was killed by his son,
Meleager. The story is related in full by Ovid (Metamorphoses,
VIII, 1.273f.). The legend is frequently referred to in the
English literature of the sixteenth and seventeenth centuries.
For example, Cleopatra, in Shakespeare's Antony and Cleopatra
(IV, xiii, ll.2-3), says of Antony in his fiery temper,

"   the boar of Thessaly
   was never so emboss'd".

   Moreover, the Latin playwright, William Gager, dramatized the story in his tragedy *Meleager*, (printed in 1592/3).

90-91. <u>scarorum iecinora...murenarum lactes</u>: MS. reads 'sacrorum'. (This is a direct quotation from Suetonius, <u>Vitellius</u>, 13.

92. <u>Adde satyras et epigrammata</u>: Doulerus is perhaps suggesting that after supper, they should be presented with 'apophoreta', the little gifts which the Romans used to give to their guests at the end of a feast, and which were generally accompanied by riddles, or puzzling epigrams. (See Petronius, <u>Satyricon</u>, 56).

92. <u>Non novi haec bellaria</u>: Anna assumes that 'satyras' and 'epigrammata' must be some new kind of delicacy.

93. <u>Volo...Iovialiter</u>: Nectar and ambrosia were considered to be the food of the gods. Doulerus thinks, therefore, that if he and his friends dine upon these, they will feast jovially -

that is to say, not only merrily, but also like Jove (Jupiter) chief god among the Romans.

95. Fabebitis...marsupium: A play on words. The author draws on the fact that the adjectives 'lautus' (sumptuous) and 'latus' (wide) are very similar in spelling, but quite different in meaning.

98. In tempore: Doulerus puns on the two meanings of 'tempus': (i) 'season', and (ii) 'time'.

100-105. Ego negligo fartum...saepe ingeritur cibus: There now follows a series of rather crude jokes, in which Nichades and Doulerus try to insinuate that the Latin 'farts' (black puddings, mincemeat, &c.) and 'turdus' (a thrush) have some connection with the English words - no longer in polite use - 'fart' and 'turd'.

lactibus: i.e. chitterlings, the smaller intestines of swine, cooked for food.

108. carnem suillam habeat altare Cereris: In Roman times, pigs were sacrificed to Ceres because they destroyed the newly planted crops. (See Ovid, Fasti, I, 1.349f.)

109. *In hoc Iudaeus sapit*: The rather strange customs and traditions of the Jewish people have always aroused great curiosity. Cf. Horace, *Satires*, I, 9, ll.69-70.

116-117. *nam...pulsat*: cf. Horace, *Odes*, I, 4, ll.13-14,

"pallida Mors aequo pulsat pede pauperum
tabernas/regumque turres..."

118. *aetate lubrica*: See above, note to Prologue, l.14.

122. *Qui...ephippiis*: There is a record of a so-called witch having ridden – not the devil – but a wealthy country yokel, whom she was trying to defraud! The title of the court case against her, which was held in London in 1594, reads,

The Brideling, Sadling and Ryding, of a rich Churle in Hampshire, by the subtill practise of one Judeth Philips, a professed cunning woman, or Fortune teller...

(See *Witchcraft*, edited by Barbara Rosen, Stratford-upon-Avon Library, 6 (London, 1969), pp. 214-18.)

125. *Si cupias, ostendent*: MS. reads 'sic cupias', but 'si' seems to make better sense here.

128. <u>quidem diabolus...cruce</u>: An old English proverb. Cf. Massinger, <u>The Bashful Lover</u>, <u>III</u>, i,

> "The devil sleeps in my pocket; I have no cross to drive him from it."

(In my quotations from Massinger, I use <u>The Plays of Philip Massinger</u>, edited by W. Gifford, second edition, 4 vols. (London, 1813)).

130- <u>Nunc...tellus</u>: A direct quotation from Horace, <u>Odes</u>, I,
131.   37, 11.1-2.

134. <u>Non ad modum sed ad modium</u>: A play on words. The author takes advantage of the fact that 'modus' (a measure) and 'modius' (a peck) look and sound very alike, but have slightly different meanings.

135. <u>Falernum, aut Caecubum</u>: These were both kinds of Roman wine.

143. <u>Colossus</u>: See above, note to II, 1.243.

148–
149.
Habent animalis suas voces,...in medio grege: This belief that animals have a language of their own, dates back to very ancient times. For example, the senate and people of Abdera, in their letter to Hippocrates, quote as an instance of the madness of Democritus, the fact that he pretends to understand the language of birds. Similarly, Porphyry, *De Abstinentia* ($\overline{\text{III}}$, 3), claims that animals do have their own language, and that men can learn to comprehend it. He lists as noteworthy examples Melampus, a famous seer in Greek mythology; the prophet, Tiresias, and Apollonius of Tyana, who, it is said, heard one swallow telling the rest, that an ass had just stumbled, spilling all its load of wheat upon the road. Philostratus, *The Life of Apollonius of Tyana*, ($\overline{\text{IV}}$, 3) relates a similar story, but states that the bird in question was a sparrow. Porphyry also adds, "a friend assured me that a youth, who was his page, understood all the articulations of birds, and that they were all prophetic. But the boy was unhappily deprived of the faculty: for his mother, fearing he should be sent as a present to the Emperor, took an opportunity, when he was asleep, to piss into his ear." The author of the Targum on Esther, says that Solomon understood the speech of birds.

150. discunt: MS. reads 'discant'.

150. per artem Apollonii: See above, note to 11.148-149.

151-152. vult...advenas: The magpie has always been looked upon as a rather mysterious bird, and many strange superstitions surround it. Its chattering, for instance, was, in times gone by, thought to be portentous: in Henry VI (Pt.3), V,vi, there is the line,

        "chatt'ring pies in dismal discords sung;"

                                        (1.48)

According to Scottish folk-lore, a magpie flying near the homestead is a sign that one of the inmates will die shortly; but in Denmark, if the bird perches on the roof of a house, it is considered an indication that strangers are coming. Doulerus is evidently acquainted with this Danish superstition. (For further information, see B. Thorpe, Northern Mythology, 3 vols. (London, 1851), II, 274).

152-
153. **vult...domestici:** In the past, the howling of a dog was regarded as ominous, foretelling death or misfortune. Bolingbroke, for example, in Shakespeare's *Henry VI* (Pt.2) I, iv, ll.16-19, says,

> "The time when screech-owls cry and ban-dogs howl,
> And spirits walk and ghosts break up their graves __"

Similarly, in *Henry VI* (Pt.3), V, vi, ll.44-6, King Henry, talking of Gloucester, exclaims,

> "The owl shriek'd at thy birth - an evil sign;
> The night-crow cried, aboding luckless time;
> Dogs howl'd, and hideous tempest shook down trees;"

In Roman times, too, howling dogs were thought to have a fatal significance. Vergil (Georgics, I, l.470) speaking of the disasters that followed Caesar's assassination, says,

> "obscenaeque canes importunaeque volucres
> signa dabant."

The superstition that a howling dog presages death, is very probably derived from Aryan mythology, where the dog is represented as summoning the departing soul. T. Fiske, in his book Myths and Mythmakers, (Cambridge, Mass., 1873), p. 36, states that, "throughout all Aryan mythology, the souls of the dead are supposed to ride on the night-wind, with their howling dogs, gathering into their throng the souls of those just dying as they pass by their houses."

153. corvus...vocat: Like the magpie, the crow was also held to be a bird of ill-omen. On account of its black plumage, it was considered to have associations with evil, and its hoarse croak was believed to foretell some sad event. Butler, in his Hudibras, (pt. 2, canto 3), remarks,

> "Is it not ominous in all countries,
> When crows and ravens croak upon trees?"
>
> (ll. 707-708)

(I quote from Samuel Butler, Hudibras, edited by T. R. Nash, 2 vols. (London, 1835).

The crow was also an infallible weather sign. Horace, Odes III, 27, ll.9-12, writes,

"antequam stantes repetat paludes
imbrium divina avis imminentum,
oscinem corvum prece suscitabo
solis ab ortu."

157- possunt...praedicere: Claims commonly made by mountebanks.
158.

159. Fortunati pileo: A reference to the popular European legend of Fortunatus. Tradition has it that Fortunatus lived in Famagusta, on the island of Cyprus. One day, whilst wandering in the forest, Fortunatus met the goddess Fortune. She promised Fortunatus that she would grant him one wish. He asked, therefore, to be made a rich man; whereupon the goddess presented him with a magic purse, which, as soon as it was emptied, replenished itself again.

With the aid of this purse, Fortunatus travelled the world. In Cairo, he was entertained by the Sultan, who showed him his many treasures. One of these was a magic cap, which had the power of transporting its wearer to any place he wished.

Fortunatus, tricking the Sultan, stole the cap and returned to Cyprus, where he lived in luxury for the rest of his days.

When Fortunatus died, his two sons, Ampedo and Andelosa, inherited the purse and the magic cap, but on account of their prodigality and recklessness, they came to a bad end. The moral of the fable is clear: seek wisdom before riches.

The longest and most complete version of the story of Fortunatus can be found in Karl Simrock's <u>Die deutschen Volksbucher</u>, vol. III, where it occupies almost 158 pages. Although the style in which the story is written would seem to indicate a comparatively modern date for the authorship, the central theme of the tale can be traced back to a much earlier period: the 'invisible cap', for example, appears in the mythology of all nations. It plays an important part in <u>Jack the Giant Killer</u>, and also in such fairy stories as <u>The Enchanted Ring</u> and <u>The Old Soldier and the Tinder Box</u>.

The earliest known edition of Fortunatus in German, appeared at Augsburg in 1509. There have been countless versions of the legend in French, Italian, Dutch and English. In 1553, Hans Sachs wrote a dramatization of the story, and in 1600, Thomas Dekker also composed a play on the same theme, which he

called Old Fortunatus. Tieck made use of the tale in his
Phantasmus, and Chamisso in his Peter Schlemihl; while
Ludwig Uhland left an incomplete narrative poem, entitled
Fortunatus and his Sons. (For further information, see E.B.,
s.v. Fortunatus; Fr. W.V.Schmidt, Fortunatus und seine Söhne,
eine Zauber-Tragödie, von Thomas Decker, mit einem Anhang, etc.,
(Berlin, 1819), and J.J.Görres, Die teutschen Volksbücher,
(Heidelberg, 1807).

160. Gygis annulo: An allusion to Gyges, a king of Lydia, who was
famous for the possession of a ring with which he could make
himself invisible. There is a legend that Gyges was once a
shepherd, who went down into an underground cave where he
discovered the hollow statue of a horse, all made of bronze
and containing a corpse, from the finger of which he stole a
golden ring. Gyges soon realized that the ring had magic powers
and could render its wearer invisible, so with its help he made
himself known to the queen of Lydia, killed her husband,
Candaules, and usurped the throne (685 B.C.). The story is told
by Plato, Republic, II, 359. (See O.C.C.L., s.v. Gyges, and
K. Flower Smith, "The Tale of Gyges and the King of Lydia",
A.J.P., 23 (1902), 261-282; 361-387).

162. **palmam**: MS. reads 'palam' again, as in the line above.

170. **Cedant arma togae**: These words are borrowed directly from Cicero, **De Officiis**, I, 22, 77.

170. **Xantippe**: i.e. Xanthippe, the wife of Socrates, who is reputed to have been a great scold. Aulus Gellius, **Noctes Atticae**, I, 17, I, says of her,

"Xanthippe, Socratis philosophi uxor, morosa admodum fuisse fertur et iurgiosa, irarumque et molestriarum muliebrium per diem perque noctem scatebat."

170. **obliviscamur**: MS. reads 'obviliscamur'.

181. **Ut concipias...tanquam equa Lusitanica**: A reference to the very ancient and widespread belief that animals can become pregnant by the wind. Homer, for instance, **Iliad**, XVI, 150ff. speaks of "- - - - - the horses that the Harpy Podargē bore to Zephyr the wind as she grazed on the meadow beside the stream of Oceanus," and ibid., XX, 221ff. "three thousand mares he had that pastured along the marshy meadow, rejoicing in their tender foals. Of

them Boreas became enamoured as they grazed, and in the semblance of a dark-maned stallion he covered them; then they conceived and bore twelve fillies".

Vergil, too, (Georgics, III, 273ff.) writes,

"ore omnes (i.e. equae) versae in Zephyrum
        stant rupibus altis
exceptantque levis auras, et saepe sine ullis
confiugiis vento gravidae (mirabile dictu)
saxa per et scopulos et depressas convallis
diffugiunt,"

Aristotle also talks of the mare being impregnated by the wind (Historia Animalium, 572 a 13ff.).

For a full discussion of this belief in wind-impregnation, see Conway Zirkle, "Animals impregnated by the wind", in Sarton's Isis, XXV (1936), 95-130.

183-164. καθαρσιν μέχρι τῶν πεντήκοντα ἐτῶν:
i.e. 'menstruation lasts until fifty'. This phrase does not occur in any of Aristotle's works, although the author of Mercurius Rusticans, through his mouth-piece Philopimus states quite firmly that it does. It is more than likely that the author's

knowledge of medicine is derived from the writings of Albert the Great (see above, note to 1.83), who, in his turn, obtained most of his information from the works of Aristotle. In his book, De Secretis Mulierum, p.16, Albert discusses menstruation, saying,

"Ad quinquaginta durat purgatio tanta".

The De Secretis Mulierum is virtually little more than a commentary on Aristotle's De Generatione Animalium, but it does have several strange additions, such as the line, quoted above, which suggests that Albert may have been acquainted with some works of Aristotle, now no longer extant.

It seems, therefore, that the author of Mercurius Rusticans, assuming that the phrase "Ad quinquaginta durat purgatio tanta," like much of what Albert says, is simply a translation of some words of Aristotle, translated it back into what he believed was the original Greek!

(I quote from Albertus Magnus de Secretis Mulierum. Item De Virtutibus Herbarum Lapidum et Animalium (Amstelodami, 1648).

185. **si maritus abstineat legumine:** Green vegetables, of course, prevent sterility, rather than cause it.

187. **Marte...mulieres:** The 'regula' referred to here, is also mentioned by Albert the Great, <u>De Secretis Mulierum</u>, p. 45. He writes, explaining it, thus,

"Postquam auctor ostendit influentiam planetarum et stellarum respectu foetus, nunc consequenter prosequitur de effectu signorum. Nota. Aries est calidus, et humidus et correspondet Veri. Ver enim est calidus et humidus, et tunc animalia maxime appetunt coitum, quia tunc augmentatur calidum et humidum gratia solis existentis in ariete, et maxime in viris tunc est appetitus. Propter hoc etiam mater ecclesia statuit jejunium magis in illo tempore restringendum quia tunc homines constricti hyeme revertuuntur ad vigorem. Unde versus,

   Marte mares, Febru̥oque canes,
  Maio mulieres.

188. **decimum:** MS. reads 'decimeum¦'

188. **organizabitur:** MS. reads 'orginazabitur.'

190. **Nisi mentiatur Albertus**: Albert the Great devotes an entire
chapter of the **De Secretis Mulierum** (De foetus formatione) to
the growth of the foetus in the womb. Pregnancy, he says,
usually lasts nine months, and the foetus grows steadily month
by month - under planetary influence. Saturn governs the
first month - arranging the matter in the womb; Jupiter - the
second month - when the foetus begins to take shape; Mars is
responsible for the development of the head and neck in the
third month, whilst in the fourth month - under the Sun's
guidance - the foetus develops a heart, and also arms, and so
on through the rest.

191. **obstetricis**: MS. reads 'obstretricis'.

197. **Tentabo, valete**: Although in the MS. no separate speech heading
is given to these words, they are obviously spoken by Caecilia,
as she is the only character to leave the stage at this point
in the scene.

199- **nam visu...basiliscus interficit**: The basilisk (sometimes called
200.
the cockatrice in English literature) was an imaginary monster,
whose eye was thought to be so deadly that it could kill by its
very look. Pliny gives a description of this strange creature in

his *Natural History*, VIII, 33, asserting that it could strike terror into all other animals with its hiss. The cockatrice is often mentioned in the plays of Shakespeare. In *Richard III*, (IV, i, ll.54-6), for instance, the Duchess cries,

> "O my accursed womb, the bed of death!
> A cockatrice hast thou hatch'd to the world,
> Whose unavoided eye is murderous."

Again, ibid., I, ii, l.150, Anne, on hearing Richard praise her eyes, exclaims,

> "Would they were basilisks to strike thee dead!"

Similarly, Sir Toby Belch in *Twelfth Night*, (III,iv,ll.185-6) says,

> "This will so fright them both that they will kill one another by the look, like cockatrices."

201. *Quam flavus est zelotypus*: In the English literature of the sixteenth and seventeenth centuries, 'yellow' was an adjective frequently used to describe jealous persons. For example, in Shakespeare's *Merry Wives of Windsor*, (I, iii, l.97) Nym sets out

to possess Ford 'with yellowness'. Beatrice, in Much Ado About Nothing, (II, i, 11.263-4), says of the Count that he is as 'civil as an orange, and something of that jealous complexion'; while in Twelfth Night, (II, iv. 11.111-14), Viola tells Orsino how her father's daughter fell in love, but her love was unrequited,

"   She pin'd in thought;
And with a green and yellow melancholy
She sat like Patience on a monument,
Smiling at grief."

205. Unus...faber: cf. Appius, ap. Sall. de Republ. Ordin. I,

"faber est quisque fortunae suae".

209. ἢ πίθι...abi: A play on words, since 'aut bibe aut abi' means virtually the same as ἢ πίθι ἢ ἄπιθι. This expression was very common amongst the Greeks: Cicero, Tusculanae Disputationes, V, 41, 118, writes,

"Mihi quidem in vita servanda videtur illa lex, quae in Graecorum conviviis obtinetur: Aut bibat, inquit, aut abeat."

212. **quicquid in buccam venit:** cf. Cicero, *Epistulae ad Atticum*, I, 12,

>"Si rem nullam habebis, quod in buccam venerit, scribito."

215. **Et diabolus...vindice:** This line is a parody of Horace, *Ars Poetica*, 11.191-2,

>"nec deus intersit, nisi dignus vindice nodus
>inciderit, "

218. **hamum illitum cibo:** cf. Lyly, *Euphues*, P.36,

>"they account it (i.e. beauty) a delicate bait with
>a deadly hook."

(I quote from John Lyly, *Euphues: The Anatomy of Wit, Euphues and his England*, edited by M.W. Croll and Harry Clemons, (London, 1916).

222. **Lupa est in fabula:** cf. Terence, *Adelphi*, 1.537,

>" lupus in fabula. "

It has been suggested that the phrase 'lupus in fabula' (the English 'talk of the devil') is derived from a play by Naevius, the subject of which was the life of Romulus, and in which, some scholars feel, a she-wolf - the wolf in the story - must have appeared, actually suckling Romulus and his brother. However, this seems rather an absurd idea, since such a scene would be practically impossible to execute on the stage. (The theory is discussed by W. Beare, in his book The Roman Stage, third edition (London, 1968), c. 4, p.39).

'Lupa' can, of course, also mean 'prostitute'. It is more than likely, therefore, - in view of Susanna's subsequent behaviour - that the word is used here with a double entendre.

223-241. <u>Domine, num opus est tibi aliquo?...et me hac nocte admittito:</u>
The following dialogue consists almost entirely of puns and word-play. Doulerus here takes on the rôle of 'clown' or 'jester', while Susanna 'feeds' him with words - the meanings of which he either plays upon, or cleverly twists. (Cf. the conversation between Olivia and the Fool in Shakespeare's <u>Twelfth Night</u>, I, v, 11.35-68).

224-
225.   **Do...dominus**: Doulerus divides the word 'dominus' into 'do' (first pers. sing. present tense of the verb 'dare', to give) and 'minus' (the comparative form of the adjective 'parvus', here used as a substantive). He then proceeds to string together any other words he can think of, that resemble 'minus' - 'munus' and 'manus' - producing the effect of a tongue-twister. It is difficult to convey the same idea in an English translation of these lines, without changing the sense somewhat.

226. **Hoc ter magis displicet**: 'Magister' is split up into two separate words: (i) 'ter' - the adverbial numeral - meaning 'three times, thrice,' &c., and (ii) 'magis' - the comparative adverb - 'more'.

226-
227.   **Num generosus?...Si tu speciosa**: Just as 'generosus' is the adjective formed from 'genus', so 'speciosa' is the adjective derived from 'species'. However, 'generosus' and 'speciosa', besides meaning 'of good birth' and 'of a particular kind' respectively, can also be used in another sense. 'Generosus', frequently indicates nobleness and dignity, while 'speciosa' often has the meaning 'beatuiful, handsome,' &c.. Hence, there is a double play on words here.

228. *Si tu matrona*: 'Matrona' is, of course, the feminine form of 'patronus'.

230. *Esne si placet astrologus?*: Susanna supposes that as Doulerus has taken hold of her hand, he is going to tell her fortune by reading her palm.

230. *almanacta*: Almanacs were very popular in the sixteenth and seventeenth centuries. They were usually published under the title *An Almanack and Prognostication made for the year of our Lord God ———*, and contained so-called prophecies about the weather, and about plagues, famines and other disasters. Frequent reference is made to these almanacs in the plays of Shakespeare: Enobarbus, *Antony and Cleopatra*, (I, ii, ll.144-5) says,

    "they (i.e. Cleopatra's passions) are greater storms and tempests than almanacs can report."

    Similarly, Prince Henry in *Henry IV* (Pt.2),(II,iv, ll.253-4) exclaims,

    "Saturn and Venus this year in conjunction! what says th'almanac to that?"

232. **Etiam nec minus...pedis**: This is Doulerus' humorous way of
saying that he knows absolutely nothing about palmistry.

233- **Etiam mea iuvencula...Milone melius**: Doulerus addresses
235.
Susanna as 'iuvencula', a term of endearment, and then goes
on to talk about her future in agricultural language: as a
heifer becomes a cow, so Susanna will grow to be a woman;
as a cow is mated with the bull, so Susanna will - in a
sexual sense - 'carry' a husband. However, the verb 'ferre'
is used here with its literal meaning, too, for the line 'et
bovem feras Milone melius', is undoubtedly an allusion to
the proverb "Milo was able to carry the bull which he had
carried as a calf". The fact that Susanna's husband-to-be is
symbolized as a bull, is also a hint that he will have 'horns',
- that is to say, be a cuckold.

236. **De hoc Hammonem consule**: Hammon was an Egyptian and Libyan
deity, worshipped in the form of a ram. This particular god
was, therefore, represented as having horns.

239. *Et sic tenebitur...sus atque sacerdos*: An allusion to the Secunda Regula Specialis concerning increasing common nouns of the third declension, in Lily, <u>Latin Grammar</u>, p.82,

"Sunt commune, Parens, autorque, infans, adolescens,
Dux, illex, haeres, exlex; a fronte creata,
Ut, bifrons: custos, bos, fur, sus, atque sacerdos."

240. *mea Sussa mea*: Doulerus implies that the name 'Susanna' is derived from the word 'sus', meaning 'a sow'.

245. *Paucis te volo*: A phrase used by Terence in <u>Andria</u>, 1.29.

247-249. *Candidior folio...lacte coacto*: These lines (except for the words 'natura dulcior una') are taken directly from Ovid, <u>Metamorphoses</u>, XIII, 1.789, and 11.795-796. In all standard editions of Ovid, 1.795 runs,

"lucidior glacie, matura dulcior uva,"

It seems, therefore, that either the text of Ovid with which the author was familiar, read 'natura dulcior una', or else an error was made here on the part of the scribe copying out the play.

251. **obsecro:** MS. reads 'observo!'

252. **amor captus oculis:** cf. Shakespeare, <u>The Merchant of Venice</u>, <u>II</u>, vi, ll. 36-7,

> "But love is blind, and lovers cannot see
> The pretty follies that themselves commit,"

~~259. Violetta: i.e. Violetta, the inamorata of the Italian poet, Lorenzo de' Medici (1448-92).~~

259. <u>Violetta, Aramanta, Rosabella:</u> Here the author may simply be listing terms of endearment commonly used by poets, or he may have in mind a particular poem or work in which these names occur. It is worth noting, perhaps, that the Italian poet Lorenzo de' Medici (1448-92) sometimes refers to his inamorata as 'my violet', i.e. Violetta.

259. <u>Dulcinea:</u> Dulcinea, of course, was the sweetheart of Don Quijote, in Cervantes' great novel, <u>El Ingenioso Hidalgo Don Quijote de la Mancha</u>, (1605 and 1615).

260. <u>Phyllis et Amaryllis:</u> In pastoral poetry, these were names often given to shepherdesses. (See Vergil, <u>Eclogues</u>, III, 1.78 and 1.81).

261. **Habeam te hac nocte usurariam**: cf. Plautus, *Amphitruo*, Prologue, 11.107-108,

> MERCURIUS: is(ie. Jupiter) amare occepit Alcumenam
> clam virum/usuramque eius corporis cepit
> sibi."

263. **Prius unda dabit flammas**: 'Sooner shall water produce flame', an expression used of anything impossible. Cf. Cicero, *Philippics*, XIII, 21, 49,

> "Prius undis flamma (sc.miscebitur)"

and Ovid, *Tristia*, I, 8, 1.4,

> "unda dabit flammas".

265. **Ad horam secundam venias**: On this occasion, it is Susanna, herself, who states at what time her would-be lover is to come to her, providing a comical contrast with her preceding conversations with Doulerus and Philopinus, in which they decided when they would visit her! Susanna is here calling Nichades' bluff!

267. <u>O impudicum et infidum muliebre genus</u>: cf. Tibullus (Lygd.), III, 4, l.61,

    "a crudele genus nec fidum femina nomen!"

268. <u>Libido venenata facie formosa latet</u>: cf. Ovid, <u>Amores</u>, I, 8, l.104,

    "inpia sub dulci melle venena latent."

269. <u>Apis...gerit</u>: cf. Lyly, <u>Euphues</u>, p.65,

    "the bee that hath honey in her mouth hath a sting in her tail."

270. <u>Cautosque...incautos necat</u>: See above, note to II, l.165.

271. <u>Caute si non caste</u>: A well-known proverb. Greene, V, p.209, says,

    "Offences are not measured by the proportion but by the secrecy: Si non caste, tamen caute: if not chastely, yet charily."

(I quote from <u>The Life and Complete Works in Prose and Verse of Robert Greene</u>, edited by Alexander B. Grosart, Huth Library edition, 15 vols. (1881-1886).).

273. **ad Graecas Calendas:** In Roman times, money that was owing had always to be paid on the first day (i.e. the Calends) of each month. However, since there were no Greek Calends, the expression 'ad Graecas Calendas' came to mean 'never'. Suetonius records that 'ad Graecas Calendas' was one of the Emperor Augustus' favourite expressions. In *Augustus*, 87, he writes,

" Cotidiano sermone quaedam frequentius et notabiliter usurpasse eum (i.e. Augustus), litterae ipsius autographae ostentant, in quibus identidem, cum aliquos numquam soluturos significare vult, 'ad Kalendas Graecas soluturos' ait."

277. Although no instructions are given here, it is obvious that at this point Philopinus makes his exit, since at 1.302 there is no stage-direction saying 'Intrat Philopinus'.

279- **Iam fremit Boreas...securo:** See Introduction, section V.
298.

304. **quasi utrem illius uterum:** The author plays upon the great resemblance in sound and appearance between the accusative cases of 'uter' (a wine-skin) and 'uterus' (the womb); the

humour is supplied by the diversity in meaning of these two words. However, the two things are similar inasmuch as they are both able to increase in size: a wine-skin swells when liquor is poured into it, and the womb expands with the growth of the foetus. (I translate 'uter' as balloon here, although, strictly speaking, this is something of an anachronism).

307. <u>At astra...mores tui</u>: MS. reads 'filia', but the accusative case seems to make better sense here. Philopinus now assumes the rôle of astrologer and, pretending to star-gaze, forecasts that Dawson will become the father of a baby daughter. It was a popular belief during the Middle Ages and later, that the positions of the Signs of the Zodiac and of the Planets with regard to the Signs, to one another, and to the Houses, exerted such a powerful influence over the affairs of mankind and the individual that it was possible to foretell what was to happen in the future by means of them, and to predict the destiny of any person by observing the conditions of the Heavens at the moment of his birth.

Philopinus also prophesies that Dawson will have a daughter because his 'mores', or constitution, points to this. Aristotle, upon whose works much sixteenth and seventeenth century medicine was based, states (<u>Generation of Animals</u>, <u>IV</u>, 2) that the physical condition of the parents at the time of conception can determine the sex of the child: older parents, he says, have a tendency to produce female offspring. Since Dawson is perhaps 'getting on in years', this may be the theory to which Philopinus is here alluding.

310–317. <u>Habebitis armum ovis...bonum</u>: See Introduction, section V.

320–321. <u>Nam devoratis...circulo</u>: Philopinus is not exaggerating when he says that the villagers of Hinksey eat more fat in a week, than the students do in the course of a whole year, for meals in hall were few and far between, and none were particularly lavish. There were only two meals a day: dinner at 11½ a.m. and supper at 5 or 6 p.m; in addition to these, there were also two small collations, regularly consisting of a pint of beer and a slice of bread. Moreover, the students were often served with 'food and meats' according to their 'rank, exertion and merit'. Consequently, the more senior members of the College, and those with higher degrees were better provided for at meal-times than the poor undergraduates! (See T. Fowler, <u>The History of Corpus Christi College</u>, pp. 50–2, and Ward, c.32.).

332. **penylesse bench**: This was the name given to a covered bench which in the past stood beside Carfax Church, in Oxford. The epithet 'penylesse' is probably derived from the fact that like similar open-air seats elsewhere, the bench was often the resort of tramps and other destitute travellers.

ACT 4

9. **adaperto capite**: 'Caput adaperire' was the Roman equivalent of taking off one's hat as a mark of respect and politeness to those higher in rank than oneself: Seneca, Epistulae Morales, LXIV, 10, writes,

> "Si consulem videro aut praetorem, omnia, quibus honor haberi honori solet faciam:equo desiliam, caput adaperiam, semita cedam:"

10. **Alisque nugis curialibus**: This is probably an allusion to the treatise De Nugis Curialium (Courtiers Triflings) written by Walter Mapes, (fl.1200), the mediaeval author and wit. It is a curious book, completely lacking in formal arrangement, and comprising for the most part legends from his native country (Wales), together with gossip and amusing tales of his life at Court. Mapes, nevertheless, shows himself to have a keen interest in, and to be well acquainted with, the

ancient classics, the christian fathers, and the current events of his own day.

(See D.N.B., s.v. Map or Mapes, Walter).

12. muscata nuce: In the sixteenth and seventeenth centuries, nutmeg was thought to have great medicinal properties, and was eaten more abundantly than it is today. Thomas Phaer, Regiment of Lyfe, (London, 1553), 6.v., says that 'to clarifie the dimnesse of the sight –

"Ye must use every daye to eate nutmigges."

15. quo communius, eo melius: cf. Ray, A Handbook of Proverbs, (London, 1666), p.45,

"Bonum, quo communius eo melius."

20. ad annos Nestoris: According to classical mythology, Nestor was the son of Neleus, and king of Pylos. He plays an important part in the Iliad, where Homer portrays him as a wise and respected, yet rather ineffectual statesman. He is always ready to counsel the leaders of the Greeks, Ulysses and Diomedes, but his advice is usually either full of platitudes, or else quite unsuccessful.

Nestor is said to have lived to a very great age. Ovid,

in Metamorphoses, XII, represents him as being more than two hundred years old. Nestor says (ll. 186-8),

"   si quem potuit spatiosa senectus
spectatorem operum multorum reddere, vixi
annos bis centum; nunc tertia vivitur aetas."

(For further information, see O.C.D., s.v. Nestor (1).).

fidicen ludit intus The hunt is up: "The hunt is up" was, according to R. Cotgrave, (A Dictionarie of the French and English Tongues (London, 1611), s.v. Resveil), the morning-song to a new bride. Some scholars have put forward the idea that this is what Juliet (Romeo and Juliet, III,v, ll.31-5) refers to, when, bidding Romeo to flee, she exclaims,

"Some say the lark and loathed toad change eyes;
O, now I would they had chang'd voices too!
Since arm from arm that voice doth us affray,
Hunting thee hence with hunts-up to the day.
O, now be gone!"

(See also Chappell, O.E.P.M., I, 86).

27. <u>quod sponte offertur vilescit</u>: MS. reads 'aufertur'; I emend to 'offertur', which seems to make better sense here. If a proverb, unknown.

30. <u>concentum bonum</u>: The author here uses the two meanings of 'concentus' simultaneously - (i) musical harmony, and (ii) agreement.

32. <u>plusquam δὶς διὰ πάσων discordes erimus</u>: A play on words: Doulerus is here trying to insinuate that the adjective 'discordes' is a compound of the Greek word 'dis' meaning 'twice', and the Latin 'chorda' - a chord, so that by this reasoning, 'discordes' means 'twice through all the chords' (i.e. a double octave in music), and is, therefore, exactly equivalent to the Greek phrase δὶς διὰ πάσων (disdiapason). However, Doulerus also hints at the true sense of 'discordes' - 'inharmonious' or 'disagreeing', - and so there is a double joke here since disdiapason in music gives rise to an extremely loud and harsh sound.

34. <u>Si pergat ludere; volumus eum deludere</u>: On account of the similarity in appearance between the words 'ludere' ('to play' - used in the sense 'to play a musical instrument') and 'deludere'

('to mock', or 'tease'), the second word seems to take on some of the meaning of the first, thereby producing a pun.

38. <u>Iniussus nunquam desistet</u>: cf. Horace, <u>Satires</u>, I, 3, 1.3,

"iniussi numquam desistant.".

40. <u>Coranto</u>: The Coranto, sometimes called the Courante, was a dance of very lively and rapid character. It was French in origin, and its name was derived from the French verb 'courir' - 'to run'. Like many other old dance types, the Coranto underwent a variety of changes in style and rhythm: in its Italian form, the Coranto's chief distinguishing marks were its incessant motion and triple time, but in France, the Coranto was a dance of duple rhythm. In the seventeenth century, it was in the country of its birth that the Coranto enjoyed its greatest vogue, reaching the peak of its popularity under Louis XIV. However, the Coranto was also danced in many other countries: Sir Toby Belch, in Shakespeare's <u>Twelfth Night</u> (I, iii,11.21-2) speaks of "coming home in a coranto." (See <u>O.C.M.</u>, s.v. Courante, and <u>G.D.M.</u>, s.v. Courante.)

40. **Spaniletto:** The Spagnoletto was an old Italian round dance, in which the male dancers clapped out the rhythm of the music with their hands against the palms of their female partners. The name of the dance suggests that it may have been Spanish in origin, dating from the period when Spain held Naples. The word 'spagnoletto' occurs in Elizabethan virginal music, attached to pieces that are either three-in-a-measure, or four-in-a-measure. (See O.C.M., s.v. Spagnoletto).

41. **Lavinianium:** There is no reference to any dance of this name in any of the standard works on sixteenth and seventeenth-century music. However, a song entitled 'From the fair Lavinian shore', - which has been attributed on manuscript evidence to the pen of Shakespeare, was, it seems, extremely popular in the seventeenth century. The music for the song was composed by Wilson, thought by some to be the Jack Wilson who acted in the plays of Shakespeare. It may well be, therefore, that the 'Lavinian', here mentioned, was a dance set to the tune of this song.

(See English Melodies from the 13th. to the 18th. Century - One Hundred Songs, edited by Vincent Jackson (London, 1910), p.92.).

41. Canarias: The Canary, a sprightly dance in three-in-a-measure or six-in-a-measure time. It has a very distinctive rhythm, the phrases all beginning on the first half of the measure, having a note of a beat and a half length. As its name suggests, the Canary probably originated in the Canary Islands, and the fact that it was thought in sixteenth and seventeenth-century England to be an old Spanish dance, performed in Spain to the music of the castanets, lends authority to this view. There are several references to this dance in the plays of Shakespeare: for example, Lafeu in All's Well that Ends Well (II, i, ll.72-4), relates how he has seen a medicine,

> "That's able to breathe life into a stone,
> Quicken a rock, and make you dance canary
> With sprightly fire and motion;"

(For further information, see O.C.M., s.v. Canaries, and G.D.M., s.v. Canarie).

43. Eandem semper canis cantilenam: cf. Dorio's words to Phaedria in Terence's Phormio, l. 495,

> "cantilenam eandem canis."

46. Si velit non tam nobis, quam ut sibi perplaceat: cf. the
Emperor Julian's remark in MISOPOGON, (BEARD-HATER) 338,

"εἶναι γάρ οἶμαι συμβαίνει τοῖς φαύλοις τήν
μουσικήν λυπηράς μέν τοῖς ἑτέροις, σφίσι
δ' αὐτοῖς ἡδίστας."

(I think it is always the case that inferior musicians, though they annoy their audiences, give very great pleasure to themselves.)

49-54. Non hinc diebus undecim...per ludos et res serias: See Introduction, section V.

56. Ex ungue leonem: cf. Erasmus, Adagia, II, 347D,

"Leonem ex unguibus aestimare ('Est...ex paucis multa, ex minimis maxima conjicere.')"

58-77. Vapores Phaebus bibit...Mihi negare potum: See Introduction, section V.

85. iam: There is an ink-blot on the MS. at this point, making the reading 'iam' doubtful.

89. **nonne iam animus tuus est in patinis?**: cf. Terence, *Eunuchus*, 1.817, where Sanga says,

   "iam dudum animus est in patinis."

90-91. **Probabo facile...patinis**: Doulerus sets out to prove by a syllogistic form of argument that the lute-player's heart 'lies in the dishes':

   PREMISE 1: ubi nummus, ibi est animus.
   PREMISE 2: At nummus est in patinis.
   CONCLUSION: Ergo animus est in patinis.

96-113. **O dulce nomen Oxonii...ut quiete redeamus domum**: The stage-directions state that Philopinus is to speak these lines - perhaps the most poetical in the whole play - "Oxonium contemplans". The audience, it seems, is to imagine that Philopinus is walking on the Hinksey Hills, enjoying the fine view of the city of Oxford, which can be obtained from their crest. The actor playing Philopinus would at this point probably come to the very front of the stage, and gaze far out over the audience, as though he were looking down from the hills, across the river, towards Oxford with its sky-line of spires and towers.

It was from the Hinksey Hills that the fifteenth century Flemish painter, Hoefnagle (1545-1601), drew what is thought to be the earliest of all known pictures of Oxford, and Turner, too, made this landscape the subject of his delightful painting, 'Oxford from Headington Hill'. (See Mallet, <u>III</u>, 218.)

97. <u>Tuumque multa turre pinnatum caput</u>: Matthew Arnold, in his poem <u>Thyrsis</u>, describes Oxford as

> "that sweet city with her dreaming spires"

108. <u>Areopagitae</u>: In ancient Greece, this was the title given to the members of the court of the Areopagus at Athens.

114-116. <u>O clara Veneris stella...Eadem vocaris Lucifer</u>: Since its greatest elongation is only 47°, Venus - the second planet in order from the sun - can never, save in high latitudes, be above the horizon for longer than three hours after sunset, and for the same amount of time before sunrise: it is, therefore, as even the ancients knew, both a 'morning star' and an 'evening star'. Cicero, in <u>De Deorum Natura</u>, II, 20, 53, writes,

"Infima est quinque errantium terraeque proxima stella Veneris, quae φωσφόρος Graece Latine dicitur Lucifer cum antegreditur solem, cum subsequitur autem "Ἕσπερος."

117-118. **exisque a Tethyos sinu...lacum:** A poetical reference to the Roman belief that when the sun set over the sea, it actually sank down into the waves. Ovid, *Metamorphoses*, II, ll.68-9, makes the Sun-God say,

"tunc etiam quae me subiectis excipit undis,
ne ferar in praeceps, Tethys solet ipsa vereri."

126. **quomodo:** MS. reads 'quodmodo'.

128. **suavitas:** MS. reads 'suaviatas'.

130-131. **Et hoc recipe...amandi:** There is no mention of any such love-potion in Ovid's *Ars Amatoria*, but Joanna, of course, does not know this.

143-144. **Est quid et ut dicis spiritus...ab Aeolo:** The author here uses the two meanings of 'spiritus' - (i) 'a spirit', and (ii) 'a blowing of air', or 'a breeze' - simultaneously. In classical mythology, Pluto was the god of the infernal regions - the abode of the spirits of the dead, and Aeolus was ruler of the winds. (See Vergil, Aeneid, I, 1.52f..)

145-146. Qui ventos congessit...Ithaca: 'Ventus' has a double entendre here: (i) 'a current of air', and (ii) 'flatulence'. These lines also allude to the tenth book of the Odyssey, where Homer describes how Ulysses and his men, as they were sailing home from Troy to Ithaca, were guests for a short time of Aeolus, lord of the winds. Before the Greeks left his island kingdom, Aeolus presented Ulysses with a skin-bag, in which he had imprisoned the force of all the winds, so that Ulysses might draw on their power, if he was becalmed during the remainder of his journey home. However, as the Greeks drew near to Ithaca, Ulysses fell into a deep sleep, and the crew, thinking that the skin-bag which Aeolus had given their king, must contain gold and silver, undid the sack. Instantly, all the winds came rushing forth and the fleet was blown far out to sea.

147-149. crudus et flatuosus cibus...unde quaerit exitum: cf. Regimen Sanitatis Salerni, (London, 1634), p.II,

"Quatuor ex vento veniunt in ventre retento,
Spasmus, hidrops, colica, vertigo quatuor ista."

149- **si loquamur apodictice...a posteriori:** A play on words: 'a
150. priori' and 'a posteriori', terms frequently used in the
field of logic and philosophy to express a judgement from
cause to effect, and from effect to cause respectively, are
here also given a second and more literal meaning, - 'from
the front', and 'from the rear'. The fact that Philopinus
employs this high-flown, scholarly language when talking
of such a low subject, adds greatly to the humour of the
speech.

151- **Triplex autem est crepandi genus...vel septicus:** 'Septicus'
161. is a doubtful reading - the hand of the writer becomes very
crabbed at this point in MS. Students of logic were taught
that all objects, or things, could be divided into various
classes and several subordinate species. Philopinus now
proceeds to apply these rules to the conception of 'crepitus'!

162- **Certe Tongilianus...Ex odore crepitus:** Possibly a reference to
163. Martial, *Epigrams*, XII, 88,

"Tongilianus habet nasum, scio, non nego. sed iam
nil praeter nasum Tongilianus habet."

164. **edictum Claudii:** The Emperor Claudius is alleged to have
contemplated an edict permitting guests to break wind and
to belch at table. Suetonius, **Claudius**, 32, says,

"Dicitur etiam meditatus edictum, quo veniam daret
flatum crepitumque ventris in convivio emittendi, cum
periclitatum quendam prae pudore ex continentia repperisset."

169. **Hoc est lac virginis:** 'lac virginis' has a double meaning
here: (i) maid's water, and (ii) mercury.

171- **Nec aversis radiis...sed te absente morior:** Doulerus addresses
172. Joanna as if she were the sun, and he - a plant, needing the
sunlight to aid its growth, and give it life.

187. **Res est ventosi plena fragoris amor:** cf. Ovid, **Heroides**, I, 1.12,

"res est solliciti plena timoris amor."

190- **O mea fragrantissima Rosamunda...soles:** An allusion to the legend
191. of 'Fair Rosamond', i.e. Rosamond Clifford (d.1176?), the
daughter of Walter de Clifford. She is thought to have been

acknowledged as the mistress of Henry II, in 1174. She was buried in the choir of Godstow Abbey, but later, in 1191 or thereabouts, her remains were moved to the Chapter House.

It is on these few known facts that the legend of Fair Rosamond is based. According to Stow, who follows Higden's version of the story, the legend related that

"Rosamond the fayre daughter of Walter Lord Clifford, concubine to Henry II (poisoned by Queen Elianor as some thought) dyed at Woodstocke where King Henry had made for her a house of wonderful working, so that no man or woman might come to her but he that was instructed by the King. This house after some was named Labyrinthus, or Daedalus worke, wrought like unto a knot in a garden, called a mase; but it was commonly said that lastly the queene came to her by a clue of thridde or silke, and so dealt with her that she lived not long after: but when she was dead, she was buried at Godstow in an house of nunnes, beside Oxford, with these verses upon her tombe:

'Hic jacet in tumba Rosa mundi, non rosa munda:
Non redolet, sed olet, quae redolere solet.'"

The story is also the subject of a ballad by Deloney, included in Percy's *Reliques*, and in 1592, S. Daniel published a poem in rhyme-royal, entitled *The Complaint of Rosamond*. Addison, too, was familiar with the legend, and composed an opera called *Rosamond*(1707). (See *O.C.E.L.*, s.v. Rosamond, Fair).

195. *Ubi sunt isti generosi generosissimi?*: MS. reads 'generosisimi.' The author employs the word 'generosus' first as a substantive, and then as an adjective, in order to produce a play on words.

206-207. *dumque antrorsum vomit...aegrare aegre tulit*: Again the author manipulates his vocabulary so as to add a touch of humour to the dialogue: there is a comical contrast between the phrases 'antrorsum vomit' and 'gemit retrorsum'; while the juxtaposition of 'aegrare' and 'aegre' constitutes a pun.

210-211. *salsa qualitas sit ingrata stomacho...ventri dixeram*: The words 'stomachus', 'ventriculus' and 'venter', have, of course, virtually the same meaning: Philopimus is simply trying to blind Dawson with science!

212- **Deus vortat olli bene...rusticel**: 'vortat olli' is an
213. example of Old Latin: the change from vo- > ve- before r,
s, and t, took place about the middle of the second century
B.C., (according to Quintilian, **Institutiones Oratoriae**, I,
7,25, the spelling of 'vert-' for 'vort-' was first
introduced by Scipio Africanus), and the demonstrative
pronoun 'olle' was later modified to 'ille'. Evidently
Philopimus, like many Romans of Cicero's day, is an advocate
of 'urbanitas' - that is, elegance and correctness in speech,
since he feigns surprise and disgust at Dawson's reversion to
archaisms, and accuses him of 'rusticitas'.

227. **Asinus nascitur non fit**: cf. the well-known saying,

"poeta nascitur non fit."

234- **ter aut novies Repetitis verbis**: Multiples of three and nine
235. had a special significance for witches and magicians, since
three is the first 'rounded' number, beginning one of the most
powerful energy forces, known as the 3-6-9 cycle. To
Pythagoreans, three was the perfect number, representing the
beginning, the middle and the end.

The fondness of witches for odd numbers can be illustrated from the works of Ovid. In *Metamorphoses*, XIV, 1.58, for example, he describes how Circe repeats her spell thrice nine times,

"ter noviens carmen magico demurmurat ore."

Again, in *Metamorphoses*, VII, 11.189-91, the importance of the number three in the practice of witchcraft is displayed by Medea's actions,

"ter se convertit, ter sumptis flumine crinem
inroravit aquis ternisque ululatibus ora
solvit"

Similarly, in Shakespeare's *Macbeth* (I,iii, 11.35-7), the three hags join hands and dance round in a circle nine times, - that is, three rounds for each witch - a charm to aid their wicked designs,

"Thrice to thine, and thrice to mine,
And thrice again, to make up nine.
Peace! The charm's wound up."

238. **ut solebat Gyges**: See above, note to III, l.160.

239. **rarescas, ut tandem evanescas**: MS. reads 'rarasces, ut tandem evenescas.'

240- **quo minus tegeris...nebula**: This is an allusion to *Aeneid*, I,
241. ll.411-14, where Vergil relates how, as they were about to enter the city of Carthage, Aeneas and his companion, Achates, were enveloped in a blanket of mist by the goddess Venus, in order to prevent their being recognised,

> "at Venus obscuro gradientis aëre saepsit,
> et multo nebulae circum dea fudit amictu,
> cernere ne quis eos neu quis contingere posset
> molirive moram aut veniendi poscere causas."

243. **Fiat!**: The words 'fiat, fiat, fiat!' always formed part of the prayers used in witchcraft and black magic (see Scot, 352).

245- **Farbus...Bumbo**: These lines are written in the form of an
247. acrostic, in which the first line reads the same across as down:

FARBUS, BUMBO, DOLON,

BUMBO, Dolon, Farbus,

DOLON, Farbus, Bumbo.

The effect produced is that of the metrical charms or rhymes, so often employed by conjurers and sorcerers.

255. **Iam...Copernicus**: A reference to the Polish astronomer, Mikolaj Kopernik (Copernicus is the Latinised form of the name), who was the first to expound the heliocentric theory of the universe, i.e. that the earth revolves in a circle about the sun; hence Philopinus' words "terrae motus".

Copernicus was born on February 19th., 1473, at Thorn in Prussian Poland. For several years he studied mathematical science at the University of Cracow, under Albert Brudzewski. Later he moved to Bologna, where he specialized in canon law, and also attended lectures on astronomy, given by Domenico Maria Novara. At Rome, in 1500, Copernicus won great renown as a lecturer, and the following year he entered the medical school at Padua, where he stayed for a further four years, until 1505, having gained in the meantime a doctor's degree in canon law at Ferrara(1503). Copernicus then returned to Poland and

resided at the episcopal palace of Heilsberg as physician
to his uncle, who was then bishop of Ermeland. After the
bishop's death, Copernicus repaired to Frauenburg, to the
cathedral of which city he had been appointed canon in
1497, and there carried out his capitular duties.

Despite his multifarious occupations, Copernicus,
nevertheless, still found time to develop an entirely new
system of astronomy. He began his great work at Heilsberg;
and at Frauenberg, from 1513 onwards, he attempted with
the few instruments he possessed, to prove his theories by
observation. The results of his research he set down in a
treatise entitled De Revolutionibus Orbium Caelestium, which
was printed at Nuremberg in 1543. The first printed copy
reached Copernicus on his death-bed, for towards the end of
the previous year he had succumbed to paralysis and apoplexy.
He died on May 24th., 1543. At first his theories were
considered merely hypothetical, but in the course of time they
came to be accepted.

The De Revolutionibus Orbium Caelestium consists of
six books. Book I deals with the heliocentric theory of the
universe in broad outline, and the evidence in support of it
is also given. The remaining five books discuss in greater
detail various aspects of the theory, such as the motion of
the earth, the precession of the equinoxes, the moon's motion

and the motion of the planets.

Prior to the publication of the Copernican theory, it was believed that the earth was the fixed centre of the universe and that the sun and the other planets all circled round it. This geocentric theory of the universe had been accepted by philosophers, theologians and scientists alike, for thousands of years, largely because it was laid down in the works of Aristotle. Admittedly, some of the ancients had thought that the earth revolved and even that it was in constant motion, but their ideas were dismissed as pure philosophical speculation. No one before Copernicus had tried to find a reasoned justification for the movement of the stars, or to work out a system (i.e. the solar system), whereby the complicated wanderings of the planets might be explained.

The great importance of Copernicus' work was that it completely changed man's outlook and ideas on the universe. Copernicus is frequently referred to as the 'Father of Modern Astronomy'. (For further information, see N.B.U., s.v. Copernic (Nicolas)).

270-272. ego in aulas principum...cognoscerem: cf. the Souldan's words about the magic cap in Dekker's play, Old Fortunatus, II, I, 1.90f.,

"By this I steale to every Princes court,
And heare their private counsels..."

(I quote from *The Dramatic Works of Thomas Dekker*, edited by Fredson Bowers, 4 vols. (Cambridge University Press, 1953.).).

279. *Et comoediam...tragoediam*: cf. Plautus, *Amphitruo*, Prologue, 11.52-5,

"...contraxistis frontem, quia tragoediam
dixi futuram hanc? deus sum, commutavero.
eandem hanc, si voltis, faciam ex tragoedia
comoedia ut sit omnis isdem vorsibus."

289. *Omnia...olet*: This is a direct quotation from Martial, *Epigrams*, VI, 93, 1.12.

302. *Toga mihi est singularis numeri...pileum*: Students were required by the College Statutes to wear the clerical dress, i.e. cap and gown, at all times - whether within the University or away from it. Once a year, the College, at its own expense, furnished each student with a gown of uniform colour, but of differing size and price, depending

upon the position which each individual student held in the College. Doulerus would, therefore, possess only one gown, and if he were to lose it, would be committing a serious breach of the College rules. (See Ward, c.28).

303-
304. Nec audeo mutare...In argentum vertere: A play on words, similar to that in I, l.81, where Philopinus speaks of turning the square into the round. Also, cf. Horace, Epistles, I, I, l.100,

"... mutat quadrata rotundis"

306-
307. Sed ego vos deducam...in numellas suas: Pigeon seems here to be under the impression that the University had its own judge, who could mete out punishment to unruly students. However, the only persons allowed to take disciplinary action against those who misbehaved were the students' own tutors, and the only punishments which they could inflict were as follows: deprivation of commons, flogging, confinement to the library with the task of copying out the most important parts of some major scholarly work, being put on a diet of dry bread and water, and finally expulsion, seldom resorted to. (See T. Fowler, History of Corpus Christi College, p.54).

309. <u>Ubi est tuus iam familiaris spiritus?</u>: All witches and sorcerers were thought to have a 'familiar', or attendant spirit. W.Gunnyon, <u>Illustrations of Scottish History, Life and Superstition</u>, (Glasgow, 1879), p.322, remarks that witches "are hellish monsters, brewing hell-broth, having cats and toads for familiars." Indeed, the cat was said to be the form most commonly assumed by the familiar spirits of witches: for instance, in <u>Macbeth</u>, I, i, 1.8, the first witch says,

"I come, Graymalkin!"

and later, (IV, i, 1.I),

"Thrice the brinded cat hath mew'd."

(Intrat ANNA): This stage-direction should read 'Intrat ANNA et IOANNA, for Joanna, in fact, left the stage at 1.292, yet at 1.313 - with no mention of her having re-entered she is present once again, taking part in the dialogue.

314. <u>Malum supervenit malo</u>: cf. Donatus on Terence, <u>Phormio</u>, 11.544-5,

...in malo aliud malum"

317. **Nostis...in infima regione?**: The phrase 'in infima regione' is used here with a double meaning: (i) 'in the lower part of the college' - the students' quarters, and (ii) 'in the Lower World' - the abode of the devil and other evil spirits.

318. **theatrum**: John Alday, translator of Boiastuaü, prided himself on being the first to use the word 'theatre' in an English book.

324. **male parta male dilabuntur**: A proverbial expression: cf. Plautus, Poenulus, 1.844, "male partum male disperit", and Cicero, Philippics, II, 27, 65,

> "Sed, ut est apud poëtam nescio quem, 'Male parta male dilabuntur.'"

Cf. too, the English saying "Ill gotten goods never prosper".

This proverb is alluded to by the King in Shakespeare's Henry VI (Pt.3) (II, ii, ll.45-6),

> "But, Clifford, tell me, didst thou never hear
> That things ill got had ever bad success?"

328. <u>Etiamsi...de pecuniā</u>: A play on words: 'credere' is used first in the sense 'to entrust', and secondly, with the meaning 'to believe'.

335. <u>coronatum Gallicum</u>: 'a French crown', a coin worth about 4s.6d. (22½p.)

336. <u>properamus</u>: MS. reads 'properaramus.'

337-
340. <u>Cordis mei custos...aquae</u>: If a quotation from classical literature, unknown.

343. <u>Imo volo, sed nolo: at iterum nolo</u>: cf. Martial, <u>Epigrams</u>, III, 90,

"Volt, non volt dare Galla mihi, nec dicere possum, quod volt et non volt, quid sibi Galla velit."

Similarly, Julia in the <u>Two Gentlemen of Verona</u> (I, ii, ll.55-6) says,

"Since maids, in modesty, say 'No' to that Which they would have the profferer construe 'Ay'."

347-
348. <u>Subit...vultus</u>: These lines are taken directly from Statius, <u>Thebaid</u>, II, ll.232-4.

ACT 5

6. **puer mihi serviens**: 'Fagging' was not unknown in the Oxford colleges of the sixteenth and seventeenth centuries. Fellows and Scholars slept two in a room, i.e. a Fellow and a Scholar together, and since there is no mention in the Statutes of bed-makers, or attendants for these rooms, it seems more than likely that the beds were made, and the rooms kept tidy by the junior occupant. Moreover, during meal-times, at the Scholars' table, the waiters were to be taken from amongst the Scholars themselves: they took it in turns - two a week - to carry out their duties. These various tasks would not have been looked upon as any more degrading than the son of a gentleman serving as a page in a great house, - a common occurrence at that time.

Later, servitors were introduced: these were poor students, (they are designated as 'serviens', or 'pauper puer' in the Buttery Books), who, having matriculated, attended on the richer students. Sometimes, of course, noblemen brought their own servants with them from home. (See T.Fowler, *The History of Corpus Christi College*, pp. 50-51).

8. **comaediae**: MS. reads 'comodiae'.

8-9. **Qui...fugant:** It was the custom, when a play was performed at a University college, for certain students to be appointed 'stage-keepers', or stewards. Their job was to ensure that the proceedings were as orderly as possible, since people flocked in large numbers to see the college plays, and those who were refused admission, often began rioting and throwing stones. The stage-keepers wore visors and brandished clubs with which to defend themselves, should the need arise; they also carried torches to guide those who had been formally invited to the performance, across the dark court-yards. It appears from these lines (8-9) that freshmen were not admitted to the plays, and that the stewards had to keep them from the doors. (For further information about the riots which took place at the time of the plays, and the precautions taken against their breaking out, see G.C.Moore Smith, *College Plays*, pp. 45-48).

10. **Doctor Forman:** i.e. Simon Forman (1552-1611), the astrologer and quack doctor. Having been left penniless at his father's death, he is said to have entered Magdalen College, Oxford, in 1573, as a 'poor scholar'. In the year 1579, Forman claimed that he possessed miraculous powers: "I did prophesy", he writes in his diary, "the truth of many things which afterwards came to pass, and the very spirits were subject to me."

Eventually, in 1583, after a very chequered career and a spell in gaol, Forman set up in business in London as an astrologer. Gradually, he built up a large, but disreputable practice, - his clientele consisting chiefly of ladies of the Court. He was imprisoned on various occasions at the instigation of medical and other authorities. In 1588, he began publicly to practise necromancy and to call angels and spirits; whilst in 1594, he embarked on a series of experiments with the philosopher's stone, and also compiled a book on magic. These activities, however, did not prevent him from being granted a licence to practise medicine by the University of Cambridge in 1603.

One of Forman's works, The Grounds of the Longitude, was published in 1591, and among his manuscripts, which came into the possession of the Ashmolean Museum, is The Booke of Plaies, which contains the earliest account of the performances of Macbeth (1610), The Winter's Tale (1611), and Cymbeline (1610/11).

In 1615, four years after Forman's death, at the trial of those accused of the murder of Sir Thomas Overbury, a book in the doctor's own hand-writing was produced as evidence. In it were discovered the names of all Forman's female clients, together with details of their intrigues with various gentlemen of the Court. Lord Chief Justice Coke was about to read aloud the contents of the book, when he noticed the name of his own wife was amongst them!

Forman is often referred to in English Literature.[1] Ben Jonson, for example, in his play, Epicene (IV, I, 148-50), mentions Forman's philtres: Daup. Eugenie remarks to True-Wit,

"I would say thou had'st the best philtre i' the world, and couldst doe more then madame MEDEA, or Doctor FOREMAN."

(In my quotations from Jonson, I use The Works of Ben Jonson, edited by C.H.Herford and Percy Simpson, 11 vols. (Oxford,1937).).

Similarly, in Richard Niccols' poem, Overbury's Vision (1616), Overbury is made to say that he often went across the river to Lambeth, where,

"Forman was, that fiend in humane shape,
That by his art did act the devill's ape."

(I quote from Sir Thomas Overburies Vision, ed. by R.N.Oxon (1616)). (See D.N.B., s.v. Forman, Simon.).

11. **per terminos categorematicos, et syncategorematicos:** These are terms used in that branch of philosophy, known as logic: 'categorematicus', i.e. categorematical, is an adjective applied in logic to a word capable of being used by itself as a term. On the other hand, 'syncategorematicus', i.e. syncategorematical, as the prefix 'syn' suggests, is the very opposite of 'categorematicus', and is used to describe a word which cannot stand by itself as a term, but only in conjunction with another word or words, e.g. a sign of quantity (like ALL, SAME, NO), or an adverb, preposition, or conjunction.

12. **Per sensum analogicum, tropologicum et similia:** viz. the figures of speech: analogy, trope and simile.

29-36. **Falsissimum est...iusserit:** That witchcraft was widely practised and believed in ('plurimi serviunt diabolo') during the sixteenth and seventeenth centuries, is clear from the large number of court cases held about this time to deal with those thought to have been dabbling in the black art, from the careful revision of the laws governing the practice of magic, undertaken in the reign of Elizabeth (see below, note to 11.39-41), and from the vast amount of literature written on the subject at this period, such as Reginald Scot's monumental work, The Discoverie of Witchcraft (1584). Contrary to what Nichades tells Pigeon - 'Paucissimi imperant (sc.diabolo)' - the fact that numerous characters in stories and legends concerning the devil, often succeed quite brilliantly in cheating and deceiving the Fiend, seems to disprove this theory.

Similarly, although Nichades assures the innkeeper that it is not necessary to make any bargain with the devil in order to enlist his aid, there were many who thought that to practise the black art effectively, one had first to come to some agreement with the Evil One: cf. Marlowe's Dr.Faustus. Scot (p.55) explains how witches made such pacts with the devil. There are, he says, two kinds of bargain: (i) solemn and public, and (ii) secret and private. Solemn and public is when the witches come together at a pre-arranged time, see the devil in visible form, and speak familiarly with him. The second type of pact Scot describes thus (p.5y),

"The maner of their private league is said to be, when the devil invisible, and sometimes visible in the midst of the people talketh with them privately, promising that if they will followe his counsell, he will supplie all their necessities, and make all their endevours prosperous: and so beginneth with small matters; whereunto they consent privilie, and come not into the fairies assemblie."

As Nichades rightly says - 'Ritibus et verbis etenim constringitur daemonis potentia' - it was also believed that the binding of an evil spirit's power could only be accomplished by uttering certain magic words (see Scot, p.347). Nichades also mentions that the black art had its good uses, too, such as healing the sick, and recovering stolen property. It is interesting to note that Simon Forman (see above, note to 1.10), an acknowledged necromancer, is said to have cured one Henry Jonson of London, of a pulmonary complaint, and to have spent a year at Quidhampton, healing 'sick and lame folk'. Forman was, moreover, an expert at tracking thieves, and discovering the whereabouts of stolen treasure by means of 'horary' speculations.

37. Haec...veteris monachi: Many mediaeval treatises on witchcraft and its evils, were, in fact, written by monks. The authors of the Malleus Maleficarum (1486), - Heinrich Kramer (Henricus Institoris) and James Sprenger - for example, were both Dominican friars. A Hammer for Witches was translated by the Rev. Montague Summers, and was first printed in 1928.

39. **Loquetur ipsa res**: cf. Cicero, *Pro Milone*, XX, 53,

"res loquitur ipsa, iudices, quae semper valet plurimum."

39. **loqui**: MS. reads 'Liqui'.

39-41. **Sed iurabis...nec aliquid alicui dicturum**: Although Nichades is only pretending to practise black magic here, he would not, nevertheless, wish Pigeon to publicize the fact, since the penalties inflicted upon anyone found, - or thought to be - dabbling in necromancy were extremely high. In the reign of Elizabeth I, for example, the laws governing the practice of witchcraft were revised: under the new Act, invocation and conjuration of evil spirits for any purpose whatsoever was to be regarded as a felony. Moreover, witchcraft, enchantment, charm and sorcery, were to be divided into three main classes: (i) bewitching to death, (ii) injury to person, goods or cattle, and (iii) looking for treasure, recovering lost property, ATTEMPTING to provoke unlawful love, or to kill, maim, or cause injury to any person. The first of these crimes was to be punishable by death; while the second and third were judged to be deserving of a combination of prison and pillory for first offenders, of death or life sentence for second offenders.

(For further information, see <u>Witchcraft</u>, edited by Barbara Rosen, Stratford-upon-Avon Library, 6, p.23).

43-44. <u>Dic vero qualis apparebit...Aut masculosi felis?</u>: MS. reads 'fellis'. There was a popular superstition in sixteenth and seventeenth-century England, that the devil and, indeed, other evil spirits, could assume many different forms (see above, note to II, 11.281-2). It was thought that they could appear not only in human guise, but also in the shape of various animals: T.A.Spalding, (<u>Elizabethan Demonology</u>, (London, 1880), p.49) writes, "the forms of the whole of the animal kingdom appear to have been at their (i.e. the devils') disposal." The notion that the toad and the cat were shapes frequently assumed by the devil is not surprising —since the former was considered evil and venomous, capable of spitting poison at all who came near it (Milton compares Satan to a toad in <u>Paradise Lost</u>, IX, 11.799-802), and the latter to be closely associated with witchcraft (see above, note to IV, 1.309). However, Nichades' suggestion that the devil might appear as a mouse - that 'wee timorous beastie' - is rather strange, unless there is some connection here with the fairy tale of <u>Puss in Boots</u>, in which the wicked ogre, boasting that he can transform himself into any animal he chooses, turns into a mouse, whereupon the cat pounces and eats him up.

46–48. *quo pingi solet...et cornibus longioribus quam tua sunt*: A stock description of the devil. As John Brand comments (*Popular Antiquities*, 3 vols.(London, 1849), II, 517-521), in every folk-tale and legend in which the devil appears, he is always represented with a cloven hoof. In pictures, too, he is seldom ever shown without one. There is a reference to the belief that the devil had a cloven foot in Massinger's play, *Virgin Martyr*: Harpax, an evil spirit, who has disguised himself as a secretary, tells Theophilus, III, iii,

> "I'll tell you what now of the devil,
> He's no such horrid creature; cloven-footed,
> Black, saucer-eyed, his nostrils breathing fire,
> As these lying Christians make him."

Butler, in his *Hudibras*, (Pt. I, canto I), writes,

> " Whether the serpent, at the fall,
> Had cloven feet, or none at all."
> (ll.183-4).

T. R. Nash, in his commentary on these lines, remarks that the curse upon the serpent, "upon thy belly shalt thou go" (Genesis, III, v, 14), indicates a loss of some privilege which he previously enjoyed. It has been conjectured that prior to the Fall, the serpent had feet, and that this is why St. Basil talks of his walking erect like a man, and having the use of speech.

The devil was usually depicted with horns because popular belief held that the shape he appeared in most often was that of a goat.

48. *cornibus longioribus quam tua sunt*: Nichades here hints that Pigeon is a cuckold.

49. *Erit pullatus...academicis*: Students, of course, wore gowns of a dark, sombre colour.

50. *Unguibus erit aduncis...hospitibus*: Innkeepers, it seems have always had a reputation for being grasping and dishonest. Horace, *Satires*, I, I, 1.29, speaks of the 'perfidus caupo', and again, ibid, I, 5, 1.4, he describes how, on his journey from Rome to Brindisi, he passed through Appi Forum, and found it 'differtum nautis, cauponibus atque malignis.'

51. **Habebit togam...literas:** Pigeon implies that students are devils in disguise. However, there is a touch of dramatic irony here, since - unbeknown to Pigeon - the part of the devil will, in the masquerade that follows, be played by a student, and therefore, in that sense, the devil '<u>will</u> sport a cap and gown'!

53. **primo ducendus est circulus:** In the practice of black magic, a chalk circle was always drawn on the ground, before the calling forth of any spirit. Inside the circle were written, in symbolical form, the names of the planets and the signs of the Zodiac (see below, note to L.55). The purpose of the circle was to ensure that the spirit, constrained to appear by the force of the symbols therein, once conjured forth, could only exert its power and influence within the area defined by the circle. The fact that Nichades draws his magic circle with charcoal - 'carbone circulu describit' - instead of chalk, suggests that he is making fun of the whole ritual! (See Scot, p.328).

(<u>Induit pileum...describit</u>): In MS. this stage-direction occurs between 1.52 and 1.53, but it makes better sense if it is placed directly <u>after</u> 1.53, and not <u>before</u> it.

54. **Agis circulatorem optime**: The author here plays on the meaning of 'circulator': usually the word is used in the sense 'mountebank' or 'quack', but since Nichades has just referred to a 'circulus', 'circulator' seems to take on some of the meaning of the latter word, so that it has in effect a double entendre: (i) 'mountebank', and (ii) 'drawer of circles.'

55. **Iam disponantur planetarum domus et pomaeria**: Inside the circle, in symbolical form, were written the names of the planets, together with the twelve signs of the Zodiac, their dispositions, aspects and government. The order in which the symbols were drawn varied according to the particular type of spirit which the necromancer wished to conjure forth. Scot gives examples of the several symbols used and their different combinations in The Discoverie of Witchcraft, p.331.

(**Ducit characteres**): In MS. this stage-direction is given *before* 1.55. However, as Nichades does not begin to carry out the actions here indicated *until* 1.55, it is clear that this particular stage-direction should be placed *after*, and not before 1.55.

(Ter pede terram concutit, candida virga capita munit): Nichades stamps on the floor three times as a sign to his accomplices waiting in the room below, that he is about to commence his 'conjuration'. He waves a wand over Pigeon's head and his own as a form of purification rite: one of the chief requirements in the practice of witchcraft was that all those taking part in the ceremony should be in a state of cleanliness and purity. This recalls, perhaps, the way in which at a Roman sacrifice, the priest would purify those present by sprinkling drops of water over them with an olive branch. This is described by Vergil, Aeneid, VI, ll.229-31,

"idem ter socios pura circumtulit unda,
spargens rore levi et ramo felicis olivae,
lustravitque viros, dixitque novissima verba."

58. ululant canes: See above, note to III, ll.152-3.

62. En nocte caeca bubo feralis gemit: cf. Vergil, Aeneid, IV. ll.462-3,

"solaque culminibus ferali carmine bubo
saepe queri..."

63-69. **Latratque trino tartari canis sono,...et regis inferni domos:**
These lines could be termed a pastiche of Underworld motifs.
Roman poets, when seeking to paint a vivid picture of the
realm of gloomy Dis for their readers, invariably mentioned
Cerberus, the triple-headed hound of hell; the three Furies;
the poor wretches, like Ixion, Sisyphus and Tityos, condemned
to eternal torment for crimes committed whilst they were alive;
the shades of the dead, 'as numerous as the leaves that fall
from the trees in autumn'; and the all-pervading darkness and
insubstantiality of the infernal regions. To describe the Lower
World in this way was a form of literary convention, and examples
of this standardized mythological representation of hell can be
found in the works of almost all the great classical writers:
see, for instance, Homer, Odyssey, XI; Vergil, Aeneid, VI,
1.268f.; Horace, Odes, III, II, 11.15-24: Seneca, Hercules
Furens, 11. 750-759, 1.783f., Agamemnon, 11.12-21. The author
of Mercurius Rusticans, therefore, had several models on which
to base his own description of the Underworld.

72-78. **Mos, flos, ros, et Tros,...Grampas, exurgas:** With the general
structure of this passage and the ideas expressed, cf. Marlowe,
Doctor Faustus, I, 3, 11.8-24,

"Within this circle is Jehova's name,
Forward and backward anagrammatis'd;
Th' abbreviated names of holy saints,
Figures of every adjunct to the heavens,
And characters of signes, and erring stars,
By which the spirits are enforc'd to rise:
Then fear not, Faustus, to be resolute,
And try the utmost magic can perform".

'Sint mihi Dii Acherontis propitii! Valeat numen triplex Jehovae! Ignis, Aeris, Aquae, Terrae spiritus, salvete! Orientis Princeps, Belzebub, inferni ardentis monarcha, et Demogorgon, propitiamus vos, ut appareat, et surgat Mephistophilis. Quid tu moraris? per Jehovam, Gehennam, et consecratam aquam quam nunc spargo, signumque crucis quod nunc facio, et per vota nostra, ipse nunc surgat nobis dicatus Mephistophilis!'

72. <u>Mos...fons</u>: This is a quotation from Lily, <u>Latin Grammar</u>, p.81, where the masculine monosyllabic nouns of the third declension are listed as follows,

"Sal, sol, ren, & splen,car,ser,vir,vas vadis,as, mas,
Bes, cres, pres, & pes, glis gliris habens genetivo:
Mos, flos, ros & tros, mus, dens, mons,pons, simul & fons,
Seps pro serpente, gryps, Thrax, rex, rex gregis, & Phryx."

73. <u>Barbara...Ferio</u>: These were the famous mnemonic lines used by the Schoolmen of the Middle Ages to summarize the teachings of Aristotle on the subject of logic. The vowels of the words Barbara...Ferio signify the nature of the major and minor premises and conclusion of the various moods of the syllogism: A - a universal affirmative, E - a universal negative, I - a particular affirmative, and O - a particular negative. (For further information, see <u>O.C.C.L.</u>, s.v. Aristotle (3)).

74. <u>Belimoth</u>: i.e. Behemoth, a Hebrew word used in the Bible (e.g. Job, XL, v.15-40) to describe all large mammalia, but more especially the hippopotamus. It may also have been the name given to a mythological, dragon type creature. (See <u>Encyclopaedia Biblica</u>, s.v. Behemoth). Here it refers specifically to the devil.

74-75. <u>per illa duodecim monstra...cum sodalibus</u>: viz. the twelve signs of the Zodiac.

76-77. <u>Per caelestem heptarchiam...Faeminarum</u>: i.e. the seven planets: Mercury, Mars, Jupiter, Saturn and Sol (male); and Venus and Luna (female). (Uranus, Neptune and Pluto were, of course, unknown until comparatively recent times, since they can only be seen with the aid of a very powerful telescope.)

77. <u>per piel et puel per hiphil et hophil</u>: Piel and pual, hiphil and hophil are terms used in Hebrew grammar to describe the Causative and Intensive forms of the verbs, respectively.

78. <u>Et trigonum et tetragono</u>: Trigon and tetragon are both terms used in astrology. T.R.Nash, in the notes to his edition of Butler's <u>Hudibras</u> (II, 67, n.7), says that "The twelve signs in astrology are divided into four trigons, or triplicities, each denominated from the con-natural element: so they are three fiery (sc.signs), three airy, three watery, and three earthy.

       Fiery   -   Aries, Leo, Sagittarius.
       Earthly -   Taurus, Virgo, Capricornus.
       Airy   -   Gemini, Libra, Aquarius.
       Watery -   Cancer, Scorpio, Pisces."

Therefore, when the three superior planets met in Cancer, Scorpio, or Pisces, a watery trigon was formed; when in Aries, Leo, or Sagittarius, a fiery one. Indeed, the meeting of the three upper planets in a fiery sign was thought, in the sixteenth and seventeenth centuries, to portend rage and contention. This idea is referred to in Shakespeare's Henry IV, (Pt.2), (II, iv, 11.253-7),

> PRINCE: Saturn and Venus this year in conjunction! what says th'almanac to that?
>
> POINS: And look whether the fiery Trigon, his man, be not lisping to his master's old tables, his note-books, his counsel-keeper."

Tetragon is the name given in astrology to the square, or quadrate aspect, of two planets when they are $90°$ distant from one another relatively to the earth.

78. Grampas: i.e. grampus, a type of killer dolphin, which breathes by a spout-hole on the top of the head. The word is also often applied to a person given to puffing and blowing, but it is evidently used here as another name for the devil.

78. **exurgas**: This was the usual command addressed to an evil spirit, when it was being conjured forth. Cf. Faustus' words in the conjuration scene in Marlowe's famous tragedy, (I, 3, 11.23-24),

"   ipse nunc surgat nobis
    dicatus Mephistophilis!"

79. *Suspicias in hoc vitro triangulo*: Scot (p.342) gives full details of how witches set about enclosing a spirit within a crystal stone. First, he says, there had to be a new moon, and all those taking part in the ritual had to wear fresh, clean clothes, and if men, to be newly shaven. They were to fast all day before the ceremony, living only on a diet of bread and water. They were also to go to Confession, and for two days prior to the conjuration, were to say the seven psalms and repeat the litany. Scot then describes the form of the prayer that was recited at such a ceremony. (For further information about the use of crystals in black magic, see above, note to II, 11.178-180).

81-82. **Volvola...feloni:** A nonsensical rhyme.

   excitatur flamma: MS. reads 'exitatur'.

85. **Extra circulum nihil est periculi:** The evil spirit's power and influence could not extend beyond the limits of the circle, and so there was no danger to those standing outside it.

86. **Foh! Nonne iam oderaris aerem faetidum:** Doubtless a bawdy allusion to the remark made by Pigeon in 1.84!

88-102. **Iterum coniuro te...Horridam sordido:** In rhythm and structure these lines could almost be a parody of Milton, *Comus*, ll.867-882, in which Sabrina, the nymph, is summoned forth with these words,

> "Listen, and appear to us,
> In name of great Oceanus,
> By the earth-shaking Neptune's mace,
> And Tethys' grave majestic pace;
> By hoary Nereus' wrinkled look,
> And the Carpathian wizard's hook;

> By scaly Triton's winding shell,
> And old soothsaying Glaucus' spell;
> By Leucothea's lovely hands,
> And her son that rules the strands,
> By Thetis' tinsel-slippered feet,
> And the songs of Sirens sweet;
> By dead Parthenope's dear tomb,
> And fair Ligea's golden comb,
> Wherewith she sits on diamond rocks
> Sleeking her soft alluring looks;"

93-94. <u>filiae Danai miserrimae</u>: A reference to the legend of the Danaids, the daughters of Danaus. They stabbed their husbands to death on their wedding-night, and as a punishment for their cruel deed, were condemned, in the Lower World, to try forever to fill with water a jar which had holes in the bottom. Aeschylus, the Greek tragic poet, made the story of the Danaids the subject of his play, <u>Suppliants</u>. (See <u>O.C.D.</u>, s.v. Danaus).

(*Exurgit Daemon, ho, ho, ho!*): The exclamation 'O ho, O ho!' was, according to George Steevens, in his edition of *The Plays of William Shakespeare*, 9 vols. (London, 1805)(I, 25, note,)constantly appropriated by the writers of the old mystery and morality plays to the devil. In Shakespeare's *The Tempest*, (I, ii, 11.349-51), Caliban, when accused by Prospero of attempting "to violate The honour of my child", replies thus,

> "O ho, O ho! Would't had been done.
> Thou didst prevent me; I had peopl'd else
> This isle with Calibans."

103. *An vigilans somnio?*: cf. Plautus, *Captivi*, 1.848,

    HEGIO: Hic vigilans somniat.

104. *Deus bone, miserere mei*: One can almost hear the impassioned pleas of the young St. Augustine in these words.

105- *Opaca...specu*: This is a direct quotation from Seneca,
106.
    Agamemnon, 11.1-2.

107- <u>Ubi colla nigris Cerberus iactat iubis...accrescens iecur:</u>
112.
    cf. Seneca, <u>Agamemnon</u>, ll.12-21,

>"nonne vel tristes lacus
>incolere satius, nonne custodem Stygis
>trigemina nigris colla iactantem iubis?
>ubi ille celeri corpus evinctus rotae
>in se refertur, ubi per adversum irritus
>redeunte totiens luditur saxo labor,
>ubi tondet ales avida fecundum iecur,
>et inter undas fervida exustus siti
>aquas fugaces ore decepto appetit
>poenas daturus caelitum dapibus graves."

118. <u>Volo, iubeo, impero</u>: cf. Juvenal, <u>Satires</u>, VI, ll.223-224,

>"hoc volo, sic iubeo, sit pro ratione voluntas:
>imperat ergo viro."

124- <u>Horror me occupat, Eriguntur comae</u>: cf. Ovid, <u>Metamorphoses</u>,
125.
    XIV, l.198,

>"me luridus occupat horror
>spectantem vultus etiamnum caede madentes."

and Vergil, **Aeneid**, IV, 1.280,

"arrectaeque horrore comae,..."

136. **A quo didicerunt Iesuitae artem suam veteratoriam:** The Jesuits did not enjoy very great popularity during the fifteenth and sixteenth centuries, largely on account of their apparent involvement in the politics and diplomacy of the day. Many kings and heads of state had Jesuits for their confessors at this time, and they soon came to wield tremendous power and influence at Court. Through their alleged involvement in diplomatic intrigue, they soon grew to be - in society's eyes - objects of hatred and envy, provoking jealousy and mistrust. Hence, they are often condemned, or satirised, as here, by the writers of the period.

137-148. **necesse est ut des iusiurandum...O dolor! Si necesse sit, faciam:** The interlude which now follows, culminating in Pigeon kissing the devil's bare buttocks, is a complete parody of the ceremony that took place when a new member was initiated into the witches' cult. The initiation usually consisted of taking a series of oaths, and denouncing various articles of faith (see Scot, p.56).

Pigeon, however, is made to swear that he will not give freshmen half measure, nor sell his serving-wenches' virtue!

139-140. <u>Scholares recentes...semiputri caseo</u>: Members of the University were always very particular about the quality and price of food, or goods, sold them by the townsmen. Whereas the majority of the people of Oxford were tradesmen and manufacturers, whose chief concern it was to keep prices as high as possible, the students were essentially a consumer body, who wanted above all cheapness, and who had no other option than to buy what they needed on the spot. The University often appealed to the Crown for protection against what it called the unjust dealing of the townspeople. (See Mallet, vols. I and II).

141-142. <u>Ancillas...redimant</u>: From this line it would appear that Pigeon's inn was also something of a bawdy-house, an idea borne out by Doulerus' description of the hostelry as a 'domus nequitiae, suburbanum prostibulum' (I, 1.180), and the mention of a 'nefastum buxi signum' and a 'fenestra rubra', or red lamp, over the door (II, 1.I)!

144. <u>osculaberis ipsum podicem cacodaemonis</u>: According to Scot (p.56), kissing the devil's bare buttocks was, in witchcraft, a way of sealing a bargain, or pact, made between witch and devil. It was looked upon as doing homage to the Evil One. Scot adds, however, that the notion is quite absurd: for whoever heard, he says of a SPIRIT having flesh, bones, sinews, hands, claws, teeth, lips and buttocks?

149. <u>Azmior, Aylitef</u>: These may be the names of certain evil spirits, or devils, although Scot does not mention them in his exhaustive list (330). It is doubtful whether there is any connection between the name 'Azmior' and the astrological term "azimuth" meaning an arc of the heavens extending from the zenith to the horizon which it cuts at right angles.

154. <u>nondum sum apud me</u>: cf. Terence, Phormio, 1.204.,

        ANTIPHO: non sum apud me.

155. <u>diabolos minorum gentium</u>: There were, indeed, several different kinds of 'devil', or evil spirit, so those who practised witchcraft believed. Some devils were thought to be more powerful

than others, but each had their own name and their own specific duty to fulfil: a list of them can be found in Scot, p.330. However, since Nichades immediately goes on to talk of satyrs, hobgoblins, dandiprats and the like, it seems that he is really referring to 'fairies' here, and not 'devils' in the true sense of the word.

156. **Qui tantum possunt ludere, non possunt laedere:** The author here plays upon the similarity in sound and appearance between the two verbs: (i) 'ludere' -'to play', or 'to sport', and (ii) 'laedere' - 'to harm'.

158. **Excutient tibi risum, non incutient timorem:** On this occasion the humour in Nichades' speech is provided by the contrast between the two phrases 'excutient tibi risum' and 'non incutient timorem'. The words 'excutient' and 'incutient', although they closely resemble one another in spelling - both being derived etymologically from the verb 'quatio', - are rendered polar opposites by the addition of the prefixes 'ex-' and 'in-'. 'Risus' and 'timor' are almost antithetical, too, and so this fact, coupled with the symmetry - verb noun, verb noun, - of the two halves of the sentence, forms both an amusing and cleverly constructed line.

159. **Panes**: According to classical mythology, these were the guardians of the countryside and fields, so called because they resembled Pan, the son of Mercury and Penelope, and the god of the woods and shepherds. They are usually represented as half man and half goat. (See O.C.D., s.v. Pan).

159. **Satyros**: In Greek mythology, satyrs were the attendants of Dionysus, the Wine-God, and were also regarded as the spirits of the woods and hills, connected particularly with the idea of their fertility. Vase-paintings show them to have been grotesque creatures in appearance, possessing in the main a human form, but with some part bestial, e.g. with a horse's tail, or the legs of a goat. The chief characteristic of the satyrs are said to have been their lustfulness and their love of revelry. (See O.C.D., s.v. Satyrs).

160. **Quos familiariter cum mortalibus versatos refert antiquitas**: cf. Catullus, LXIV, ll.384-386,

> "praesentes namque ante domos invisere castas
> heroum et sese mortali ostendere coetu
> caelicolae nondum spreta pietate solebant."

161. **haec poetarum numina**: Pans and satyrs figure prominently in the pastoral, lyric and occasional poetry of the Augustan period and of the Late Empire, e.g. Vergil, *Eclogues*, X, 11.26-7; Horace, *Odes*, I, I, 1.31, and II, 19, 1.4; Statius, *Silvae*, II, 2, 11.105-6. The poet Ausonius, writing in the fourth century A.D., also paints a delightful picture of these strange little creatures sporting on the river-bank, in his poem, *Mosella*, 11.170-4,

> "hic ego et agrestes Satyros et glauca tuentes
> Naidas extremis credam concurrere ripis,
> capripedes agitat cum laeta protervia Panas
> insultantque vadis trepidasque sub amne sorores
> terrent, indocili pulsantes verbere fluctum."

162. **Fayries**: In sixteenth and seventeenth-century England, believing in fairies was very much in fashion, especially among country-people, and many traditions and superstitions grew up around them. Several of these are, of course, embodied in Shakespeare's *A Midsummer Night's Dream*.

162. **Mammets**: The word 'mammet' is derived from Mahomet, the name of the god worshipped by the Mohammedans. It originally meant an idol, but later came to mean doll, or puppet, or even a person of grotesque appearance or costume. 'Mammet' is used here, however, in the sense of 'fairy'. Cf. Lyly, *The Mayde's Metamorphosis*, II,

> IOCULO: What Mawmets are these?
> FRISCO: O they be the Fayries that haunt these woods.

(I quote from *A Collection of Old English Plays*, edited by A.H.Bullen, 4 vols. (New York, Benjamin Blom, Inc. 1964) I).

163. **Bugges**: In the sixteenth century, 'bugge', or more commonly, 'bug', was another name for a hobgoblin, or bogeyman. In Thomas Matthew's translation of the Bible (1537), for instance, Psalm XCI, v.5, is rendered into English thus, "Thou shalt not nede to be afraied for any bugs by night." 'Bug', therefore, has, on this occasion, been used to translate the Hebrew phrase, 'terror of the night'.

163. **Apesfaces**: An 'apesface' was probably another kind of goblin. This may be what Caliban is referring to in *The Tempest*

(II, ii, 11.8-10), when he says of Prospero's spirits,

> "For every trifle are they set upon me;
> Sometime like apes that mow and chatter at me,
> And after bite me;"

163. <u>Hobgoblins inferioris ordinis</u>: In Shakespeare's time, a hobgoblin was thought by the superstitious to be a mischievous, tricksy imp, or sprite. Hobgoblins were frequently called Puck, or Robin Goodfellow, since 'hob' was the diminutive form of Robert or Robin, and so 'hobgoblin' was equivalent to Robin the Goblin. Burton, in his <u>Anatomy of Melancholy</u> (Everyman's Library (London, 1961) I, p.193), writes, "A bigger kind there is of them (i.e.spirits) called with us hobgoblins, and Robin Goodfellows, that would in those superstitious times grind corn for a mess of milk, cut wood, or do any manner of drudgery work."

164. <u>Dandiprats</u>: i.e. dwarfs, or pigmies, said to be about three spans (approx. $2\frac{1}{4}$ft.) in height.

164. **Mop et eius progenies**: According to Joshua Poole, *The English Parnassus*, (London, 1657), (s.v.Fairies), Mop was the name of one of the ladies-in-waiting at the fairy court of King Oberon and Queen Mab. 'Progenies' possibly refers not so much to her descendants, as to her sister maids-of-honour ('progenies' is often used in the sense of 'tribe', or 'clan', in mediaeval and renaissance Latin), who, Poole tells us, were called: Hop, Drop, Pip, Trip, Skip, Fib, Tib, Tick, Pink, Pin, Quick, Gill, Im, Tit, Wap, Win and Nit!

165. **Seu Panes, aut Manes, seu satyri vel fityri**: The assonance in this line adds greatly to its effectiveness.

    Panes: See above, note to l.159.

    Manes: In Roman thought, the 'Manes' were the deified souls of the departed, or the shades of the dead. As the 'Di Manes' they also became identified with the Di Inferii, the rulers of the Lower World. They were regarded as benevolent spirits. (See O.C.D., s.v. Manes).

    satyri: See above, note to l.159.

fityri: Probably a word of the author's own invention. There is no reference to 'fityrs' in any of the standard works on folklore, or fairy mythology. Perhaps the author had in mind some creature that was half fairy - 'fi', and half satyr - 'tyr'. The name, however, rhymes well with 'satyr', and that is the author's main concern here.

166. Seu lares aut lemures aut Penates vocamini: Again it is the repetition of certain sounds - in this case 'es' - which contributes to the success of the line.

lares: In Roman times, this was the name given to the household gods. Their images often stood on the hearth in a little shrine, or in a chapel called the 'lararium'. (See O.C.D., s.v. Lares).

lemures: The ghosts of the dead. Unlike the Manes, these were considered maleficent spirits, which had to be exorcised, when, as was commonly supposed, they visited the homes of the living on the 9th., 11th. and 13th. May, the festival of the 'Lemuria'. The ceremony is described by Ovid in Fasti, $\overline{V}$, 1.419f.. (See also O.C.D., s.v. Lemuria).

Penates: In Roman religion, the Penates were the spirits of the store-cupboard. They occupied a place in the atrium of every early Roman house, and like the 'lares', were also regarded as protectors of the household. (See O.C.D., s.v. Penates).

167-168. **Qui dormientium brachia...notis:** Fairies were thought to be great lovers of cleanliness, and it was said that they would punish anyone found keeping a dirty or slovenly household, by pinching them black and blue. This idea is referred to by Ben Jonson in his ballad, Robin Goodfellow,

> "When house or hearth doth sluttish lie,
> I pinch the maidens black and blue,
> The bed clothes from the bed pull I,
> And lay them naked all to view."

169-171. **Qui iunctis manibus...Nigricans arescit:** According to popular superstition, dancing was a favourite pastime of the fairies. It was believed that they always danced at night and usually in a ring. Mistress Quickly in Shakespeare's The Merry Wives of Windsor (V, v, 11.63-66),

"And nightly, meadow-fairies, look you sing,
Like to the Garter's compass, in a ring;
Th' expressure that it bears, green let it be,
More fertile-fresh than all the field to see;"

The fairies' moonlight roundelays were thought to be responsible for the little circles of brighter green grass which are sometimes found in pasture-lands and fields, and hence called fairy rings. These are now known to be caused by the outspreading propagation of a certain species of mushroom, by which the ground is fertilized for a richer next crop. However, many strange superstitions clustered around the phenomenom of the fairy ring during the sixteenth and seventeenth centuries: it was, for example, regarded as highly dangerous to step inside such a ring, lest one should fall subject to the fairies' power; on the other hand, those who dwelt in a house built on the site of a former fairy ring, enjoyed - it was said - great prosperity and good fortune.

Fairies were also accused of wearing the grass away completely with their midnight revels ('tritumque gramen pedibus Nigricans arescit'). Cowley, in his *Complaint*, (stanza 6, l.22), remarks,

> "Where once such fairies dance, no grass does
> ever grow."

(I quote from <u>The Complete Works in verse and prose of
Abraham Cowley</u>, edited by the Rev. A.B.Grosart, (New York,1967).

171-
173. <u>qui media de nocte luditis...Ignemque vivum</u>: As already
mentioned (note to ll.167-168), fairy-folk were generally
portrayed as being firm advocates of cleanliness and order.
Consequently, those housewives who believed this superstition,
endeavoured to keep their homes spotlessly clean and tidy,
always to have a fire burning in the hearth, and to keep plenty
of pails of fresh water in the kitchen. It was thought that,
at dead of night, when the rest of the world was sleeping, the
fairies entered the homes of mortals to inspect them, and if
they found them dirty and in disorder, punished those
responsible. Robert Herrick, in his <u>Hesperides</u>, writes in a poem
'The Fairies',

> "If ye will with Mab find grace,
> Set each Platter in its place:
> Rake the Fier up, and get
> Water in, ere Sun be set.

Wash your Pailes and clense your Dairies;
Sluts are loathsome to the Fairies:
Sweep your house; Who doth not so,
Mab will pinch her by the toe."

(I quote from <u>The Poems of Robert Herrick</u>, edited by L.C.Martin(London, 1965)).

175. <u>Adeste tripudiantes cum musica</u>: The fairies' love of music, both in dancing and singing, can be illustrated from the folk-lore of most European nations. Shakespeare has frequent references to the fairies' fondness for music in <u>A Midsummer Night's Dream</u>: Titania, for instance, when preparing to retire to her leafy bower, says to her followers (II, ii, 1.1),

"Come now, a roundel and a fairy song;"

Later (III, i, 11.143-5), she tells Bottom,

"I'll give thee fairies to attend on thee;
And they shall fetch thee jewels from the deep,
And sing, while thou on pressed flowers dost sleep;"

176. **quum Oberon reginam duxerat:** Oberon will, of course, always be chiefly associated with the play, <u>A Midsummer Nights' Dream</u>, but neither the name Oberon, nor his rôle as the king of the fairies, were Shakespeare's own invention. Oberon appears for the first time in literature in the old French romance of <u>Huon de Bourdeaux</u>, and he is also identified with Elberich, the dwarf king, in the German tale of Otnit, which is included in the Heldenbuch. The name Elberich, on passing into French, became first Auberich, then Auberon, and eventually Oberon, the most familiar form. Spenser, in the <u>Faerie Queene</u> (II, I, 6), mentions him, when talking of Sir Guyon,

> "Well could he tourney and in lists debate,
> And knighthood tooke of good Sir Huons hand,
> When with king Oberon he came to Faerie land."

Again, in the same poem (II, 10, 75), Oberon represents in an allegorical fashion, Henry VIII. Elficleos had two sons,

> "   of which faire Elferon
> The eldest brother did untimely dy;
> Whose emptie place the mightie Oberon
> Doubly suppiide, in spousall, and dominion."

(I quote from <u>The poetical works of Edmund Spenser</u>, edited by J.C.Smith and E. de Selincourt, (London, 1912)).

'Oberam, King of Fayeries' also figures in Robert Greene's play, James the Fourth; while one of Jonson's masques is entitled, Oberon, the Faery Prince.

178- Nec nauseam vobis sordida supellex creet...lautior pascat
179. cibus: A further allusion to the fairies' love of cleanliness and propriety.

182. quam lepidos ludos video: The alliteration of 'l' and 'd' sounds is particularly effective here in conveying Pigeon's excitement at what he has just seen.

183. De his narrare solebat avia prolixas fabulas: Old women and children were thought to be especially susceptible to 'seeing fairies': the author of "Round About Our Coal Fire" writes - according to J. Brand (Pop. Antiquities, 3 vols. (London, 1849) II, 477, n.4) - "My grandmother has often told me of fairies dancing upon our green, and that they were little creatures clothed in green."

187. tetrius, quam Avernus: i.e. Lake Avernus, which is situated near to Puzzuoli, and which in ancient times was thought to lie close to the entrance to the Underworld. According to classical mythology, the vapours rising off the lake were so poisonous

that they killed even the birds flying over it.

188. <u>non exprimit sepe lingua, quod imprimunt oculi</u>: An effective line, relying chiefly for its impact on the contrast, yet balance, between the two phrases 'exprimit lingua' and 'imprimunt oculi'. 'Imprimunt' is particularly forceful here, and seems to echo the view, commonly held in the sixteenth and seventeenth centuries, that the eye was the most powerful organ of sense: what one <u>saw</u> was thought to be more indelibly printed on the mind, than what one heard. Hence, the Puritans often criticized stage-plays which depicted immorality and violence because they felt that these had a corrupting influence upon the spectators: "If thy eye offend thee, pluck it out," (Matthew, <u>XVIII</u>, v.9).

189. <u>archidiabolum mugientem et rugientem</u>: The two present participles 'mugientem' and 'rugientem' are put to good use here: not only are they onomatopéic, but they also rhyme, adding greatly to the humour and effectiveness of Pigeon's description of his satanic majesty.

193. <u>Ὦ παντοκράτορ- Michadem</u>: Ὦ παντοκράτορ
is an expression frequently found in the Bible: cf.
Revelations, I, v.8.

194. <u>manus</u>: MS. reads 'manam'.

197. <u>Tullius non magis est familiaris Lentulo</u>: The two men here
referred to are, of course, Marcus Tullius Cicero, the great
Roman orator and writer, and his friend, P. Cornelius Lentulus
Spinther. However, in the course of his consulship (64-63 B.C.),
Cicero also had dealings with another Lentulus - P. Cornelius
Lentulus Sura - and was instrumental in putting him to death
for his part in the Catilinarian conspiracy (see Sallust,
<u>Bellum Catilinae</u>.) It may well be, therefore, that Philopinus
is here taking advantage of Pigeon's ignorance of Roman history
in order to crack a rather subtle joke.

200-201. <u>perdidi plus quam duos bonos angelos...tres malos angelos</u>:

A pun on the two meanings of 'angelus': it is used first in the
sense of 'angel', i.e. an English gold coin, worth about 6s.8d.
(33½p.), in use between the reigns of Edward IV and Charles I,
and so called because it had the figure of St. Michael, the
archangel, engraved upon it; and secondly, with the meaning of
'a spiritual being', here alluding to the 'pueri antiquos

imitantes', whom Pigeon has just been watching. The play on words is reinforced by the addition of the adjectives 'bonus' and 'malus', which can be applied equally successfully to 'angelus' used in either of the senses mentioned above.

202. **cum Vespasiano facile resarcias damnum ex lotio**: Suetonius (<u>Vespasian</u>, 23) to illustrate the Emperor Vespasian's keen sense of humour, relates how, when his son Titus criticized him for putting a tax on public conveniences, Vespasian held a coin from the first payment up to his nose, asking whether he found the smell of it offensive. Titus replied that he did not, whereupon his father exclaimed, "Yet it comes from urine!"

"Reprehendenti filio Tito, quod etiam urinae vectigal commentus esset, pecuniam ex prima pensione admovit ad nares, sciscitans num odore offenderetur; et illo negante: "Atqui", inquit, "e lotio est."

234. **Ad exitum laetum iam producitur noster iocus**: One of the chief characteristics of comedy was, according to the ancients, its happy ending. Evanthius, <u>De Fabula</u>, IV, 2, writes,

" in comoedia mediocres fortunae hominum, parvi impetus periculorum laetique sunt exitus actionum..."

236-
237. **moresque hominum varios Perspeximus:** Comedy was also thought to 'mirror' life. Donatus, *De Comoedia*, V, 3, states that Cicero (in a work no longer extant) described comedy as a

"poema sub imitatione vitae atque morum similitudine compositum."

(See also note to Prologue, l.17.)

237-
238. **hos autem iuveniles dolos Iuvabit olim meminisse senili cathedra:** cf. Vergil, *Aeneid*, I, l.203,

" forsan et haec olim meminisse iuvabit."

EPILOGUE.

By adding an epilogue to his play, the author of Mercurius Rusticans is departing from the laws for the writing of comedy laid down by the Romans and Greeks, and is following those of the Elizabethan theatre. It was customary for Roman comedy to come to an abrupt end - as soon as the plot had been successfully unravelled, or mistaken identities discovered - with one of the characters asking the audience to give their applause. In Terence's Phormio (1.1055), for example, the 'cantor' turns to the spectators, and says: "vos valete et plaudite"; similarly, in the Amphitruo of Plautus, Amphitruo (1.1146), addresses the members of the audience thus: "nunc, spectatores, Iovis summi causa clare plaudite."

In England, however, throughout the sixteenth and seventeenth centuries, up until the 1700s, it was quite common for plays - particularly those performed at Court - to have a concluding epilogue. The epilogue was usually between twenty and thirty lines long, and was spoken by one of the chief characters in the play: Prospero delivers the epilogue in The Tempest, Rosalind in As You Like It, while in A Midsummer Night's Dream, the task falls to Puck. Very often the epilogue was little more than a conventional apology for

the inadequacies of the performance and a request for
applause. Sometimes, however, - as in the case of this
particular epilogue - it took the form of a commentary,
either witty or scathing, on the politics and social
conditions of the day. The best epilogues in the English
theatre were undoubtedly those written by Dryden (1631-1700)
and Garrick (1717-1779).

In <u>Mercurius Rusticans</u>, it is the Genius Academiae
who speaks the epilogue: since it was he who opened the
play (Prologue, ll.I-30), it is appropriate that he should
be the one to close it. The greater part of the epilogue is
an attack upon those who criticize the behaviour of University
students, and who disapprove of academic drama in general, but
the fact that this rebuke is couched in what can only be
described as metaphorical and lyrical language, gives it a
certain poetic quality.

As he speaks, the Genius Academiae moves, almost
imperceptibly, from one image to another: first (ll.1-6), he
presents the audience with a graphic court-room scene: the
students stand in the dock, falsely accused by the townspeople
of Oxford, of being drunk and disorderly, of practising black
magic, and of being wanton and mischievous. The effect of this
is heightened by the use of such words as 'arguit', 'obiiciantur'
and 'crimina'.

In ll.6-7, there is a fleeting glimpse of the countryside: the fresh milk poured into the unwashed churn, immediately turns sour, while amongst the nodding flowers, the evil-looking spider lazily weaves its web.

At l.8, we are ushered back into the court to hear the Genius Academiae, who now assumes the rôle of judge, pronounce sentence - <u>not</u> on the students, but on their accusers: 'Non leviter expiandum scelus', he says, 'nec iniuria levis Academiae, mihique'.

Line 9 finds us on Mount Olympus, where Apollo, god of poetry and music, is preparing to vent his wrath against those who in any way threaten, or try to harm his protégés.

In l.10, those who have by their slander successfully killed the good name of the Oxford students, are depicted as a group of relatives greedily awaiting the reading of the will after one of their number has died: they learn - too late - that their inheritance is 'misera vita'.

Later (ll.17-18), we see babes in arms suddenly metamorphosised into little, wizened up, old men, and young men turning grey overnight.

At l.23, the image of the court-room and the judgement seat is again repeated when the Genius Academiae mentions the word 'tribunal'.

For two lines (ll.26-7), the University becomes a huge tree of knowledge, - 'Vigeat...crescat...floreat'.

Finally, in l.28, the University is seen as the eye of some huge Cyclopic giant (a metaphor for the continent of Europe), - a ray of light and hope in a sea of mental darkness and obscurity.

These images - some of them very unusual - following close on one another, are extremely effective: they transform what would otherwise have been a conventional type epilogue into a fine piece of poetry, whilst their vividness and colour sharpen considerably the attack which this closing speech is intended to convey.

1-6. <u>Querela vetus...Totis Athenis</u>: An allusion to the feud between the University students and the townspeople of Oxford, which lasted for several centuries. Scholars frequently drank to excess; brawled in the streets; caused riots, and their low behaviour often broke the bounds of decency and law. It seems, though the Genius Academiae, of course, would be the last to admit it, that the laymen of Oxford had a valid case against the clerks. The charge of practising black magic, however, is an unusual one, for although some Oxford men, e.g. Simon Forman, did turn to the black art, after leaving University, there is, as far as can be ascertained, no record of anyone found dabbling in necromancy whilst still a student. (For further information about the conflict between the students and the townspeople of Oxford, see above, note to Prologue, ll.3-5, and Mallet, <u>History of the University of Oxford</u>, vols. I and II).

6-7. <u>pura sic vas acidum Corrumpet</u>: cf. Horace, <u>Epistles</u>, I, 2, l.54,

>"Sincerum est nisi vas, quodcumque infundis
>arescit."

7. <u>et flos araneo venenum dabit</u>: It was once universally believed that spiders were poisonous. Consequently, Shakespeare in his plays <u>Cymbeline</u> (IV,ii, l.91) and <u>Richard III</u> (I, ii, l.19) places them in the same category as vipers and toads. Similarly, in <u>The Winter's Tale</u> (II, i, ll.39-40), Leontes declares,

>"There may be in the cup
>A spider steep'd."

Again, Richard II (III, ii, ll.12-17) setting foot on dry land once more, after a long sea voyage, addresses the soil of England with these words,

"Feed not thy sovereign's foe, my gentle earth,
Nor with thy sweets comfort his ravenous sense;
But let thy spiders, that suck up thy venom,
And heavy-gaited toads, lie in their way,
Doing annoyance to the treacherous feet
Which with usurping steps do trample thee;"

9. *irato sed vivant Apolline*: An imitation of a poetic commonplace often used by Roman writers. Cf. Horace, Satires, II, 3, 1.8, "iratis natus paries dis," ; ibid., I, 5, 1197-98, "lymphis iratis exstructa"; ibid., II, 7,14, "Vertumnis...natus iniquis", and Juvenal, Satires, X, 1.129, "dis ille adversis genitus fatoque sinistro."

11-12. *Quod si aliquibus...canis displiceant haec ludicra*: While the majority of the members of the University were keen and enthusiastic supporters of college plays, there were those – especially during the latter part of the sixteenth century and first half of the seventeenth century – who adopted a Puritan attitude towards academic drama, and who felt that the ban on professional acting ought to be extended to the University stage. (See Boas, pp.227-48).

15-17. **Inconstans hominum genus Spernit quod olim petiit,...
Confundit aetates:** cf. Horace, *Epistles*, I, I, ll.97-100,

> "   quid, mea cum pugnat sententia secum,
> quod petiit spernit, repetit quod nuper omisit,
> aestuat et vitae disconvenit ordine toto,
> diruit, aedificat, mutat quadrata rotundis?"

19-23. **At vos benignae, animae candidissimae...non ad tribunal voco:**
A plea for indulgence. Cf. Prologue, ll.27.28.

25. **Huic academiae fausta comprecatus omnia:** It was once the custom, at the close of a play, or of the epilogue, for the actors to kneel down on the stage and offer prayers for the Sovereign, the nobility, the clergy and even the commoners. Hence, the dancer, in the epilogue to Shakespeare's *Henry IV*, (Pt.2), (ll.13-16) exclaims,

> "Bate me some, and I will pay you some, and, as most debtors do, promise you infinitely; and so I kneel down before you - but, indeed, to pray for the Queen."

Since this is a play about University life, performed by students of the University, before other members of the University, it is fitting that the Genius Academiae should at this point pray for the University, and for all those who teach and learn therein.

26-27. **Vigeat et crescat...et moribus bonis**: The Genius Acadamiae expresses the hope that the University, like the mustard seed in the parable in St. Matthew's Gospel (XIII,v.31), - which was the smallest of all seeds, but which grew into a tree so large that its branches could provide shelter for the birds of the air - will, from its small beginnings, increase in size and reputation, and come to be renowned throughout the whole world. This hope was not in vain: today, Oxford is still one of the greatest universities in the world, and down the ages students of many different nationalities have passed through its colleges.

26. **octavum miraculum**: i.e. 'the eighth wonder (sc. of the world)'. The Seven Wonders of the ancient world were, of course: the Pyramids in Egypt; the statue of Zeus at Olympia; the Mausoleum at Halicarnassus; the Temple of Diana at Ephesus; the Colossus of Rhodes; the Pharos at Alexandria, and the Hanging Gardens of Babylon. Of these Seven Wonders only the

Pyramids now remain.

28. **Oculusque unicus Europae Polyphemicae**: A very unusual metaphor. 'Polyphemica' is the adjective derived from Polyphemus, the name of the one-eyed giant, or Cyclops, who was blinded by Ulysses (Odyssey, IX).

29. **Habeatur a Chinensibus**: To an author writing at the end of the sixteenth, or very beginning of the seventeenth, century, before the discovery of Australia, China would seem like 'the other side of the world': for the name and reputation of the University of Oxford to have reached as far as China would be fame indeed! Although Marco Polo had brought back to Europe the first eye-witness accounts of China as early as the thirteenth century, the Orient still held a certain mystery and fascination hundreds of years later. The author of <u>Mercurius Rusticans</u>, talking through his mouthpiece, the Genius Academiae, appears to look on the Chinese in much the same way as Horace does on the "rigidi Getae" (<u>Odes</u> III, 24, 1.11), or the "Britannos hospitibus feros" (<u>Odes</u>, III, 4, 1.33): in other words, they are a strange, distant people, with whom he, himself, has had no direct contact - what he knows of them has been reported to him by others. In fact, the manner in which the

Genius Academiae speaks of Oxford's great renown spreading throughout the world, is very reminiscent of some passages of Augustan Age poetry, where writers prophesy that the glory of Rome will extend to the ends of the earth.

29-30. **nec orbis latius Aut diutius extendatur, quam eius decus:** The mention of the then known world growing ever wider is very appropriate here, since the years 1492-1650 are often referred to as the Great Age of Discovery. Ship-building and navigation methods in Europe had so improved by the close of the fifteenth century, that longer voyages of exploration were made possible: Columbus reached America in 1492, Vasco da Gama reached India in 1498, and Magellan crossed the Pacific and sailed round the whole world in 1521. Close on the heels of Columbus, the Portuguese penetrated deep into the heart of Brazil, and the Spanish attempted to cross the continent, which separated them from the treasures of the East. In 1513, Balbao crossed the Isthmus of Panama, and shortly afterwards, Hernando Cortés conquered Mexico, and arrived at the Gulf of California. The English and the French secured strongholds in North America, and together with the Dutch, endeavoured to discover a North-West

Passage in the Arctic as a route to China. By the year 1650, the existence of all the continents, with the exception of Antarctica, had been proven.

31-32. **His precibus meis...claro manibus incussis sono:** The conventional request for applause, found at the close of all Roman comedy, and much Elizabethan drama. Cf. Plautus, *Mostellaria*, 1.1181,

"spectatores, fabula haec est acta, vos plausum date."

and Shakespeare, *The Tempest*, Epilogue, 11.9-10,

"But release me from my bands
With the help of your good hands."

CHANGES OF PUNCTUATION

Prologue

Line No.	Reading of this edition	MS.
1	academiae,	academias
4	ortus,	ortus
	status,	status
5	convenit.	convenit,
9	diem,	diem
13	protulit:	protulit,
14	lubricae,	lubricae
16	dolus,	dolus
17	speculo,	speculo
18	facta,	facta
	similia.	similia:
23	negotiis:	negotiis,
24	hilares,	hilares
	saturnii:	saturnii
25	nascitur,	nascitur
26	facile.	facile
27	oculis,	oculis
28	frontibus.	frontibus

Act I

Line No.	Reading of this edition	MS.
1	pater,	pater
5	scripserit:	scripserit
8	tempestivitas!	tempestivitas.
9	malum:	malum,
12	infestis,	infestis
21	Ha, ha, he!	Ha, ha, he,
23	sordidum.	sordidum:
24	metum,	metum
25	micans,	micans
26	volens,	volens
27	cumulo.	cumulo,
29	incurvans,	incurvans
30	coniicit.	coniicit,
31	uno.	uno,
33	Ha, ha, he!	Ha Ḧa he.
35	charissime!	charissime
36	dies!	dies.
	laetior!	laetior.
37	laetissimus!	laetissimus:
39	Posteritas:	Posteritas,
	probe.	probe

40	heus! Dic,	Heus dic
42	meus.	meus
43	impedit,	impedit
45	meretrix,	meretrix
46	editur:	editur,
47	Deest, amici, pecunia,	Deest Amici pecunia,
48	Pish!	Pish.
50	est:	est,
51	nihili.	nihili,
52	passerum,	passerum
57	iocos.	iocos
58	rogas?	rogas
61	otii.	otii
62	loqui,	loqui;
67	reiicit!	reiicit.
69	iter:	iter
70	optima,	optima
80	Heigh!	Heigh,
	Oxonium!	Oxonium,
	Hincksy!	Hincksy:
83	circuli.	circuli,
85	vita.	vita,
	pecunia?	pecunia,

86	denarios:	denarios
88	genio,	genio
89	cerebrum;	cerebrum
90	capiamus.	capiamus
91	cito!	cito.
93	vocabimur:	vocabimur.
	Primus, Secundus, Tertius.	primus secundus Tertius.
95	Michades,	Michades
97	Philopinus,	Philopinus
98	partes.	partes
99	dery,	dery
	dery!	dery.
	dery!	dery.
100	Ambulemus!	ambulemus.
101	Hospes!	Hospes,
	Hoe!	hoe,
102	ades!	ades.
103	vocites,	vocites
106	Oh,	Oh
	uxor:	uxor
108	pluit,	pluit
110	placet:	placet
112	soliti;	soliti

114	antiquitus,	antiquitus
115	studia,	studia
116	studiis.	studiis
117	aliquid;	aliquid
118	incipiam.	incipiam
	forum,	forum
119	favorem,	favorem
120	furorem,	furorem
121	diligo!	diligo
122	diligas,	diligas
123	haurias,	haurias
	ha,ha,he!	ha ha he:
124	Ha, ha, he!	Ha ha he
	Ha, ha, he!	ha ha he
	Dum cantamus ha, ha, he!	dum cantamus ha ha he
125	profundum,	profundum
126	rotundum,	rotundum
127	iucundum,	iucundum
128	fundum!	fundum
129	reversas,	reversas
130	meretrix,	meretrix
131	mersas.	mersas

132	merulae!	merulae.
	Tibi, Roberte,	Tibi Roberte
	larynx!	larynx
134	Quaeso,	Quaeso
	tace.	tace
135	moriar;	moriar,
137	frigore,	frigore:
138	popinam.	popinam,
139	abortivum,	abortivum:
140	titubans,	titubans
142	ferat.	ferat,
143	corrumpitis;	corrumpitis,
144	domi:	domi,
146	remedium.	remedium
149	mihi,	mihi
	nupseram!	nupseram,
151	vires,	vires
	verberarem!	verberarem.
153	ebrium!	ebrium.
155	posthac,	posthac
	agam!	agam.
156	sordidula!	sordidula,

157	cavete,	cavete
	Oxonii!	Oxonii,
158	Vicini,	Vicini
	Oxonii!	Oxonii,
159	tu,	tu
	loquacior,	loquacior
	tace!	tace,
160	anseribus!	anseribus.
161	est:	est;
	uxoribus!	uxoribus.
162	Cavete, mariti,	Cavete mariti
	uxoribus!	uxoribus,
163	volumus.	volumus:
164	facitis?	facitis
165	oppidi!	oppidi,
166	patibulo!	patibulo,
167	doddy,	doddy
	loquar,	loquar
168	stoole!	stoole
169	caelum!	caelum,
170	ungerem!	ungerem.
171	progenies!	progenies.

173	simiae!	simiae,
174	potes,	potes
	trifurcifer!	trifurcifer.
175	fluvio,	fluvio
176	vehi.	vehi
177	amplius!	amplius,
	crucem!	crucem
178	immortale!	immortale,
	rixando!	rixando,
179	vincitur!	vincitur.
180	Heus,	Heus
	puer!	puer,
	prostibulum,	prostibulum
181	dedecus?	dedecus.
182	latronum,	latronum?
183	mendicantium?	mendicantium
185	Oh,	Oh
	est!	est.
187	verissime!	verissime,

Act 2

Line No.	Reading of this edition	MS.
2	est.	est
7	garrulam!	garrulam,
12	ego	Ego.
	exeo.	exeo
13	ἔλου.	ἔλου
19	muro?	muro
20	muro?	muro
21	redimendam!	redimendam
22	aliud;	aliud
25	saltat!	saltat
30	laborare!	laborare.
	laborare:	laborare
36	rubram.	rubram
45	advenistis,	advenistis
47	placet?	placet.
	placet.	placet,
48	bibere?	bibere:
	cito!	cito
53	frangam.	frangam,
59	feras.	feras
61	aliquid:	aliquid

62	l,	l.
	50,	50.
	i,	i.
67	Dawson?	Dawson.
	agricola.	agricola
68	es?	es.
	liberos?	liberos.
70	Ah,	Ah
	tellus:	tellus
72	sodales,	sodales
74	circulo.	circulo
75	agricola,	Agricola
76	horreo!	horreo
77	Vulcane,	Vulcane
	domi.	domi
78	deditis.	deditis
79	colimus.	colimus
81	odor.	odor
83	miracula.	miracula
86	mihi.	mihi:
	mihi.	mihi:

91	somniant.	somniant
98	Pish!	Pish.
101	reponito.	reponito,
105	exeas!	exeas
107	unica.	unica,
112	similiter?	similiter,
113	academico.	Academico,
117	potui!	potui.
120	he!	he,
121	placeat.	placeat,
129	Ioanna,	Ioanna
	mei,	mei
130	incrementum!	incrementum,
132	Virgo,	virgo
	regna.	regna;
133	serio.	serio,
136	amares.	amares,
139	candida.	candida,
142	Infandum, regina,	Infandum Regina
146	periculum.	periculum

150	cantites.	cantites
152	periculum.	periculum,
158	nomen.	nomen
169	sponsa?	sponsa.
171	Hymen!	Hymen.
176	periscelidis.	periscelidis
177	Ioanna,	Ioanna
183	clauditur.	clauditur
185	omnibus.	omnibus,
186	Elysios!	Elysios;
187	curo.	curo,
188	nepenthes!	nepenthes
195	modo:	modo
196	pulchrior.	pulchrior
197	charitatis.	charitatis
	vis?	vis
198	meum.	meum
200	intelligant.	intelligant,
201	academici?	Academici:
	mali.	mali:

209	trahas.	trahas
232	subtilior.	subtilior
236	equus.	equus
239	levissimas!	levissimas.
240	contigit:	contigit,
242	reverentia.	reverentia
243	Molossum:	Molossum,
	Holoo! Holoo!	holoo, holoo,
244	reverentia.	reverentia
245	remedium!	remedium.
246	sequi.	sequi
249	grano.	grano,
	porco.	porco
251	apprehenderet:	apprehenderet
252	mordet:	mordet
	talionis,	talionis
253	agit;	agit
254	porcus:	porcus,
256	canis:	canis.

257	facinus?	facinus:
259	iniuria?	iniuria;
260	geometrice:	Geometrice,
265	necessitatis,	necessitatis
266	tertium:	tertium
269	experiri.	experiri
282	solet,	solet
283	mali.	mali
285	nigrior!	nigrior
293	viatoribus.	viatoribus:
294	quaeso,	quaeso
301	intelligis,	intelligis;
	vocas,	vocas
304	mihi, agricola,	mihi Agricola
306	fecisses!	fecisses
311	he!	he,
312	trabe.	trabe:
313	segete:	segete,
316	simul!	simul.

Act 3

Line No.	Reading of this edition.	MS.
5	patet,	patet
6	suam,	suam
7	Ho!	Ho:
12	Ho!	Ho:
13	Ho!	Ho:
15	sordet,	sordet
17	Ho!	ho:
18	Ho!	ho:
19	latronibus,	latronibus
28	pocula.	pocula
30	chartam!	chartam
31	accingamur!	accingamur
32	gratias!	gratias.
33	usquebach allas,	Usquebach Allae
40	coincidunt.	coincidunt
42	tetrastichon:	Tetrastichon
46	lupulos!	lupulos:
47	pöemata!	pöemata;
51	cito!	cito.
53	nicotianus;	Nicotianus

54	fumus:	fumus
56	foret!	foret:
57	poeta!	poeta,
59	foret!	foret:
60	Ha, ha, he!	Ha ha he.
61	disputabile,	disputabile
63	gratia:	gratia.
68	barbatus,	barbatus
69	barbatus.	barbatus
71	septipedes,	septipedes.
72	pueri,	pueri.
	vimineam,	vimineam
73	sentina,	sentina.
76	indet,	indet
77	eris!	eris
78	vituperetur;	vituperetur:
79	laudetur;	laudetur
83	Caietanum,	Caietanum
84	seraphicos,	Seraphicos
85	Hah!	Hah:
	caena?	caena
	Hoh! Hospita!	Hoh; Hospita.

89	Phuh!	Phuh:
97	tempore.	tempore
103	mihi,	mihi
	vocibus.	vocibus
104	laetibus,	laetibus
109	nostra:	nostra
111	Filia,	Filia
117	pulsat.	pulsat:
118	lubrica?	lubrica
119	affectio.	affectio
124	amplissime.	amplissime,
128	crumenis,	crumenis
129	Quaeso, mi hospes,	Quaeso mi hospes
131	Heigh!	Heigh.
133	congium:	congium
134	modum,	modum
	Tibi, mi faber,	Tibi mi faber.
135	Falernum,	falernum
	Caecubum!	Caecubum:
136	pocula:	pocula,
142	aves.	aves

146	discatis, dubito.	discatis dubito;
147	auribus;	auribus,
149	grege;	grege
153	vocat.	vocat
154	experientia,	experientia
157	foret:	foret;
158	praedicere,	praedicere
160	illud,	illud
164	invisibilem.	invisibilem
165	vis,	vis
166	uxor!	uxor;
167	hodie?	hodie,
169	morio!	Morio
170	togae!	togae:
	O Xantippe,	O Xantippe
172	maxime,	maxime
175	medici!	Medici.
176	bene,	bene
178	medico.	medico
182	contextu:	contextu.
	Graecus	graecus

185	brevi,	brevi
	legumine;	legumine,
186	regulam:	Regulam.
191	noverat,	noverat
194	electuarium,	Electuarium.
195	petis,	petis
196	fides.	fides;
	Tentabo. Valete.	Tentabo, valete.
200	interficit!	interficit
203	Sed, amabo,	Sed amabo,
205	faber.	faber
207	periculo:	periculo
209	ἡ ἔμιϐι,	ἡ ἔμιϐι
212	venit,	venit;
	risus!	risus.
213	nugis,	nugis
	Michades.	Michades,
216	est:	est
217	hospitio,	hospitio
220	facilem.	facilem;
222	ecce!	ecce,
	fabula!	fabula,
	incipiam:	incipiam,

224	manus,	manus
229	dilectum.	dilectum
231	dicere,	dicere
232	pedis.	pedis
242	Phi!	Phi;
243	repulsam:	repulsam;
	duodecimam.	duodecimam,
244	clanculum.	clanculum
251	Sis, obsecro, benigna,	Sis obsecro benigna
252	Phi!	Phi,
255	Hei ho!	Hei ho,
257	oculos,	oculos
258	meam.	meam
261	usurariam!	usurariam
262	Phi!	Phi,
265	clanculum.	clanculum
267	genus!	genus
268	latet;	latet
269	gerit;	gerit,
270	necat;	necat,

272	serio,	serio
278	otiosi:	otiosi
280	curo:	curo
281	rapide,	rapide
283	ding,	ding
	dere,	dere
284	sedere!	sedere
286	curo:	curo
287	misere,	misere
291	curo:	curo
292	turbine,	turbine
293	securo.	securo
296	curo:	curo
297	grandine,	grandine
298	securo.	securo
300	venia,	venia
301	benignior:	benignior
303	Roberte,	Roberte
306	possib̦le.	possib̦le
310	ovis,	ovis

311	bovis,	bovis
312	ovis,	ovis
314	fartum,	fartum
315	partem,	partem
316	fartam,	fartam
318	solet:	solet
319	Hincksey!	Hincksey,
	Hincksey!	Hincksey:
320	qualibet,	qualibet
321	circulo!	circulo.
324	pastor,	pastor
	luderes;	luderes
326	Exangue	Exangue,
	vino,	vino:
	musica,	Musica
327	scholastici,	scholastici
329	bibant,	bibant
332	domum!	domum
333	Hoh!	Hoh,
	musicus!	Musicus

Act 4

Line No.	Reading of this edition	MS.
1	filiam,	filiam
3	pares.	pares,
5	iocis.	iocis,
8	gerere,	gerere:
11	Hoh!	Hoh,
	Ancilla!	ancilla,
	Proma,	proma
12	nuce!	nuce.
13	Salve,	Salve
	promiseram.	promiseram
15	maxima:	maxima.
	quo	Quo.
19	exhauriam.	exhauriam
	dictum:	dictum
25	Hoh! Quis	Hoh, quis
27	vilescit.	vilescit,
29	desinas,	desinas
	veniam,	veniam
	obsecro.	obsecro
32	erimus.	erimus

33	veniam,	veniam
	quaeso.	quaeso
34	ludere,	ludere;
	deludere.	deludere
35	Audite, quaeso,	Audite quaeso
38	desistet.	desistet:
43	crucem!	crucem
44	hinc!	hinc,
	Hincksy!	Hincksey.
	Domini,	Domini
50	principem,	principem
54	serias.	serias
55	Oxoniensibus,	Oxoniensibus
56	Sed, st, st: ex	Sed. St, St: Ex
61	folium.	folium:
63	facies,	facies
79	cauponarium:	cauponarium,
81	aliquid, obsecro.	aliquid obsecro
82	Hem,	Hem
	tibi.	tibi
84	abi,	abi

85	Oh,	Oh
86	Hospes,	Hospes
	certam?	certam
87	voluptate,	voluptate
89	neges,	neges
90	patinis,	patinis
92	recreat.	recreat,
93	quaeso,	quaeso
95	domum!	domum.
97	caput,	caput
101	iterum,	iterum
107	veniam,	veniam
119	poculum,	poculum
120	torqueor,	torqueor
123	fatear,	fatear
128	suavitas.	suavitas
132	amo!	amo:
133	despiciam,	despiciam.
139	domini,	domini
	filia!	filia:
142	quaeso,	quaeso
	dicite.	dicite

143	filiam,	filiam
144	Asolo,	Asolo
147	habeto: crudus	habeto. Crudus
149	apodictice,	apodictice
150	posteriori.	posteriori
154	vocale,	vocale
155	species,	species
156	parem,	parem
158	duplici:	duplici;
159	grave,	grave.
	bassum,	Bassum.
160	naso,	naso
167	lucri.	lucri
168	Tu, Doulere,	Tu Doulere
169	formidetis!	formidetis.
170	Quaeso,	Quaeso
174	aliquem:	aliquem
176	sponsam, Doulere:	sponsam Doulere,
	abiit;	abiit,
178	generositas.	generositas
183	Poh! Non potes avelli;	Poh, non potes avelli,
184	Abait,	Abait
	est.	est
185	Quaeso,	Quaeso
189	aloes.	Aloes

192	Foh! Quam meas!		Foh, quam meas
198	invisibilem,		invisibilem;
199	lepidissimum,		lepidissimum.
204	aliquid.		aliquid
211	dixeram.		dixeram
213	dubites,		dubites
214	patrem.		patrem
215	artibus,		artibus
216	memorem!		memorem
217	Sed, Nichades,		Sed Nichades
219	conditione:		conditione
222	ceremoniis:		ceremoniis
224	manu,		manu
225	asinus.		Asinus
226	asinum?		Asinum
229	annulum.		annulum
232	oportet.		oportet:
233	annulus.		annulus,
237	annulus		annulus.
239	penitus.		penitus,
243	tu, Roberte Dawson, Cupio. Fiat.		tu Roberte Dawson Cupio: Fiat
244	Fiat.		Fiat,

247	Bumbo.	Bumbo,
248	Ecce,	Ecce
	mirum!	mirum,
	Abiit!	abiit
	Evanuit!	evanuit
	Inanis	inanis
	cathedra!	cathedra
249	video.	video
250	Quaeso,	Quaeso
	vides,	vides
253	auriculam?	auriculam.
254	movente!	movente:
260	partus,	partus
	fortiter.	fortiter
261	proripis,	proripis
	me,	me
262	loco!	loco:
265	charissime,	charissime
266	cupias,	cupias
268	corporeus!	corporeus.
269	verbera:	verbera
271	heroicos luderem,	Heroicos luderem
272	cognoscerem:	cognoscerem
273	aliquo.	aliquo
	proculdubio,	proculdubio

275		domum!	domum,
		ludificant.	ludificant
276		Valete,	Valete
		mihi.	mihi
278		dolos,	dolos
281		fortuna	fortuna,
		bonis:	bonis
282		meo,	meo
285		pedere.	pedere
288		sponsa, gaudeo	sponsa Gaudeo
		incolumem.	incolumem
289		Foh!Omnia	Foh omnia
291		relinquere.	relinquere
292		amor.	amor
304		Oxonii.	Oxonii
305		nominibus?	nominibus
306		academiae,	academiae
307		suas.	suas
308		lenone!	lenone
311		craterem!	craterem
316		cratere:	cratere
318		hospitem.	hospitem
320		dies!	dies.
321		supellectils,	supellectilis.
322		abiit!	abiit.

322	abiit.	abiit,
324	Hic,	Hic
	dilabitur!	dilabitur.
	dilabuntur.	dilabuntur
325	cognoscere,	cognoscere;
326	caverem!	caverem.
327	ponite!	ponite,
	numeretur,	numeretur
	scholastici!	scholastici.
330	numerato.	numerato:
	insuper.	insuper,
333	efficiet,	efficiet.
339	redeo!	redeo:
340	aquae!	aquae:
342	proximi.	proximi
344	mater.	mater
345	volo.	volo;
346	rosas!	rosas
348	vultus.	vultus
349	valeas, dilectissima.	valeas Dilectissima
350	Vale,	vale
	Doulere.	Doulere,
351	Vale,	Vale
	Vale,	Vale
	domina	Domina.

Act 5

Line No.	Reading of this edition	MS.
6	serviens,	serviens
	carnifex,	carnifex
10	Forman,	Forman
11	categorematicos,	categorematicos
12	similia.	similia
15	fiducia.	fiducia,
19	remanere:	remanere
	quaeso,	quaeso
25	pepegistis.	pepegistis
26	fiet,	fiet
27	colloquamur.	colloquamur
38	narras.	narras,
40	mean,	mean
44	felis,	felis?
	teterrima?	teterrima.
45	felis,	felis
46	solet:	solet
48	sunt.	sunt
49	academicis.	Academicis
50	hospitibus.	Hospitibus

51	literas.	literas
52	amat.	amat
53	operi:	operi,
54	optime.	optime
55	pomaeria.	pomaeria
56	alterum,	alterum?
57	placeat?	placeat.
58	crepat!	crepat.
63	sono!	sono,
67	incolas,	incolas
70	eloquere:	eloquere,
71	purgatorium.	purgatorium
	infernum!	infernum
72	mus,	mus
	dens,	dens
	mons,	mons
	pons,	pons
75	sodalibus;	sodalibus
77	puel,	puel
	hophil,	hophil
81	pagloni,	pagloni
83	bone!	bone,
	sum!	sum

84	alteram!	alteram
85	periculi.	periculi,
86	Foh!	Foh,
87	meum.	meum
88	te,	te
90	pendulos,	pendulos
91	baratari,	barathri
92	dolii,	dolii
94	miserrimae,	miserrimae
95	crus,	crus
99	Surge,	Surge
	ros,	Ros
100	os,	os
102	erumpe.	erumpe,
103	somnio?	somnio,
	Ubi sum?	ubi sum
104	bone,	bone
	miserere mei!	miserere mei
105	loca,	loca
106	specu,	specu
114	dic,	dic
	mendacio,	mendacio

117	omnibus,	omnibus
118	velociter,	velociter
121	cito!	cito.
122	videas, hospes,	videas Hospes
	nuntium.	nuntium;
123	tuum!	tuum.
124	est!	est.
	bone!	bone,
125	oculi!	oculi.
127	memoriae,	memoriae
129	ho!	ho.
130	nescit,	nescit
132	esse.	esse
133	necesse.	necesse
134	memini,	memini
143	iurabis,	iurabis
144	cacodaemonis.	Cacodaemonis
146	facias,	facias
148	dolor!	dolor
	sit,	sit
150	descendas!	descendas.
151	ulterius, hospes,	ulterius Hospes
153	aspicere?	aspicere.

154	Nequaquam,	Nequaquam
155	gentium,	gentium
157	gestibus,	gestibus
159	Satyros,	Satyros
161	numina,	numina
162	Mammets,	Mammets
169	cingitis,	cingitis
174	fugite.	fugite
176	duxerat.	duxerat,
177	choros,	choros
181	omine!	omine.
182	he!	he
	video!	video,
187	barathrum.	barathrum,
189	rugientem;	rugientem,
192	redditum!	redditum
193	Nichadem!	Nichadem,
	crede,	crede
194	manum,	manum
195	tenebris.	tenebris
197	Lentulo:	Lentulo,

203	cervisia,	cervisia
205	apud	Apud.
	mingunt.	mingunt
212	domum,	domum
213	familiaribus,	familiaribus
214	choro.	choro
216	fuere,	fuere
217	habuere,	habuere
219	iocus, iocus!	iocus iocus.
220	potavere,	potavere
221	audivere,	audivere
223	dedere,	dedere
224	sumpsere,	sumpsere
226	lusere,	lusere.
227	purgavere,	purgavere
229	duxere,	duxere
230	ostendere,	ostendere
232	he!	he,
	Iterum, domini,	Iterum domini
237	gratis:	gratis,
244	grave.	grave

Epilogue.

Line No.	Reading of this edition	MS.
2	necromantiae:	Necromantiae
11	censoribus,	Censoribus
24	vale,	vale.

BIBLIOGRAPHY

BEARE, W., *The Roman Stage. A short History of Latin Drama in the Republic*, third edition (London, 1968).

BERNARD, E., comp., *Catalogi librorum manuscriptorum Angliae et Hiberniae in unum collecti cum indice alphabetico* (Oxford, University Press, 1697).

BOAS, F.S., *University Drama in the Tudor Age* (Oxford, 1914).

CHAPPELL, W., *Old English Popular Music*, 2 vols. (London, 1893).

COOPER, T., comp., *Thesaurus Linguae Romanae et Britannicae, 1565*, English linguistics, 1500-1800, 200 (Menston, 1969).

FOSTER, J., comp., *Alumni Oxonienses: The Members of the University of Oxford 1500-1714...Being the Matriculation Register... alphabetically arranged, revised and annotated*. Early series, 4 vols. (Oxford, 1891-2).

FOWLER, T., *The history of Corpus Christi College, with lists of its members*, Oxford Historical Society, 25 (Oxford, 1893).

HARBAGE, A., *Annals of English Drama 975-1700* (London, 1964).
—— 'A Census of Anglo-Latin Plays', *P.M.L.A.*, 53 (1938), 624-9.

HUDDESFORD, W., comp., <u>Catalogus Librorum Manuscriptorum...A. à Wood:</u> <u>being a minute catalogue of each particular contained in the</u> <u>Manuscript Collections of A. à Wood deposited in the Ashmolean Museum</u> <u>at Oxford</u> (Oxford, 1761).

LILY, W., <u>A short introduction to grammar (commonly call'd the</u> <u>Accidence)...and of the Latin tongue. Followed by Brevissima</u> <u>institutio. (Corrected and enlarged by Erasmus and others)</u> (?London, 1719).

MADAN, F., comp., <u>A Summary Catalogue of Western Manuscripts in the</u> <u>Bodleian Library at Oxford</u>, 7 vols. (vol.II is in two parts), (Oxford, Clarendon Press, 1953, 1895-1953).

MALLET, C.E., <u>A history of the University of Oxford</u>, 3 vols. (London, 1924-27; reprinted New York, 1968).

MUSTARD, W.P., ed., <u>The Eclogues of Baptista Mantuanus</u> (Baltimore, The Johns Hopkins Press, 1911).

NARES, R., comp., <u>A glossary of words, phrases, names and allusions in</u> <u>the works of English authors, particularly of Shakespeare and his</u> <u>contemporaries</u>, new edition by J.O.Halliwell and T. Wright (London, 1905).

ONG, W.J., *Ramus, method and the decay of dialogue. From the art of discourse to the art of reason* (Cambridge, Mass., 1958).

OTTO, A., comp., *Die Sprichwörter und Sprichwörtlichen Redensarten der Römer* (Leipzig, 1890).

SCOT, R., *The Discoverie of Witchcraft*, introduction by H.R.Williamson (Arundel, Centaur Press, 1964).

SMITH, G.C.MOORE, ed., *Club Law: a comedy acted in Clare Hall, Cambridge about 1599-1600* (Cambridge, University Press, 1907).
--- *College Plays performed in the University of Cambridge* (Cambridge, University Press, 1923).

TILLEY, M.P., comp., *Elizabethan proverb lore in Lyly's 'Euphues' and in Pettie's 'Petite Palace', with parallels from Shakespeare*, University of Michigan publications; language and literature, II (New York, 1926).

WARD, G.R.M., trans., *The Foundation Statutes of Bishop Fox for Corpus Christi College A.D. 1517, with a life of the founder* (London, 1843).

WOOD, ANTHONY à, Athenae Oxonienses. An exact history of all the writers and bishops who have had their education in the University of Oxford, to which are added the fasti, or annals of the said university, new edition by P. Bliss, 4 vols. (London, 1813-20).

---The Life and times of Anthony Wood, antiquary, of Oxford, 1632-1695, described by himself. Collected from his diaries and...papers by Andrew Clark, Oxford Historical Society, 19, 21, 26, 30, 40 (Oxford, 1889-1899).

---Survey of the antiquities of the city of Oxford. Composed in 1661-66 by A. Wood, edited by A. Clark, 3 vols., Oxford Historical Society, 15, 17, 37 (Oxford, 1889-1899).

General Works of Reference

Allgemeine Deutsche Biographie

Cambridge History of English Literature

Cambridge Modern History

Chambers's Encyclopaedia

Dictionary of Greek and Roman Biography and Mythology

Dictionary of National Biography

Encyclopaedia Biblica

Encyclopaedia Britannica

Grove's Dictionary of Music and Musicians

Nouvelle Biographie Universelle

Oxford Classical Dictionary

Oxford Companion to Classical Literature

Oxford Companion to English Literature

Oxford Companion to French Literature

Oxford Companion to Music

Oxford English Dictionary

Victoria History of the Counties of England

For Product Safety Concerns and Information please contact our EU
representative GPSR@taylorandfrancis.com
Taylor & Francis Verlag GmbH, Kaufingerstraße 24, 80331 München, Germany

www.ingramcontent.com/pod-product-compliance
Lightning Source LLC
Chambersburg PA
CBHW050521300426
44113CB00026B/952